Rhetoric and Reality on the U.S.—Mexico Border

Commentary from Leaders in the Rio Grande Valley, Texas

"Dr. Fleuriet does the Valley great justice in that she understands from the ground up the nuances of life along the US/Mexico Borderlands. She understands how decisions are made in the minds of a proud yet humble people who many times are faced with putting a meal on the table or paying the rent and trying to take care of their health now and for the future. She understands the very core of what it takes to survive and still smile when a child is born. She understands the hope that everyone aspires to achieve despite the obstacles of making enough money to flourish and survive. She has done her work and painted a beautiful picture of the proud Americans, albeit struggling, in our region."

—Paula Gomez (health care administrator and advocate)

"This book is an excellent example of the importance of perspective and the value of acquiring the 'whole story' throughout our journey in life. *Rhetoric and Reality* is uniquely written by interweaving anthropology and sociology to change the narrative of a national story and stereotype that has been politicized for personal gain. The author's perspective as a native of South Texas further illustrates the value of experiences in challenging a national narrative. *Rhetoric and Reality* is exquisitely written to illuminate the rest of the story of the U.S.-Mexico Border and has the potential to advance the body of knowledge on the importance of "suspending judgement" and challenging national rhetoric. This book is superb!"

—Dr. Arturo Cavazos (superintendent)

"This book is a must read. *Rhetoric and Reality* adds to an already growing body of anthropological work on the suffering and inequality prevalent along the U.S.-Mexico border, and distinguishes itself by providing a critical synthesis of the lived experiences of leading voices in the borderlands region. It is due time a book like this counters the negative news coverage and political commentary surrounding the Rio Grande Valley—a diverse and unique region, unlike any other."

—Filemon Vela (political leader)

K. Jill Fleuriet

Rhetoric and Reality on the U.S.—Mexico Border

Place, Politics, Home

K. Jill Fleuriet
Department of Anthropology
The University of Texas at San Antonio
San Antonio, TX, USA

◆

ISBN 978-3-030-63556-5   ISBN 978-3-030-63557-2   (eBook)
https://doi.org/10.1007/978-3-030-63557-2

Cover illustration: Isabel Pavia/Moment/Getty Images and grandriver/E+/Getty Images

This Palgrave Macmillan imprint is published by the registered company Springer Nature Switzerland
AG
The registered company address is: Gewerbestrasse 11, 6330 Cham, Switzerland

For Hazel

Foreword

Dr. Jill Fleuriet begins her book with the 1857 order from President McKinley appointing a commissioner to survey and mark out upon the land the dividing line between the United States and the Republic of Mexico. She explains that ever since, generations of politicians, journalists, and all of us who tell stories have been about the business of "bordering." Then she teaches us what bordering means; there, the adventure in learning begins. Fleuriet's fascinating book identifies and humanizes the social processes that define (border), reinforce (reborder), or challenge (deborder) difference. Her extensive research teaches us ways to think about what our instinct has always driven us to do, as exemplified in my own family.

Dr. Fleuriet and I are both daughters of *El Valle*, the Rio Grande Valley of south Texas. My father was born in Monterrey, Mexico, and came to the United States as a legal resident alien to escape the ravages of the Mexican Revolution. He carried a "green card" every day of his life to prove his legal standing in the United States. His job with Pan American World Airways and *Compania Mejicaña de Aviación*, required that he cross the border daily. He was perfectly bilingual, bicultural, and biliterate. He straddled the border in all ways. He respected his country of origin, his roots, and his native language, but he loved living in the United States. As a member of the next generation, I grew up in Brownsville. I thought everyone was bilingual and could convert *pesos* into dollars, kilos into pounds, and kilometers into miles in their heads. My father and I spent our lives debordering.

A few years ago, I went to the cemetery where my grandparents were buried in Harlingen. I remember going there as a young girl, but I had not returned in many years. There was a Texas Historical Commission plaque just a few feet from where my grandparents were buried. In part it read, "This cemetery originally was divided into sections for babies, Blacks, Anglos, and Hispanics." Placemaking, in this case, the separation of people even after they have died, recreated and defined.

Fleuriet's research meticulously tells the story of how a society takes an imaginary line drawn by a treaty and makes it socially significant through human behavior. This "bordering," she teaches us, was no accident. We define "us" and "them" through distinction of nationality, language or dialect, citizenship, ethnicity, taxation, healthcare policies and opportunities for a quality education. For that treaty's imaginary line to become socially significant, it had to be physically and socially molded—indeed, continually reinforced, by human behavior. One of the stories told over and over in our mother's family was how the Mexicans were only allowed to swim in the public pool one day a year; the next day the pool was drained and cleaned. Once again, bordering.

The second half of Fleuriet's book expertly contrasts how people *deborder*, the ways in which we try to erase boundaries and ideas of difference. She chronicles with precision the story of how the leadership in the Rio Grande Valley joined forces to aggressively push back to "flip the script" and surface the power of regional thinking, planning, and acting to help lead to the establishment of The University of Texas—Rio Grande Valley. Authenticated with over a hundred interviews with Valley leaders, Fleuriet weaves their individual voices throughout her book to argue that their purpose was to shed prevailing identities that marked the region and her people as something to be "controlled and feared." Instead, these border leaders have begun to co-create a regionalism that should be used as a national model for how communities working toward a shared goal can achieve great purpose.

I had the privilege to help lead the expansion of higher education in the Rio Grande Valley for 32 years. At every commencement, I would attest that it was my fervent hope that the next generation of graduates would build bridges, not walls, between our two countries and around the world. Each time, on hearing those words, the audience would break into spontaneous applause. I believe it was because they heard "*de voz alta,*" out loud what was in their own hearts. I believe they left our campus with the intention of spending their lifetime in that noble pursuit.

Fleuriet's vivid work provides wise counsel as she teaches, challenges, and gives hope. Her book is exceptional and should be required reading in undergraduate classes in journalism, history, Latino studies, and leadership. And, it comes to us at just the right time to serve as an important resource for civic leaders, activists, families, and neighbors across the globe who are reexamining our notions of borders.

Brownsville, USA
2020

Julieta Villarreal García, Ph.D.
President, former
The University of Texas at Brownsville
Professor of Communication
The University of Texas Rio Grande Valley

Acknowledgments

This book happened because of other people. I am profoundly grateful and humbled by their support. The book began and ended with my parents, Randy and Gerry Fleuriet, my husband, Bill Spedding, and our daughter, Hazel Spedding. We have had "the border" conversation in every possible medium: over the dinner table, the phone, text, email, and social media; while folding laundry, making dinner, and doing yard-work; during daily walks in San Antonio and holiday walks in Harlingen; through comments inserted into drafts; and referrals to more people to talk to and books, articles, and Valley media to read. I can't begin to count the times I began emails to my father, Randy Fleuriet, with "Ohhh, Editor…," and phone calls to my mother, Gerry Fleuriet, with "Mom, tell me about…". During daily dawn walks with our dogs, as I juggled a coffee mug and dog leash, I'd blearily say to my spouse, Bill Spedding, "so, I was thinking…" and talk out yet another idea for the book. Through my daughter, Hazel, I saw the Valley through the eyes of a visiting granddaughter and a new generation. Hazel reminded me of my Valley experiences before the advanced degrees and academic research questions as well as gave me fresh ways to think about the region.

Without each of you— your endless patience, insights, and encouragement, I could not have done this. That is no hyperbole. Thank you.

To my Honors College colleagues at The University of Texas at San Antonio, especially Sean Kelly and the academic team of 2018 and 2019, Alegra Lozano, Brent Floyd, and Kalia Glover: you gave me the precious gift of time to write. Alegra, Brent, and Kalia, you definitely "had my back."

To my Anthropology colleagues at The University of Texas at San Antonio, especially Jamon Halvaksz, Michael Cepek, and Patrick Gallagher: your thoughts on methods, space and place theory, and book writing came at pivotal times. I have the great fortune of working in a department of highly collaborative, dynamic, and committed intellectuals. The Department of Anthropology funded several research trips, and UTSA's Institute for Health Disparities Research supported a research assistantship related to the project.

To the former and current Anthropology students with whom I have worked in the years spanning this project, especially Milena Melo, Nikky Greer, Will Robertson, Jess Reid, Mari Castellano, and Itzel Corona: you inspire me with how you think. For those of you who have continued into the academy of higher education, you are among my most trusted professional colleagues. Milena and Nikky, so many of our conversations about our homes and our discipline have influenced my work.

To the family and friends across my networks, particularly Julieta García, Paula Gomez, Peg Graham, Elena Marin, Sister Angela Murdaugh, Barbara and Joel Barks, Heide Castañeda, Asia Ciaravino, Kari, Ken, Matthew and Nikki Fleuriet, Brad Hawkins, Billy Handmaker, Kristi Meyer, Betul Ozmat, John Phillip Santos, Tara and Brian Schwegler, and Barbara and Tom Wynn: our discussions about ideas of home, narrative, place, the Valley, and subjectivity helped me connect my own story of the Valley and my work with larger histories of our borderlands.

I owe an additional debt of gratitude for the intellectual guidance of my academic mentors in graduate school in the mid-1990s through the early 2000s, Drs. Bohdan Kolody and Clifford Barnett. Their practical ethical orientations to their work showed me that working in the academy of higher education can and should lead to change. Bo was also there at a critical point in my personal life, and he made sure I remembered what I could do. His support has been unconditional, and I have tried to emulate him as a professor and mentor. Cliff and his wife, Zelda Barnett, kept me grounded during a time when it would have been easy to forget why I went to graduate school in the first place.

To Mary Al-Sayed at Palgrave MacMillan: from the first exploratory conversation in a mostly empty book room toward the end of a Society for Applied Anthropology conference to the final manuscript, you believed in the importance of the border story as much as I did. I am also very thankful for the helpful, incisive comments of anonymous reviewers and the keen eye of Suzanne Elizondo. They made the book better.

And most especially to the dozens and dozens of Rio Grande Valley leaders who participated in the project or have surrounded me since I was a child: I am indebted to you. I listened and learned. You have taught me what collaboration, creativity, and compassion can accomplish. Together, you chart a path for our nation.

Contents

List of Figures

List of Tables

1

Introduction

Taken from "Report on the United States and Mexican Boundary Survey"

From the Personal Account of Major W. H. Emory

On the 15th August, 1854, I received from the President of the United States ... the appointment of commissioner "to survey and mark out upon the land the dividing line between the United States and the Republic of Mexico ... " (Emory, 1857, p. 22).

WASHINGTON, August 1, 1856

To the Senate and the House of Representatives of the United States:

I communicate to Congress, herewith, the report of Major W. H. Emory, United States Commissioner, on the survey of the boundary between the United States and the republic of Mexico, referred to in the accompanying letter of this date from the Secretary of the Interior.

FRANKLIN PIERCE

(President Franklin Pierce, cited in Emory, 1857, p. v)

© The Author(s), under exclusive license to Springer Nature Switzerland AG 2021
K. J. Fleuriet, *Rhetoric and Reality on the U.S.—Mexico Border*,
https://doi.org/10.1007/978-3-030-63557-2_1

This book is about thinking critically about assumptions behind news stories and political discourse about the U.S.–Mexico border. It is also about listening to alternative stories about our southern border that could help us think differently about issues relevant to our nation: our identity, our policies regarding immigration and health, and our resource allocation. I trace the national story and the local story about one place along the U.S.–Mexico border, the Rio Grande Valley of south Texas. Each story about the U.S.–Mexico border acts as a kind of *place-making*, or discourse and action that build contours of a space with identifiable characteristics, characters, values, and plots. Place-making in borderlands necessarily deals with defining or erasing social difference. The current U.S.–Mexico border was imagined during the Treaty of Guadalupe Hidalgo in 1848. It then had to be created. In 1854, American President Pierce commissioned Major W. H. Emory to officially demarcate the new U.S.–Mexico borderline with a boundary survey. Policies and practices reinforcing national differences followed.

Put another way, the U.S.–Mexico border was an imaginary line, drawn up by a treaty. In order to become socially significant, it had to be physically and socially inscribed by human behavior. Such behavior is called *bordering*. Bordering processes define "us" and "them," whether through claims of difference through nationality, language or dialect, citizenship, ethnicity, taxation and health care policies, or a whole host of other ways in which we determine who belongs and who does not. *Bordering* and *rebordering* are constantly occurring. They are conscious and unconscious processes of language, behavior, laws, and actions that are frequently messy and complicated. One example is U.S.–Mexico border fencing, or "the wall." Both the physical barriers and arguments for and against them are bordering and rebordering processes. They are claims of what the border means, what it is supposed to keep out, and what it is supposed to let through. There is little agreement among these claims. There is a third term: *debordering*, or the ways in which we try to erase boundaries and ideas of difference. When we talk about national geopolitical borders, we are also talking about the social processes that define (border), reinforce (reborder), or challenge (deborder) them.

As a nation, we most often think of the U.S.–Mexico border as one static place different than the rest of the United States, but really, where does the border end? How far north into the United States or south into Mexico do you have to go to leave "the border"? In this book, I contrast stories of place-making that largely (but not always) reborder the U.S.–Mexico border as a singular place of difference and threat, e.g., national media and political stories of the border in the 2010s, and those that largely (but not always) deborder the U.S.–Mexico border, e.g., the story of the border told by leaders in the Rio Grande Valley. In more common parlance, leaders in the Rio Grande Valley are attempting to flip the script on the national story of the U.S.–Mexico border. Social practices of re/bordering create boundaries around an idea, a place, or a group of people. Social bordering and rebordering are things people do and say to create and reinforce beliefs that the U.S.–Mexico borderlands are porous and in need of control. Debordering, by contrast, suggests the opposite: the United States borderlands with Mexico are not infused with difference and threat, but rather with similarity to the rest of the United States and distinct potential to improve the nation. The debordering I talk about in this book is not suggesting a lack of geopolitical borders, i.e., promoting so-called "open borders." It is first and foremost a social process of shedding identities that mark the region as something to be controlled and feared.

In the first half of the book, I trace how the Rio Grande Valley in national media in the 2010s became a place that symbolized the whole of the U.S.–Mexico border. I use approximately 780 media stories as data. These stories border and reborder the south Texas region and, by extension, all of the U.S.–Mexico borderlands as faraway failures of American projects of health care, economy, and immigration. I argue that dominant American understandings about the southern border, especially south Texas, are rooted in the very old idea of the Global South. The Global South is a term that lumps together regions, communities, and other groups of people that have borne the brunt of colonialism and, more recently, globalization. The Global South is mostly a suite of wholly negative attributes, and it stands in contrast to the Global North, or those countries and the constellation of economic and political power that led and benefitted from colonialism and globalization. The Global South/North relationship is patterned by a certain discourse, or ways of thinking, talking, and acting that reflect assumptions about who has what kind of economic, political, and social capital. Those assumptions include the Global North as more civilized, educated, sophisticated, and wealthy—the Global South, the opposite.

In many ways, Americans use the same implicit ideas about the Global North to talk about the urban centers of the United States (say, Chicago, Dallas or New York City) and the Global South to talk about the U.S.–Mexico borderlands and the people who live there. Implicit assumptions about the people who live in the Global South impact national policy and, by extension, funding for national security, health care, education, and crime (Nevins, 2010 [2002]). The circulation of ideas about the Rio Grande Valley, "the border" writ large, during the 2016 presidential election illustrates the depth and durability of the Global South version of the border. Of course, the U.S.–Mexico borderlands are not so simple, and neither are our urban interiors. Yet, these ideas percolate in our national imagination, often unquestioned until they bubble over into extreme language or behavior, such as hate speech during the 2016 election season or the racial violence of the El Paso Walmart shooting in 2019.

In the second half of this book, I analyze a very different story about the U.S.–Mexico borderlands. It challenges the Global South rhetoric about the U.S.–Mexico border by debordering one south Texas region. This important alternative border story is drawn from the experiences and voices of over 110 Rio Grande Valley leaders in economy, health care, education, philanthropy, activism, law enforcement, politics, and journalism gathered over four years of research in the region. Identified by community members as people of influence, these leaders work with and speak to state and national audiences. They have an active, vested interest in reconfiguring the national narrative about the borderlands. These leaders are on the front lines, fighting to reframe the national story about the border during an era when the region is central to national political discourse and policymaking.

Valley leaders strategically and rhetorically deploy a new border story to remake, or deborder, the region as a model by which to address the challenges of our nation's future. Valley leaders tell a story of these south Texas borderlands that tries to erase perceptions of negative differences between the borderlands and the rest of the United States. Their stories construct borderlands as a place of dynamic innovation, growth, and potential in health care, education, and the economy that represent classic American values of ties to the land, hard work and entrepreneurialism. They attach a very specific American idea of home to the region. Home is a complex, rich idea, full of strengths and weaknesses but above all, personal relationships. Sometimes, their stories also inadvertently contribute to the national generalizations of "the border."

As a whole, though, how leaders tell the story of the Valley pushes back against the implicit assumptions of the borderlands as a gateway to the Global South. They describe life in the Rio Grande Valley as rich with cultural capital, resilience, and creativity in the face of barriers erected by state, national, and international politics and histories. They emphasize how Valley communities partner across social differences, whether national, ethnic, class, or geographic, to tackle problems that face both the region and nation. They suggest that these partnerships can be a national model. This project of debordering is explicitly political. As such, leaders leave out some stories that complicate their border ideal. I detail these silences, too. I compare leaders' stories to grassroots efforts that also reframe the southern border of the United States as home, as a national resource of expertise, and as the future. In these strategic retellings, our southern border simultaneously becomes a classic American ideal of home and a new rendering of our nation whose core and strengths reside in our peripheries and along our borders, especially our southern border with Mexico.

I want something very specific for this book. I would like the book to be accessible to two audiences: people from all walks of life interested in the U.S.–Mexico borderlands and students in undergraduate college classrooms across the United States. I would like our nation to recognize and assess its own assumptions about the places we denigrate, especially when "the border" and immigration through our southern borders are most commonly used for national political agenda on both sides of the aisle. I would like my work to demonstrate how anthropology can make us think productively about places we initially think of as different or faraway. I hope this book can contribute to ongoing efforts by borderland communities and scholars from the Gulf of Mexico to the Pacific Ocean who seek to change the narrative, to flip the script, about the U.S.–Mexico border during a time in our country when we seem more intent on using ideas of differences to deepen our problems than to attend to them.

Works Cited

Emory, W. H. (1857). *Report on the United States and Mexican boundary survey* (Vol. 1). Washington, DC: Secretary of the Interior.
Nevins, J. (2010 [2002]). *Operation gatekeeper and beyond: The war on "illegals" and the remaking of the U.S.-Mexico boundary.* New York: Routledge.

2

Home and Faraway Places

Some things will change, some things, never … it's been 18 years since I left Heaven … this place I love has got a little bigger … I'm home, everybody, I'm home. (lyrics about the Rio Grande Valley from "I'm Home" by Bo Garza, 2015)

There used to be a moment when I knew I was home. It happened when I returned by car. I would be driving down U.S. Highway 77 in deep south Texas and cross the Willacy County line. Suddenly, soaring palm trees appeared in the median. Nothing else really changed in the landscape. The scrubby south Texas ranchland still bordered both sides of "77." The turkey vultures soared high overhead or sat on fence posts contemplating roadkill. The big, white, puffy clouds stretched out over power lines and wind farms. But those palm trees, they meant home.

When I hit that line of Washingtonia palms, I entered the Rio Grande Valley of south Texas, the four southernmost counties of Texas. This is "the border" that has dominated news stories on and off since 2014 about changing patterns of unauthorized immigration from Latin America, health care shortages, and political debates about national security. The almost 2,000 mile U.S.–Mexico border is not truly generalizable. Yet, in

© The Author(s), under exclusive license to Springer Nature Switzerland AG 2021
K. J. Fleuriet, *Rhetoric and Reality on the U.S.—Mexico Border*,
https://doi.org/10.1007/978-3-030-63557-2_2

national media and political rhetoric, the phrase "the border," refers to a singular idea and place of difference and danger, and this area of south Texas has been the exemplar in national media in the last decade. Even in my opening above, I conjured a very specific image of the "southernmost counties of Texas": hot, dusty, and rural. My image reinforces a notion of difference with urban metropolises such as New York City, Dallas, Chicago, Los Angeles, Atlanta, or Miami.

National rhetoric about the U.S.–Mexico border is most evident in comments by national political leaders and in mainstream news media. Most often, that rhetoric treats the U.S.–Mexico border region as one faraway place whose poverty, corruption, immigration, violence, and smuggling threaten the United States. National stories in the 2010s about the U.S.–Mexico border and the Rio Grande Valley in particular had more to do with American political and public conversations about militarization, securitization, and immigration than a comprehensive analysis and understanding of life in borderland communities. Militarization, securitization, and immigration have, in fact, shaped a decade's worth of "border" news. The late 2010s were a time when the American president used these ideas to justify the longest government shutdown in U.S. history, a declaration of National Emergency to fulfill a campaign promise to build more physical barriers between the United States and Mexico, threats of border closures to a foreign government and trade partner, and fundamental changes to immigration policies.

This is what this book explores: why we as a nation tell certain kinds of stories about places and people and why it matters to listen to alternative stories. I focus on the U.S.–Mexico borderlands region with a case study of one area on one side of the geopolitical borderline, the Rio Grande Valley of Texas. Few Americans who live outside "the Valley" think of the south Texas border region as a dynamic source of economic, educational, and health care innovation for the state of Texas and the nation. In mainstream news, the Texas–Mexico borderlands get slapped with all sorts of negative images that cannot convey the complexity of the region and its strengths. It is presented as a place rife with corruption. State and national media and public discourses about the Rio Grande Valley suggest an image of the Valley as a site of unchecked immigration, rampant poverty, drug running, and poor health (Fleuriet & Castañeda,

2017)—and little else, though occasionally, a "hunter's paradise." Sometimes, stories pop up about the popular Spring Break tourist venue of South Padre Island, hurricanes that slam the Texas coast, or the unique birding ecologies and migratory flyways in the Valley. Mostly, though, the Valley is wrapped in narratives of a dangerous place.

Some elements of the national story about "the border" do reflect some defining aspects of life in the Rio Grande Valley. People in the Rio Grande Valley of south Texas are more likely to live in poverty with significantly less access to health care than the rest of Texas. Changing federal response to immigration, especially in the 2010s, has led to more and visible police and military presence. The region has rural swaths. South of Corpus Christi for a good 70 miles, the region is mostly ranchland belonging to historic landowning families of Spanish, Mexican, and American descent. The ranchland is inhospitable but magnificent. Low lying scrub brush, mesquite trees, and cactus stretch as far as the eye can see. Then, my palm trees begin at the entrance to Willacy County on Interstate 69, the new version of U.S. 77.

The Valley as rural, poor, and surveilled is not so much inaccurate as replete with erroneous assumptions and incomplete information. In the Valley, there are about 1.4 million people living in dense cities such as Brownsville, McAllen, Edinburg, and Pharr (U.S. Census Bureau, 2019). There is tertiary hospital care even in smaller cities like Harlingen. There is a thriving tourism industry for Canadians, Americans, and Mexicans at South Padre Island. The Valley is world-renowned for its diversity of resident and migratory birds. It has underground punk rock music scenes; vocal activist communities united around topics of immigration and sustainability; internationally and nationally recognized universities, colleges, community colleges and technical schools; long-standing legacies of award-winning elementary school chess, middle school robotics and high school drama, dance teams and bands; a growing art scene that tackles issues of social justice and inequality; and close-knit economic and social networks with its sister cities across the Rio Grande River that yield tens of billions of dollars in gross domestic product per year. Flows of people, goods, and capital between the United States and Mexico are an essential part of life in the Valley as in any U.S.–Mexico borderlands region.

What if we thought of places like the Valley as the future rather than as a failure? What if we thought critically about why we tell the stories we tell about ourselves, our homes, and each other? What can we learn? We tell stories about our homes as a way to define ourselves; we tell stories about other places to define other people and communities in relation to ourselves. Cultural, political, and economic currents shape what stories we tell about places, as well. Ultimately, this book is about documenting those currents as well as what is missing in those stories and offering a different, richer story about this one section of the U.S.–Mexico borderlands that could fundamentally shift how we think about the whole region from Brownsville to San Diego. This book is about how we can change dominant stories about ourselves and others.

When I began thinking about this book in 2014, I was more interested in how the national version of the border threw up roadblocks to regional work to improve Valley communities. I first wanted to analyze the tension between state and national perceptions of the border and contrast those stories with the work local leaders were doing to improve well-being in their communities. I was tired of reading and hearing stories with tropes about a place beset with problems decontextualized from history and politics and without internal assets. I wanted to understand how our ideas of a place shaped or hindered efforts to improve that place. I did not foresee how a distorted national idea of the border, with the Valley as its emblem, would so profoundly shape national immigration policy and deployment of federal resources in a few short years.

As Donald Trump's presidential campaign began in 2015, I became deeply concerned that a businessman in the 2010s could use a specific rhetoric about Mexican immigrants and the border as a treacherous place to propel him into our highest national office. In some basic ways, Trump's use of the border was nothing new. American presidents over the last 150 years have used the idea of the border as a means to enact national economic, security, and military agendas. The dominant stories about Mexican immigrants have been replete with negative and patently false stereotypes for decades, a way of national scapegoating during times of economic stress (Chávez, 2001, 2008; Nevins, 2010 [2002]; Ono & Sloop, 2002). But Trump wove stories about the border as an economic and social menace with threads of xenophobia, nationalism, and racism in ways that were new. Trump's use of tired but apparently effective stereotypes comingled with an enduring image of the U.S.–Mexico border, especially the south Texas border, as remote but especially hazardous to the nation. Then came efforts by President Trump to end Deferred Action for Childhood Arrivals and his successful action separating immigrant children from their parents. Soon thereafter came the government shutdown of 2018–2019 as the president's negotiating tool over the funding of more "Wall." The Trump administration worked hard to convince the American public that there was a security and humanitarian "crisis" at "the border," later "the southern border." It was the longest government shutdown in American history. After several weeks of the shutdown, President Trump addressed the nation on Tuesday, January 8, 2019, stressing his belief in the need for a border wall. He said,

> My fellow Americans: Tonight, I am speaking to you because there is a growing humanitarian and security crisis at our southern border .... But all Americans are hurt by uncontrolled, illegal migration. It strains public resources and drives down jobs and wages .... Our southern border is a pipeline for vast quantities of illegal drugs, including meth, heroin, cocaine, and fentanyl.... Over the years, thousands of Americans have been brutally killed by those who illegally entered our country, and thousands more lives will be lost if we don't act right now. This is a humanitarian crisis — a crisis of the heart and a crisis of the soul.... [A]s part of an overall approach to border security, law enforcement professionals have requested $5.7 billion for a physical barrier. At the request of Democrats, it will be a steel barrier rather than a concrete wall. This barrier is absolutely critical to border security. It's also what our professionals at the border want and need. This is just common sense. (Trump, 2019)

Two days later on Thursday, January 10, 2019, President Trump traveled to McAllen, Texas, where Rio Grande Valley leaders told him in no uncertain terms that there was no "crisis" (Jervis, 2019; Martinez, 2019; Schallhorn, 2019). Valley leaders were honest. They identified the logistical hurdles and resulting human costs of our legal system pertaining to unauthorized immigration and the asylum seeking process that could strain local governments. They were concerned about conditions of overcrowding. But, they said, there was not an imminent immigration crisis, and if there were, the crisis described in presidential speeches and tweets would not be remedied by a wall or other physical barrier extension along the U.S.–Mexico border. Later, in April of 2019, Immigration and Customs Enforcement began dropping off asylum seekers in groups of several hundred at a single community location. This did become unmanageable, ultimately to crisis proportions in terms of immigrant health and well-being. That President Trump labeled the border a crisis much earlier and for other reasons was soon lost in ensuing public debates about humanitarian care of such large numbers of asylum seekers.

During these years, my perspective on my research project shifted. I still wanted to know not only how dominant ideas about a place enable or disable efforts to improve it, but also where these ideas came from, how they were woven into media and political discourse, and how people from the borderlands resisted (or reproduced) them. I started to think about how the stories we tell about places profoundly shape our nation. I wondered how the story of one region, the borderlands, became a soundbite that carried so much meaning about who we believe ourselves to be as a nation. I also wanted to know who could change the story. To put it in anthropological terms, I wanted to document how rhetoric about "the border" becomes a story and how the story circulates, with particular attention to how people from the primary referent place react and produce their own stories about themselves and their home. I wanted to know why debordering happened and how debordering could create ideas of similarity rather than difference when it seemed, instead, a national trend to retrench beliefs about difference.

Anthropology

So many aspects of our personal experiences and social identities shape how we understand places like the U.S.–Mexico borderlands. For me, one of those is my professional identity as an anthropologist. Anthropology is, quite simply, the study of humans. Within anthropology, I am a cultural anthropologist. In cultural anthropology, we study how humans make meaning, share meaning, act on meaning, and change meaning. In this book, I consider the meanings of the Rio Grande Valley and the U.S.–Mexico borderlands. Valley meanings are nested in national discourses about "the border." Meaning is often like this, wrapped up in other meanings. Meanings can change from person to person, depending on their social positions and individual experiences. The meaning of the Valley for Texas Governor Abbott will be different than that of a national legislator from the Valley, the mayor of a large Valley city, or the executive director of a shelter that feeds the hungry in the Valley. One of my professional tasks as a cultural anthropologist is to figure out how meanings are similar and different based on social categories, how they shape our experiences and vice versa, and how these meanings get passed around. Questions for this book revolve around what "the border" means to Valley leaders, in national news stories, and in national political discourse in the United States. My perspective is also one of many different academic and personal forays into understanding the U.S.–Mexico borderlands. Historians, sociologists, political scientists, geographers, Mexican-American Studies scholars, creative writers and other artists, among so many other disciplines, study what makes the border "the border." Throughout the book, I will bring in ideas from different disciplines and creative writers to supplement and extend my anthropological analysis.

Anthropologists look at how meaning is created, how it travels, and how it changes. Valley leaders are an essential voice in spreading different stories about the region whether through media efforts or smaller scale efforts. Examples include the president of The University of Texas Rio Grande Valley talking to the chancellor of The University of Texas System and his Board of Regents; the head of Brownsville's Economic Development Council meeting with Elon Musk about a potential SpaceX rocket launch site; or U.S. Representative Filemon Vela, Jr., writing an open letter to President Trump criticizing his plans for a border wall. My focus on Valley leaders is intentional, but I also walk a fine line with my focus. Except for the exemplary work of Josiah

Heyman in the El-Paso-Ciudad Juarez border region (e.g., Heyman, 2012a, 2012b; Heyman & Symons, 2012), rarely are borderlands' leaders included in social science research about border regions. More often, social scientists highlight voices of marginalized communities and for good reason. Voices from marginalized communities are often ignored but should be pivotal to efforts to reduce suffering and improve well-being. Experiences of people from marginalized communities can point to problems in our legal, economic, political, and social systems as well as solutions to them.

Valley leaders occupy positions of privilege relative to other Valley community members. Their perspectives as leaders consciously and unconsciously influence how, why, and when they tell their border story. At the same time, *any* borderland voice could be considered marginal, inasmuch as these voices are rarely integral to the national conversation that impacts daily lives in border regions vis-à-vis policies on immigration, international trade, and national security. Valley leaders were the primary group in the 2010s fighting to flip the script until the groundswell of Valley community efforts in 2018 and 2019 (see Chapter 9). I am also interested in highlighting local expertise evidenced by community-recognized leaders, in part because it is so often not central to the national story. Nevertheless, meanings of place and rhetorical techniques of Valley leaders should not be generalized to other Valley groups, such as those who live in poverty or the shadows of unauthorized immigration status.

Early work of mine mentioned but did not focus on local efforts to reduce inequalities or challenge their root causes. My prior anthropological research focused on how meanings of gender, citizenship, ethnicity, and healthcare shape the pregnancy and prenatal care experiences and birth outcomes of low-income Latina women living in the borderlands (e.g., Fleuriet 2009; Fleuriet & Sunil 2015, 2016). Over time, I came to realize that my focus, while committed to improving community health and health care for women in the Valley, also reinforced certain ideas of the Valley: poverty, poor health, and unauthorized immigration. To be sure, these issues are central to the Valley experience in many significant ways, but their relationship is more complex. Unauthorized immigration does not have to equate with poverty and poor health. The American system of citizenship and employment are larger factors in poverty and poor health of unauthorized immigrants than the actual geographic space of the Valley. Local efforts to improve health outcomes are numerous. For example, local Valley community, educational, economic, and philanthropic efforts have made tremendous improvements in population health and care for chronic illness, such as farmers' markets available to all incomes and small clinics strategically placed to diagnose diabetes and offer realistic lifestyle changes to manage the disease. Bike and walking trails in Valley cities alongside community policing efforts make a movement-based lifestyle more possible for more people across socioeconomic lines. The new University of Texas Rio Grande Valley has a medical school with significant training and outreach for local communities.

At the same time I was reevaluating my work, a few things happened that paved the way for this book project. In the fall of 2015 as Donald Trump was emerging as a political force, I was reading two books. I was reading Salman Rushdie's *Two Years Eight Months and Twenty-Eight Nights* (2015) for pleasure as I was teaching another book, *Theory from the South* by Jean Comaroff and John L. Comaroff (2012), at The University of Texas at San Antonio. Together, these books helped me understand why Donald Trump's verbal attacks on Mexican immigrants and the U.S.–Mexico border region seemed to resonate with so many Americans. For me, Rushdie's book was a story about the stories we tell as nations that shape our reality and can tear apart or reinforce the social order.[1]

Theory from the South (Comaroff & Comaroff, 2012) crystallized my thoughts on my growing discomfort with the stories many scholars and the larger American public told about the U.S.–Mexico borderlands. *Theory from the South* is not about the borderlands, but rather the relationship between Africa and what Comaroff and Comaroff call "Euro-America," and their argument has global application. The Comaroffs argue that those of us who live in the Global North, common shorthand for northern countries where wealth concentrates and who

---

[1] Of course, the novel is so much more than this. A quick internet search for reviews on the book will give the reader a better summary than I can provide here.

control low-wage labor and resources in southern countries, have too long thought of people in the Global South as living their lives in reaction to our (presumed better) political, economic, and social directives. What if, the Comaroffs suggested, "everyone else" was the source of solutions to the problems "we" created, such as the ever-increasing wealth gap, environmental destruction, corruption, and ethnic conflict? What if "we" listened to "them," people from regions automatically dismissed as peripheral to political and social power in our global economy? Their argument clicked with my experience with the Valley. My course preparation notes for that week in our graduate seminar are sprinkled with "Valley"; "U.S. and Valley? Yes!"; and "U.S. MX border." As I continued to write my research articles on pregnancy and prenatal care in the Valley, I found myself asking: where were the stories about Valley expertise and novel problem-solving? Why weren't they being told and shared as models for the rest of the country struggling with issues of health care access and efforts to make health care interventions sustainable in people's lives? As a nation, we were narrowing an idea about the border that was increasingly afield from my realities. Why wasn't I actively telling a different story?

What I Hope for This Book

I believe we need national conversations and slow, careful thought about our borders now more than ever. In this book, I write to the interested public and undergraduate students from within my discipline, Anthropology, but not to it, during a tumultuous time in the United States. In 2019 when I completed the first draft of this book, President Donald Trump was in his third year of office with an avowed isolationist approach, treating the U.S.–Mexico borderlands as a geopolitical line to be guarded from dangerous and violent foreigners. He was one of many presidents who have used the U.S.–Mexico border as a political pawn. In his rhetoric, there was little to no consideration of the border except as an uncontrolled entry point for people and things that endanger personal and national security. Community life, individual people's lives, fragile environments, an economic driver for one of the most powerful states, and a source of innovation and creativity in an atmosphere of declining state investment in infrastructure were noticeably absent in his political discourse but also in our commonplace, national renderings of the U.S.–Mexico borderlands.

My work dovetails with academic conversations about borders and borderlands, border rhetoric, place-making and concepts of home, and the sizeable and increasing research on daily life on both sides of the U.S.–Mexico border. I will frame each chapter in concepts derived from that literature, and I will demonstrate how my argument extends these conversations. But, my hope is that more people than anthropologists read this book, and that means I will not use standard academic conventions in writing. When an anthropologist writes a book, she can write it in several ways. The most common anthropological book is written in professional, disciplinary-specific language and structure. These are books by anthropologists written for other anthropologists. My book is not that book. Another approach to writing an anthropological book is to illustrate how anthropology can help shift the way we as a society think about a social problem, using the perspective of the communities the problem affects. This kind of book is called an "applied" or "engaged" book. Applied books can be written for different audiences: the general public and/or target audiences, such as policymakers, undergraduate students, and the interested general public. Mine is an applied book for those audiences but can also be read as part of a larger discussion among academics about how and why we tell stories about borders.

The Book's Narrative

In the chapters that follow, I trace an idea of one place through stories. I begin from the premise that there is not just one story of any place and from the anthropological commitment to understanding a place through the perspectives of the people who live there. I also position myself as a certain kind of insider/outsider. I am from the Valley but I no longer live there. My family and friends do, and I have conducted research with Valley leaders and communities since 1996. In my work as a professor, a current resident of San Antonio, Texas, and as an administrator in higher education, I am exposed to state and national narratives about the Valley in particular ways. They often reinforce negative generalizations that we see in national news stories about the Valley. The Valley and its people are regularly seen as "less than." My current position in my field of higher education in Texas shapes how I approached this project. My personal and professional past and present are one thread of the stories that I analyze. I weave my stories into the analysis, because my personal and professional overlap in the work that I do. I agree with Luzelma Canales, a Valley leader in education, as quoted in Taylor (2018): "Let us begin to tell our own story of the Valley. We don't need for somebody to come study us. We can study ourselves. We can tell our own story." My story is but one, and my primary focus is on national and other local stories about the region.

I will chart Valley stories in the nation's imagination as seen through almost eight hundred news stories and contrast them with local leaders' stories about the Valley. Stories often have five elements: characters, setting, plot, conflict, and resolution. National news stories about the Valley and Valley leaders' stories differ in each of these story elements. More than anything else, there is one dominant, negative story about the Valley in national news, yet Valley leaders tell stories that are rarely unilaterally positive or negative. The contrast between local stories of Rio Grande Valley leaders and national news stories will test the common ways many Americans think about our southern borderlands. Taken together, these stories are a reminder that understanding a place is impossible through one story or through privileging the negative alone (Adiche, 2009).

The book is divided into three parts. The first part, Chapters 1 through 3, introduce the book's narrative arc, argument, methods, and analytical approach. The second part, Chapters 4 and 5, tells the national story about the U.S.–Mexico borderlands in the 2010s, which used the Rio Grande Valley as the exemplar "border." In Chapter 4, I consider the primary stories told about the Valley, including its setting and communities, as represented in national news stories. In Chapter 5, I offer an anthropological explanation for the durability of the national misrepresentation for the Valley using news stories about the Valley during the rise of Donald Trump to the American presidency as a case study.

My argument in these chapters is that our national rendering of the southern border, especially south Texas, draws from a deep history of place-making rhetorical techniques to characterize the southern border in need of external intervention and control. "The border" has become a specific device in American media and political wrangling to border and reborder, a process of making or reinforcing social, economic, and cultural boundaries in our nation, that mirror historical discourse associated with colonialism and Western expansionism in the United States.

The last part of the book is Chapters 6 through 9. In these chapters, I tell the Valley story from the lens of leaders' understandings and experiences in educational, health care, economic, political, philanthropic, activist, law enforcement, and media sectors in the Valley. I argue that these leaders are engaged in a focused project to upend the popular idea of the south Texas borderlands by debordering, or breaking down assumed differences between the U.S.–Mexico borderlands and the rest of the United States. In Chapter 6, Valley leaders tell their own stories of the Valley: home, heritage, and as a major driver of new models for the nation, all by virtue of being next to Mexico. Framing the region as home in terms that resonate with the American ideal of home as family, land, and history remakes the borderlands into iconic America. At the same time, leaders suggest that the region is unique and pivotal to addressing common challenges of health care, economy, and education because of its constant flow of ideas, identities, goods, and capital with Mexico. In Chapter 7, I explore these regional challenges from the perspective of its leaders, including their views on the mischaracterizations in national news stories. Leaders do not ignore enduring challenges but contextualize them with accomplishment, opportunity, and resilience. Weaknesses are understood primarily as inevitable results of a state and nation that cannot get past their stereotypes. In Chapter 8, I present the story of The University of Texas Rio Grande Valley (UTRGV) as the most commonly told story by leaders in the mid and late 2010s to emphasize the strengths and potential of the region. Especially important, the UTRGV story represents another political intervention by leaders: borderlands can be places of partnerships across historical and national difference and division. New social formations can emerge, such as the bicultural, binational, and bilingual public research university, beneficial to a national economy dependent on international relations and trade.

In Chapter 9, I conclude with an analysis of other recent efforts to change the story about the Rio Grande Valley and its representations as the U.S.–Mexico border in our national imagination. I argue that producing knowledge about our borderlands impacts us all, and Valley leaders invite us to know our southern border in a very different way. Production of knowledge about the border should be a conversation with borderland communities, especially when national policies and politics about our borderlands and its communities exacerbate racial violence and suffering, such as unequipped and overcrowded detention centers and declining funding for public services for the disenfranchised. A retelling of the Valley story as a model for our nation may be more important now than ever before.

Works Cited

Adichie, C. N. (2009, July 10). The danger of a single story. *TEDGlobal*. TED.

Chávez, L. R. (2001). *Covering immigration: Popular images and the politics of the nation*. Berkeley: University of California Press.

Chávez, L. R. (2008). *The Latino threat: Constructing immigrants, citizens, and the nation*. Stanford: Stanford University Press.

Comaroff, J., & Comaroff, J. L. (2012). *Theory from the South or, how Euro-America is evolving toward Africa*. Boulder: Paradigm Publishers.

Fleuriet, K. J. (2009). Pregnant, uninsured, and undocumented: Prenatal care for immigrant women in south Texas. *The Applied Anthropology, 29*(1), 4–21.

Fleuriet, K. J., & Castañeda, H. (2017). A risky place? Media and the health landscape in the (in)secure U.S.-Mexico borderlands. *North American Dialogue, 20*(2), 32–46.

Fleuriet, K. J., & Sunil, T. S. (2015). Reproductive habitus, psychosocial health, and birth weight variation in Mexican immigrant and Mexican American women in south Texas. *Social Science and Medicine, 138*, 102–109.

Fleuriet, K. J., & Sunil, T. S. (2016). Stress, pregnancy, and motherhood: Implications for birth weights in the borderlands of Texas. *Medical Anthropology Quarterly, 30*(1), 60–77.

Garza, B. (2015). I'm Home [recorded by B. Garza]. On *That's Who I Am*.

Heyman, J. (2012a). A voice of the US southwestern border: The 2012 "we the border: Envisioning a narrative for our future" conference. *Journal of Migration and Human Security, 1*(2), 60–75.

Heyman, J. M. (2012b). Constructing a "perfect" wall: Race, class, and citizenship in US-Mexico border policing. In P. Barber & W. Lem (Eds.), *Migration in the 21st century: Political economy and ethnography* (pp. 153–174). New York and London: Routledge.

Heyman, J., & Symons, J. (2012). Borders. *A companion to moral anthropology* (pp. 540–557). Hoboken: Wiley.

Jervis, R. (2019, January 10). As Trump visits border, McAllen residents ask: What crisis? *USA Today*. Retrieved January 10, 2019, from https://www.usatoday.com/story/news/politics/2019/01/10/trump-visits-border-mcallen-residents-ask-what-crisis/2535007002/.

Martinez, G. (2019, January 11). President Trump went to a border town to prove they need a wall. Residents say otherwise. *Time*. Retrieved January 13, 2019, from http://time.com/5499188/mcallen-residents-not-supporting-border-wall/.

Nevins, J. (2010 [2002]). *Operation gatekeeper and beyond: The War on "illegals" and the remaking of the U.S.-Mexico boundary*. New York: Routledge.

Ono, K. A., & Sloop, J. M. (2002). *Shifting borders: Rhetoric, immigration, and California's proposition 187*. Philadelphia, PA: Temple University Press.

Rushdie, S. (2015). *Two years eight months and twenty-eight nights*. New York, NY: Random House.

Schallhorn, K. (2019, January 10). Trump visits Texas border town amid push for wall: What to know about McAllen. *FOX News*. Retrieved January 13, 2019, from https://www.foxnews.com/politics/trump-visits-texas-border-town-amid-push-for-wall-what-to-know-about-mcallen.

Taylor, S. (2018, May 6). *RGV FOCUS: Henceforth, the Valley will tell its own education story*. Retrieved October 4, 2018, from Rio Grande Guardian: https://riograndeguardian.com/rgv-focus-henceforth-the-valley-will-tell-its-own-education-story/.

Trump, D. J. (2019, January 8). *President Donald J. Trump's address to the nation on the crisis at the border*. Retrieved January 13, 2019, from Remarks,

Briefing Statements, The White House: https://www.whitehouse.gov/briefi
ngs-statements/president-donald-j-trumps-address-nation-crisis-border/.

U.S. Census Bureau. (2019, July 1). *Quick facts: Starr County, Texas; Willacy County, Texas; Hidalgo County, Texas; Cameron County, Texas.* Retrieved January 7, 2020, from United States Census Bureau: https://www.census.gov/quickfacts/fact/table/starrcountytexas,willacycountytexas,hidalgocount ytexas,cameroncountytexas/PST045219.

3

How We Tell the Stories We Tell

I feel like every story that I do, I have to introduce the Valley, especially when I am writing more regionally or nationally. Because people don't know …. They don't have a sense of the cultural or physical geography of what I'm writing about …. If people do have a template, it's often not the correct template. I'm constantly having to give them the template.—Rio Grande Valley journalist

The Rio Grande Valley: Shifting Industries, Shifting Social Orders

Technically, the Rio Grande Valley is not a valley. The Valley is a river delta in the South Texas Plains and Gulf Coast Texas Plains. From April to October, humid, subtropical heat can sap your energy. November to March are milder, drawing "Winter Texans" by the tens of thousands each year for three to six month stretches. Our four lower Valley counties—Willacy, Cameron, Hidalgo, and Starr, border the northern Mexican state of Tamaulipas (see Map 3.1). The borderline was drawn along the Rio Grande River (in Mexico, the Rio Bravo del Norte) in the

© The Author(s), under exclusive license to Springer Nature
Switzerland AG 2021
K. J. Fleuriet, *Rhetoric and Reality on the U.S.—Mexico Border*,
https://doi.org/10.1007/978-3-030-63557-2_3

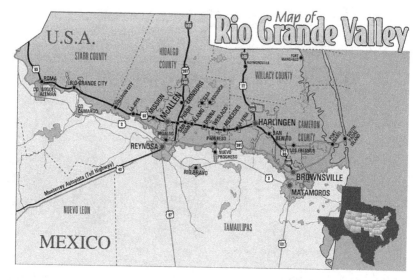

Map 3.1 The Rio Grande Valley of Texas: Starr, Hidalgo, Willacy, and Cameron counties

1848 Treaty of Guadalupe Hidalgo (Pletcher, 2010). These four Valley counties span approximately 4,300 square miles, roughly twice the size of Delaware (Vigness & Odintz, 2010). Ranchland has been a constant in the Valley landscape for centuries, but land tenure laws and outright theft of land complicate the history of ownership. Initially, socioeconomic class was the primary social division, though poverty and Mexican heritage were routinely conflated. The railroad and citrus and cotton crops arrived in the early twentieth century, bringing wealthier non-Hispanic whites and a primarily race-based social order (Bowman, 2016; Nájera, 2015). Urban sprawl in late twentieth and early twenty-first centuries, due notably to growth in service and international production industries, crowded out agricultural fields and ranchland along the east-west highways. Today, the almost million and a half people live mostly in cities. This is no dusty borderlands portrayed in countless Hollywood films and news stories.

Just what constitutes life in the "Rio Grande Valley of South Texas" depends on your perspective. Definitions of the Valley can vary by the importance placed on different variables, such as environmental features, especially access to Rio Grande water; metropolitan growth due to international trade, such as the port and bridge expansions after the North American Free Trade Agreement (NAFTA); or a mix of cultural, geographic, and border patrol boundaries that draw more interior lines in the sand. Some would argue that Zapata County should be included in the lower Rio Grande Valley with Willacy, Cameron, Hidalgo, and Starr because of Falcon Lake. Falcon Lake stretches more than 30 miles from just north of Roma in Starr County well into Zapata County. It is the last large body of water before the Rio Grande River flows into the Gulf of Mexico. Others would add Laredo, another 45-minute drive from Zapata, as part of the Rio Grande Valley because of its interconnected state and binational commerce and culture. In this book, I include the four southernmost counties, but my data collection was largely focused on Hidalgo and Cameron counties, the most populous of the four.

Most in the Valley would agree that Cameron, Willacy, Hidalgo and Starr counties are central to the environmental, cultural, and economic space that we call the Rio Grande Valley (see Map 3.1). The southern borders of Cameron, Hidalgo and Starr extend 100 miles up the Rio Grande River (Vigness & Odintz, 2010). Hidalgo and Cameron Counties are the most populous at 865,939 and 432,908 in 2018, respectively (U.S. Census Bureau, July 2019). In 2018, the most populous cities were McAllen (143,433 people), Edinburg (98,665) and Pharr (79,707) in Hidalgo County and Brownsville (183,392) and Harlingen (65,436) in Cameron County (U.S. Census Bureau, July 2019). McAllen, Edinburg, and Pharr have adjacent borders, constituting the McAllen-Edinburg-Pharr Metropolitan Statistical Area, while Brownsville and Harlingen are two constituents in the Brownsville-San Benito-Harlingen Metropolitan Statistical Area. The Valley Hispanic population percentage estimate in 2018 was 91% (U.S. Census Bureau, May 2019).

In this chapter, I detail primary considerations of perspective as I explain my approach to collecting and analyzing different kinds of border and Valley stories. Perspective influences any analysis of the Rio Grande Valley region. Valley folks are the first to be critical of our home, but we are also the first to defend it. Even so, there is not a single internal narrative about our region. How we analyze our region reflects our "subject positions": those identities that shape how we see and interact with the world. Common identities in the United States that we assign to people and ourselves are gender, ethnicity/race, sexual orientation, socioeconomic class, religious affiliation, nationality and citizenship, and age. For example, I am a heterosexual, non-Hispanic white woman born in the United States who grew up in an upper middle class family in Harlingen, Cameron County, Texas, in the 1970s and the 1980s. I went out of state for college and graduate school, returning to be a professor of Anthropology at The University of Texas at San Antonio. My suite of identities is relatively rare in the Valley and privileged. I experienced and still experience the Valley very differently than someone who regularly encounters poverty, racism, or exclusion based on citizenship status or ethnic identity. I also understand the Valley differently than my parents, who grew up in the region during the 1940s and 1950s. Although different identities and experiences mean people in the Valley have different ideas about the region, it is also fair to say that those of us from the Valley are quick to identify our common community when the Valley is criticized by people who have little to no experience living there.

The Border, the Valley, the Nation: Why Border Stories Matter

The U.S.–Mexico border in the 2010s emerged again in national news and political rhetoric as a kind of place where no one would really want to live. The U.S.–Mexico border was falling into the same trope as downtown Detroit after the recession of 2008, rural Pennsylvania after the steel mills closed, and Appalachia when the coal economy waned. There are national implications to the stories we tell about places like these. Living through the 2016 presidential election in the United States and Donald Trump's subsequent presidency made it easy to see how our national understanding of the U.S.–Mexico borderlands shapes our national politics, allocation of federal funding, immigration policy and treatment of asylum seekers and unauthorized immigrants, and even constitutional debates over presidential vetoes and declarations of national emergency. "The border" or, later, "the southern border" encapsulated political and social beliefs about people, places, and the United

States among Democrats and Republicans alike. American ideas about the U.S.–Mexico borderlands have been entangled with ideas about immigration, Mexico, and Mexican Americans for generations (Abrajano & Hajnal, 2015; Nevins, 2010 [2002]). Negative beliefs about immigration, especially if migrants are unauthorized and from Mexico, significantly influence political party affiliation and voting among white voters in the United States and predict state decreases in public funding for education, health and welfare when the Latino/a[1] population initially increases (Abrajano & Hajnal, 2015). American ideas about the border and immigration are pulled from many sources, but news media and politicians are primary (Abrajano & Hajnal, 2015; DeChaine, 2012; De Genova, 2012; Heyman, 2012b; Nevins, 2010 [2002]; Wilson & Hastings, 2012).

In the 2010s, the Rio Grande Valley became the nation's reference for "the border," much like San Diego did during Operation Gatekeeper in the 1990s under President Clinton (Nevins, 2010 [2002]). In part because of Operation Gatekeeper and historic migration pathways from Central America into the United States, the Valley saw a significant increase in border crossings in the mid-2010s. News outlets and politicians cited the Valley for immigration stories during the increase of Central American families crossing to claim asylum but also in reference to the political platform of Donald Trump. The Valley was the common example for a vicious legal battle over reproductive rights and abortion services that headed to the United States Supreme Court. It was also the region regularly referenced in stories about a multiyear Federal Bureau of Investigation corruption sting during the 2010s. Through each of these events, the Valley became the dominant border reference and representation for the United States during the decade.

Analyzing the national stories of the Rio Grande Valley provides a lens by which to ask questions of our nation about our southern borderlands. Why do we tell the stories we tell of the U.S.–Mexico borderlands? How much do they represent borderlands life? What do they assume and why?

---

[1]There are other terms, such as Latinx and Chicana/o/x. In the book, I use different terms at various points in order to reflect what terms are used by the texts I reference or by the leaders whose words I cite.

What do they miss and why? What are other stories that could be instructive for our nation? I answer these questions by using media analysis and ethnographic research methods. My hope is that we can learn to think more carefully and critically about the assumptions and generalizations we make about people and places and to listen to other possibilities.

How I Collected and Analyzed Stories

I documented the stories told about the Rio Grande Valley in the news and the contrasting stories told about the Rio Grande Valley by the people who live there and lead it. My goal was to put news and leaders' stories into conversation and to privilege Valley leaders' meanings of the Valley rather than news media and political rhetoric produced outside of the Valley. I conducted a news analysis of Valley stories in mainstream metropolitan news media in the Valley, the state, and nation. My anthropological methods for news analysis were systematic collection and analysis of themes and narrative construction of news stories about the Valley from 2010 through August 2017. The 2010–2017 date range includes several significant national news events that reference the Valley and corresponded with my ethnographic data collection period. My anthropological methods with the Valley leaders were rooted in ethnography, including participant observation, or the long-term immersion of the researcher in the target community; interviews; focus groups; and collection of cultural texts.

The National Story: Media Analysis of National News Stories About the Rio Grande Valley

To understand Valley representations in our national imagination, I systematically analyzed national news stories from January of 2010 to

August of 2017 that referenced the Rio Grande Valley.[2] I used this specific timeframe for several reasons. First, the timeframe encompassed the bulk of my participant observation and ethnography beginning early in 2015 through the summer of 2017. Second, the timeframe for the news stories included recent events in which the Valley figured predominantly: the passage of the Affordable Care Act in 2010; the passage of Texas House Bill 2 in 2013 that restricted abortion care and subsequent appeals of certain provisions to the United States Supreme Court through 2016; Drug Enforcement Administration (DEA) and Federal Bureau of Investigation (FBI) investigations in 2013 and 2015; and the dramatic increase of Central American families and unaccompanied children crossing into the United States at the Rio Grande Valley and claiming asylum, which began in 2010 and peaked in 2014. Stories, of course, have lasting effects; the ways in which we think about places are embedded in our past interactions with the place. For most in the United States, these national news stories constitute their only exposure to the Rio Grande Valley of Texas. These stories become the background by which most Americans contextualize messages about the region, such as those conveyed in the 2016 and 2020 presidential elections.

For the news analysis, I included major mainstream media outlets in national markets, including ABC, CBS, Fox, MSNBC, *The New York Times*, National Public Radio (NPR), *USA Today*, *The Wall Street Journal* and *The Washington Post*. Except for the *The Wall Street Journal*, I accessed each of these media outlets through Nexis Uni, an extensive academic database or its older interface, Academic Universe LexisNexis. The Nexis Uni database for the outlets often included multiple forms of media, such as print, online, and transcripts from television news shows (see Table 3.1). *The Wall Street Journal* was accessible behind a paywall and had its own search engine.

I searched for the verbatim phrase "Rio Grande Valley" and "Texas." I excluded obituaries, opinion-editorials, and sports pieces that were score or drafting reports. The search yielded 780 articles (see Table 3.2). I used qualitative content analysis (e.g., Honey, 2013; Lincoln, 2014; Udupa,

---

[2]An earlier analysis of a slightly different database informed my approach (Fleuriet & Castañeda, 2017). For that analysis, I am indebted to Dr. Heide Castañeda and several research assistants, including Mari Castellano, Itzel Corona, Milena Melo, and Ryan Logan.

Table 3.1 National news sources: Shows and editions

Media outlet	Media database name on Nexi Uni	Editions and shows
ABC	ABC News Transcripts	20/20
		Good Morning America
		Nightline
		Primetime Live
		This Week
		World News Sunday
CBS	CBS News Transcripts	48 Hours
		60 Minutes
		CBS Evening News
		CBS Morning News
		CBS News Sunday Morning
		Face the Nation
CNN	CNN Transcripts	CNN Anderson Cooper 360 Degrees
		CNN At This Hour
		CNN Cuomo Prime Time
		CNN Early Start
		CNN Erin Burnett Outfront
		CNN Inside Politics
		CNN International
		CNN Morning News
		CNN New Day
		CNN Newsroom
		CNN The Lead with Jake Tapper

Media outlet	Media database name on Nexi Uni	Editions and shows
		CNN The Situation Room
		CNN Wolf
		CNN Your Money
		HLN
Fox	*Fox News Network*	Beltway Boys
		Cavuto Business Report
		Fox Files
		Fox News Sunday
		Hannity & Colmes
		Special Report with Brit Hume
		The Crier Report
		The Drudge Report
		The O'Reilly Factor
MSNBC	MSNBC and MSNBC.com	11th Hour with Brian Williams
		Abrams Report
		All In with Chris Hayes
		Hardball
		Jerry Nachman
		MTP Daily
		NBCNews.com
		Phil Donahue
		Politics Nation
		Press Vs Buchanan

(continued)

Table 3.1 (continued)

Media outlet	Media database name on Nexi Uni	Editions and shows
		The Beat with Ari Melber
		The Last Word with Lawrence O'Donnell
		The Rachel Maddow Show
National Public Radio	National Public Radio: Transcript[a]	All Things Considered
		Morning Edition
		Talk of the Nation
		Weekend Edition
The Associated Press	The Associated Press	Print edition and online articles
The New York Times	The New York Times	Print edition and online articles
USA Today	USA Today	Print edition and online articles
The Wall Street Journal	(Direct search on website)	Print edition and online articles
The Washington Post	The Washington Post	Print edition and online articles

[a]Nexis Uni launched in 2018. With the help of research assistants, I had conducted a prior search and theme analysis on the older interface, Academic Universe Lexis Nexis. I independently repeated the search on Nexis Uni to find that all sources had greater yields on Nexis Uni, except National Public Radio (NPR). Therefore, the NPR results are from Academic Universe Lexis Nexis, and all other media results are from Nexis Uni (excluding the *The Wall Street Journal*)

Table 3.2 Article counts by source and year, N = 780

Source	2010	2011	2012	2013	2014	2015	2016	2017 through August	Total
ABC Transcripts	0	0	0	0	5	0	0	0	5
The Associated Press	10	12	11	19	86	20	22	24	204
CBS Transcripts	1	1	3	0	10	0	1	2	18
CNN Transcripts	3	3	0	0	25	2	5	10	48
Fox News Network	1	1	0	1	35	5	2	9	54
MSNBC and MSNBC.com	2	1	0	4	31	2	2	0	42
The New York Times	12	16	16	24	62	9	10	26	175
National Public Radio	0	3	6	4	19	11	4	16	63
USA Today	0	3	2	8	18	4	4	2	41
The Wall Street Journal	3	3	3	8	21	7	10	9	64
The Washington Post	4	2	1	4	30	7	12	6	66
Total	36	45	42	72	342	67	72	104	780

2012) with iterative coding (e.g., Luque, Bowers, Kabore, & Stewart, 2013) to identify story themes that repeated across news pieces. I coded each title and each article for all years and sources for repeated themes. I began with a priori topical themes, or concepts, that were principal in academic research on the borderlands as well as in my personal and professional experience in the Valley. If, as I read each article, a new theme appeared, I would include it in the theme list.

I followed the same analytical approach to understand the local story with data from interview transcripts and notes; participant observation fieldnotes; and cultural texts, such as local Valley reports, presentation transcripts and media, and magazines.

The Local Story: Interviews and Focus Groups

Valley leaders, whether activist, faith leader, or CEO, are simultaneously interested in talking about the topic of Valley representation and very tired of doing so. Most met with me initially because of personal and professional networks. Invariably, the conversation would begin with "how's your [mom/dad/brother] doing?" or we would talk about either our overlapping high school experiences or, in the case of older leaders, experiences I may have shared with their children. We would catch up on family before we headed into my interview topics. That is, we traced our Valley lineages. Leaders kept talking to me in large part because they are devoted to our region and were frustrated by the incomplete, negative external image of the Valley. Often, after I said I was interested in how they ran up against or countered dominant ideas of the Valley, I did not have to provide any further explanation. Leaders would launch into the most common misunderstandings they faced. For example, during high-level job recruitment conversations in business, health care, and education, job candidates or their spouses expressed fear that their children would be kidnapped off Valley streets by drug cartels or encounter drug-related shootings on a regular basis. While telling versions of this story, more often than not, Valley leaders would throw up their hands and roll their eyes.

I interviewed 91 Valley leaders and journalists and conducted four focus groups with 23 emerging leaders during 2015 through 2017 and a brief period again in 2019. I identified potential interview participants by first classifying influential sectors in community life: education, health care, economy/business, government and law enforcement, philanthropy, advocacy, journalism, and nonprofit social services. Then, I talked to community members and read the newspapers to identify a starting list of people in each sector recognized for their influence. Once I identified a potential participant, I would talk to friends about the leader's reputation in their specific sector, such as education, as a way to triangulate. Reputation in the Valley is a mix of both professional and personal behavior. As my network grew with each interviewee, I would also ask for recommendations for additional leaders from the interviewees themselves. I followed up with leaders who were recommended repeatedly as respected and influential in their sectors. I continued to interview until I reached and went past data saturation. That is, my data was complete when I was no longer getting new stories or themes within stories about the Valley. I reached data saturation around 80 interviews spread across the target sectors but continued to confirm. All but two interviews took place in the Valley. I met leaders at their workplaces, homes, restaurants, coffee shops, or for walks around the community. I continued the conversation for as long as the leader wanted, meeting with each leader between one and four times. Interviews lasted between one and six hours with an average duration of around two hours. Many informal conversations during social and community events like farmers' markets, fundraisers, or community award ceremonies or random encounters in places such as grocery stores, coffee shops, or restaurants complemented the formal interviews. Two additional meetings were in Austin to interview a state journalist and a Valley leader serving in a governor's administration.

My conversations with Valley leaders revolved around these topics: leaders' "Valley story," or how their families came to the Valley and their paths to leadership in their sectors; the external meanings of the Valley that they regularly encounter and their responses to them; an analysis of the strengths, weaknesses, and opportunities in their sector and in the region as a whole; their expectations for their sector in the future and their hopes for the Valley in the future; and analyses of common media themes in national stories about the Valley. Focus group topics revolved around group discussions on similar topics.

Valley leaders included current and former mayors; current and former elected state and national officials; current and former appointed city, county and state officials; current chiefs of police and their high ranking officers; current CEOs and Executive Directors of hospitals and community health care centers as well as doctors and county health directors; current executive management in philanthropic granting, community organizations and nonprofit social services; community activists in housing, health care, immigration, and education; business women and men currently involved in economic development boards, Valley-wide mentoring and workforce initiatives, and chambers of commerce; community college, college, and university senior administrators and professors, preK-12 school board members and superintendents; religious leaders and their teams; and current Valley and state-level publishers, editors and journalists in largely mainstream news media production.

Valley leaders varied in their history with the region. Some could trace their families' regional roots back hundreds of years to original Mexican city founders, Spanish land grants, or ranch workers on those land grants. Others' families arrived after the Treaty of Guadalupe Hidalgo of 1848, whether from Mexico or the interior United States, but before the citrus, sugarcane, and cotton industries were established in the late 1800s and early 1900s. Some came as a direct result of marketing in the Midwest to non-Hispanic white farmers for agricultural industries developing in the 1910s and 1920s. Others grew up as migrating farm workers and settled as adults in the Valley. Many who grew up in the Valley left for college and returned for family and job opportunities. Some leaders came to the Valley as adults, accompanying spouses or parents or coming for business opportunities for themselves; these leaders were more likely in higher education with a few notable exceptions in law enforcement, business, and politics.

Leadership in the 2010s in the Valley was more likely to be older, male, and non-Hispanic white (Table 3.3). Among the 91 people I interviewed, the average age was fifty-five, 64% (58) were male, and 53% (46) were non-Hispanic white. Leaders' highest educational attainment

Table 3.3 Demographics of participants, $N = 114$

	Established leaders (91)	Emerging leaders (23)
Average age	55 years	35 years
Age range	30–82 years	24–42 years
Gender	33 (36%) women	13 (57%) women
	58 (64%) men	10 (43%) men
Self-identified ethnicity[a]	35 (40%) Hispanic	11 (49%) Hispanic
	46 (53%) Non-Hispanic White	9 (39%) Non-Hispanic White
	6 (7%) Other	2 (9%) Other
Education[a]	5 (6%) High school, some college, or associate's degree	4 (17%) High school or associate's degree
	25 (29%) Bachelor's	10 (44%) Bachelor's
	22 (25%) Master's	5 (6%) Master's
	30 (35%) M.D., Ph.D., J.D.	2 (2%) J.D.
Originally from the Valley	49 (54%)	13 (65%)

[a]sums may not equal total or 100% due to missing data

varied from 29% (25) with a Bachelor's degree, 25% (22) with a Master's degree, and 35% with a terminal graduate degree (Ph.D., M.D., and J.D.). Forty-nine (54%) leaders were originally from the Valley, colloquially referred to as "Valley natives." Valley counties are between 85 and 95% Hispanic. While the leadership is still disproportionately non-Hispanic white, it is a dramatic change from the 1970s. Through the 1970s, public leadership in each sector, except nonprofit social services and religious life, was almost uniformly non-Hispanic white. As a result, today's leaders see ethnic representation as moving in the right direction. They focused more frequently on age and gender as key issues to address in representative leadership. As a result, I wanted to understand how younger, emerging leaders might see the Valley. I worked with a Hispanic female leader recognized across the Valley in higher education, in order to organize a focus group of five increasingly influential people across the Valley. I worked with a non-Hispanic white female leader in business development and arts and culture to arrange two more focus groups of emerging leaders from across the Valley. Finally, we conducted a fourth focus group with Harlingen-specific emerging leaders to see if meanings of the Valley changed when we talked with leaders from one city. Focus group participants had an average age of 35; 57% (13) were women, and 49% (11) were Hispanic. Their highest formal educational attainment varied from 44% (10) with a Bachelor's degree, 6% (5) with a Master's degree, and 2% (2) with a terminal degree (J.D.). Thirteen (65%) focus group participants were originally from the Valley.

The Local Story: Participant Observation

In addition to interviews and focus groups, I conducted participant observation to understand daily life as a Valley leader. Participant observation is a method in Anthropology and related disciplines whereby the anthropologist lives as much as possible as a member of the community of interest, in order to try to understand the community as an insider might. I lived with my parents each time I went to the Valley. Between 2015 and 2017, I drove the eight-hour round trip to the Valley 22 times to interview leaders and journalists and participate in Valley life. Each trip lasted between two and ten days. My elementary-then-middle school-aged daughter went with me to the Valley on some weekends, and my husband and daughter went with me during Spring Break, Thanksgiving, and winter holiday breaks. I easily fell back into the rhythms and connections of home: walks with my dog around the neighborhood or along the *resaca* (a particular kind of channel for water overflow, storage, and irrigation that dots the Cameron County landscape); coffee and meals with friends and family; visits with my bed-ridden grandmother; Saturdays at farmers' markets and in revitalized downtown market days; attendance at fund-raising events, annual events, award dinners, and major personal events such as graduations and funerals; and outings to the beach, birding centers, and wildlife refuges. I also caught up with friends at various formal events, such as my 25-year high school reunion, and a weekend where a high school friend and I drove from the Gulf of Mexico to Laredo, stopping at places recommended by participants as a way to understand the region today. In the summer of 2017, I spent an additional two weeks co-leading an anthropological field school with UTSA students about health and the environment in the Valley. Each Christmas season, I ate fresh tamales made by family friends, bought fireworks for New Year's at Mr. G.'s, headed out to hunting camps to visit with family, caught up with old friends when I ran into them at the grocery, Starbuck's, or restaurants, visited museums and the outlet malls for after-Christmas sales, and bought bags of citrus from Diana's Nursery & Patio, our ritual family stop in Lyford on our drive back to San Antonio.

In essence, participant observation for this project was an extension and expansion of what I already do in the Valley but with an added emphasis on spending time in and around leaders' common locations, events, and conversations. I also attended two public meetings in McAllen and Edinburg with politicians and other Valley leaders facilitated by journalists from the *Texas Tribune*, or "Trib," a highly respected Austin-based news outlet that focuses on state economics and politics. The Trib's events were part of a larger series of journalist-facilitated roundtables all over the state, culminating in the annual Texas Tribune Festival at The University of Texas at Austin campus. The Trib Festival hosts similar roundtables with Democratic and Republican elected and appointed officials and nonprofit leaders. I attended the Trib Festival in 2016, sticking close to the panels on border issues. One border security panel consisted of Valley politicians and law enforcement representatives, and another on higher education featured the new president of The University of Texas Rio Grande Valley. Each Trib event was a chance to see how mainstream journalists, state politicians, and other people of state-level influence, as well as Valley leaders, talk publicly with each other about the idea of the Valley and the border.

The Local Story: Collection of Cultural Texts

From 2015 through 2019, I also gathered a diverse, large quantity of cultural texts that were used as promotional or report materials about the Valley by Valley leaders or their organizations, targeted to larger audiences, such as state legislators, The University of Texas System, tourists, and potential businesses. These included regional economic analyses and forecasts as well as reports and policy statements by The

University of Texas Rio Grande Valley, school districts, health care facilities, philanthropy organizations, chambers of commerce and economic development corporations, and nonprofit activist and social justice organizations. I gathered print and virtual materials from offices of the state demographer, comptroller, and workforce commissions as well as from state and national elected officials and presidential candidates that portrayed the Valley region. Other texts included educational materials about the Valley from local and regional museums, nature centers, and parks; regional publications such as *RGVLead* that connects employers and educators; and promotional materials from tourism offices. On social media, I followed local and state news media, Valley organizations and groups, and friends and family from the region. As the Rio Grande Valley reemerged as the primary focal point and illustration in national and political discussions about "the border" in the fall of 2017, I kept an additional repository of news stories on the Rio Grande Valley that I encountered through print, radio, social media, and television outlets. My interest in cultural texts was twofold. I wanted to learn as much as I could about the current Valley, and I wanted to understand how different constituencies in the region portrayed the Valley. These texts constitute another source of data in my analysis.

I conducted an additional, brief period of official data collection when the Valley and the border exploded back onto the national scene during the 2018–2019 government shutdown and the 2019 National Emergency declaration. I participated in "RGV Day at the Capitol" in Austin in February 2019 with hundreds of Valley leaders. Arranged by the Valleywide RGV Partnership, leaders from economic, education, health, political, activist, and other sectors rode buses to Austin to spend a day formally lobbying for the Valley with legislators from across the state. The lobbying was focused on promoting the region, often by debordering with examples of our centrality to the state's economy and novel, successful interventions in population health and education that could benefit the state and nation. During RGV Day at the Capitol, I had the opportunity to catch up with leaders I had interviewed as well as meet and talk with new ones. I observed how we crafted our messages to individual legislators from different parts of Texas and how they responded. After RGV Day, it was time to finish writing, and I

knew how the book would end. I would emphasize not only the importance of understanding the Rio Grande Valley on its own terms but also
the importance of understanding how rapidly our southern borderlands
change and develop. To assume the U.S.–Mexico border can be captured
from faraway in a single moment of time in a single place is folly.

Doing Anthropology at Home, Studying up, and Reflexivity

My participant observation was relatively easy. This is unusual but
understandable. Most anthropologists spend significant amounts of time
establishing rapport and gaining entrée into a community. Leaders in
particular are often too busy and too leery of outsiders to give them any
real access. However, I am not an outsider. In addition to growing up
in the Valley, I am "fourth generation Valley," which means the first
generation of my family to live in the Valley were all four sets of my
great-grandparents. That matters in establishing rapport, especially in
a community used to "parachuting researchers or philanthropists" that
descend with pre-identified problems to fix with pre-identified solutions. Three generations of Piles and Fleuriets (my father's family) and
Haires and MacPhersons (my mother's family) before me have been
committed to raising families and working in our community. My grandfather MacPherson began his pharmacy in our hometown of Harlingen
in the early 1930s. As a white man hailing from the Midwest and Canada
in the first half of the twentieth century, he did not at first understand
the heavy racism toward Hispanic people that permeated business in the
Valley. He charged Hispanic community members and visiting African
American railroad workers the same price for medicine as he charged
non-Hispanic whites. According to him, he was just following standard
business practice as he knew it. His business flourished without initial
recognition as to why. He later provided office space free of charge to
both a new community health center for people without insurance and
Planned Parenthood at a time when both were considered even more
controversial than today. My mother was one of his three daughters and
the only one still in the Valley.

My mother has been deeply involved in leadership in community service and public education, emergency medical services, arts and culture, and family services since the mid-1970s. She was part of the teams that brought the first emergency mobile intensive care services serving a coalition of communities in Cameron County and developed the first cultural arts celebration of artists and musician in our town. For decades, she has served on multiple community boards, including the Girl Scouts of Greater South Texas and Family Emergency Assistance. She quietly fought for desegregating the Junior League, a women's service organization, and Cotillion, a Southern tradition of grooming and presenting high school-aged girls and boys. She is now in her mid-70s and has been an elected member of the Harlingen Independent School District School Board for over 20 years. My father was a lawyer who conducted pro bono work in civil law on the weekends and for community organizations, such as the first women's health center. Long before Title IX, he started a citywide softball league for girls in elementary through high school that continues today. He put the Valley on the radar of elite private colleges decades ago, executing the first reception for college representatives from Duke, Rice, Stanford, and each of the Ivy League schools, to gather and talk to top Valley students. My brother was a state representative in the Texas Legislature in the early 1990s. My family, then, has consisted of involved community leaders for some time. Their networks were essential to my success in data collection with Valley leaders.

I have been returning to the Valley to work as an anthropologist with community health centers since 1996. I grew up in Harlingen with one set of grandparents two blocks to the east and the other set of grandparents two blocks to the west. In 1990, I graduated from Harlingen High School and left for Harvard College in Cambridge, Massachusetts. I could not have felt more out of place on Harvard's campus. In large part, I did not know the ways of talking, moving, and acting in elite, urban spaces of the northeastern United States. I received many comments about how "different" I was: my accent, my home, my background. That was the first time I remembering thinking of the Valley as something "other than" the rest of the United States. Decades later, I would read *Belonging* by bell hooks (2008). An African American woman from the rural South, hooks left for Stanford for college and then work in New York City. She writes about how other Americans thought of the rural South as something backward, odd, and negative. Her words clicked with my experience despite our very different subject positions. In college and graduate school, I struggled to reconcile my childhood with my new peers' ideas and academic research about the U.S.–Mexico borderlands, especially south Texas. Their perception carried the weight of social or intellectual status but seemed limited and the place they described, diminished.

The idea of the Valley as a distinct cultural space simmered throughout my undergraduate years, but my academic pursuits were in biological anthropology, not cultural anthropology. During my time as a Master's student at San Diego State University, my mentor, Dr. Bohdan Kolody, introduced me to the academic study of health and health care inequalities that plague border areas—and he taught me how to think about those inequalities critically across local, state, national, and international scales. He encouraged me to return to the Valley to better understand and explore those inequalities. That return to the Valley as a cultural anthropology graduate student in 1996 coincided with my awareness of the strength, power, and innovation of Valley leaders. I realized my college-born idea of the Valley as "exotic" or "other" was flatly inaccurate, reflecting my privilege, location, and peers at the time.

My first research project in cultural anthropology in the Rio Grande Valley grew out of family networks, too. My father introduced me to Dr. Elena Marin, a pediatrician and leader in community health care in the Valley. With Dr. Marin, I began to really see and understand the leadership and excellence in the Valley. Dr. Marin is the executive director of Su Clinica Familiar, the women's and family health clinic with whom my father worked and for which my grandfather provided office space in its infancy. Dr. Marin helped grow Su Clinica into an award-winning, nationally recognized primary community health center serving Cameron and Willacy counties. Dr. Marin not only encouraged me to pursue my research on reproductive health outcomes with the Su Clinica community but also led me to Sister Angela Murdaugh. Sister Angela, a member of Texas Women's Hall of Fame, is known throughout the Valley as the woman who helped cut the maternal mortality rate in half in

Hidalgo County. Trained as a certified nurse midwife, Sister Angela built an alternative birthing center in Weslaco, Texas, in 1972. Holy Family Birth Center used one of the earliest forms of health care that incorporated the woman and her family directly into care. She introduced payment-in-kind and sliding scale structures so the poorest and uninsured women had access to high-quality prenatal care. Her staff went to women's homes to drive them to appointments and, after birth, to have appointments in their homes. Midwives came from all over the country to train under Sister Angela, one of the mothers of American midwifery.

After my first research project on reproductive health in 1996, I went on to earn my doctorate in Anthropology studying borderlands health care inequalities in northern Baja California, Mexico. In 2003, I received my Ph.D. from Stanford University and accepted a position as an Anthropology professor at The University of Texas at San Antonio (UTSA). San Antonio is at the northern tip of south Texas, a short four hour drive to Harlingen. I often tell people that San Antonio was as close as I could get to home at the time with the kind of job I wanted, which was being a professor at a public university with an explicit commitment to the south Texas region. My primary research began again in the Valley. I have made the San Antonio to Harlingen drive countless times for work and family. I have met and worked with many Valley leaders, and I realize now that I have been surrounded by Valley leaders throughout my life.

Valley leaders come from different ethnic identities and economic backgrounds as well as different forms of community engagement, from activism to traditional economic development activities. Some are "Valley natives." Others are not. Some were born into wealth, others, poverty. They have lived through different shades of classism and racism in different parts of the Valley, both urban and rural. As a group, they have fought long and hard against these and other forms of inequalities in the Valley. They have advocated for a voice in state and national political discourses that affect our region. Their political persuasions are more likely to be socially conservative and fiscally liberal, but by no means does this represent everyone. They are local, state, and national leaders in education, health care, finance and economic development, politics, law enforcement, philanthropy, nonprofit social services, and activism. Despite working with such leaders every time I conducted a new research project through 2014, I did not conduct research about them. I was more interested at first in the production of inequality and difference in the Valley, not the fight against assumptions in public and political spheres that shaped that inequality and difference.

In 2014, more and more stories about the Valley as "the border" appeared in national news. The stories seemed to be only about corruption, human and drug smuggling, and poverty. Meanings of "the border" and "the Rio Grande Valley," when it popped up in national news, were almost uniformly negative. The news rarely, if ever, treated the Valley as a complex place with a cadre of leaders in diverse sectors with diverse viewpoints that worked toward solving problems with creative, novel approaches. The omission of these stories in national news reproduced the worn-out trope of the Valley and border (excepting San Diego) as backwater outposts or forgotten places. I started to imagine a project that did not whitewash the problems of the Valley as a region but also told of the successes, novel approaches, and sense of home that permeate the lives of people in the Valley.

In some ways, my research in the place where I grew up can be classified as "native anthropology," and my work with Valley leaders can be considered "studying up." I am uncomfortable with both of these terms, and my discomfort is an important consideration for my data analysis in this book. The concept of native ethnography[3] came about at a time when my academic discipline of anthropology was struggling with its identity. As an academic discipline, we are largely a product of colonialism, Western state efforts and early American initiatives to study communities that the nation encountered through expansionism and imperialism. Early on, our job was to document the assumed-to-be-very-different cultural practices of "others" in places we perceived as distant. As our discipline matured, we started to question our role and colonial legacies in our methods, theories, and writing. We realized how our work was predicated on studying that which we automatically defined as different and how our work had an inherent bias toward our own norms and values. We justly criticized ourselves for trying to speak for other

---

[3]Narayan (1993) provides a good early review of the development and complexities of the concept.

people in terms and concepts that fit our own culture. Native ethnography arose as a possible intervention and reflexivity as another. A third was to study our own culture with the same tools and questions and among those with more social, political, economic power, i.e., so-called "studying up" first coined in the early 1970s (Nader, 1972).

Native anthropology is a relatively straightforward concept. Someone from the community becomes an anthropologist who then studies within their own community. The idea was that native anthropologists would diversify the discipline by providing new ways of thinking through anthropological questions, methods, and theories. Reflexivity is a regular dialogic process during fieldwork where you ask yourself repeatedly what you know, how you know it, what gets included in your data and analysis and what does not, in order to identify bias. For example, in my work, who exactly is a leader? Of those, to whom did I have access and to whom did I not? How do their positions as leaders affect the responses they gave me? How does my Valley, demographic, or academic background (or all three) impact how leaders talked to me? Studying up is where anthropologists work with people who make decisions that influence communities, such as Wall Street investment bankers (Ho, 2009), decision-makers in mining companies (Duarte, 2010), or a Japanese advertising agency (Moeran, 1996).

Here is why these terms are important, if not entirely accurate, to my work in the Rio Grande Valley and borderlands. Native anthropology is a concept that helps recognize that I have different access to Valley leaders because of my personal and professional backgrounds in the region than would an anthropologist coming in from another part of the country or world. This is true. The reason I could do this project was because of my social capital through my family, friends, and my work in the Valley. Out of about 125 invitations to participate in the project, I had only about 10 leaders not respond; no one said "no" outright. Most definitely, my insider status was the cause of such a high participation rate of very busy people, not all of whom are that interested in anthropology. But, "native" also suggests I can represent more of the Valley than I can. There is no way my status as someone from the Valley who works in the Valley lets me personally represent anyone other than myself. Given how long the region was inhabited first by indigenous groups and then by Mexicans, I would not claim "native," either.

A better term for what I do is "anthropology at home" (Nordquest, 2007; Peirano, 1998). In particular, anthropologists whose home is the United States must be as attuned to questions of who produces knowledge and ideas about what is right and wrong and who is "in" and "out" as much as if we were working in some foreign locale (Maskovsky, 2009). Other anthropologists and sociologists from the U.S.–Mexico borderlands have also focused their careers on research in their home regions, and many others began working in the borderlands when their jobs as professors took them there. The latter have lived and worked so long in the borderlands region that they, too, in many cases are doing anthropology at home. Most applicable to my arguments in this book are those anthropologists who have analyzed how and why certain social relationships form, persist, or change in the U.S.–Mexico borderlands, such as citizenship, class, ethnic and gender identities, and the way those influence well-being. Principal among such works are Chad Richardson's Borderlife Project in the Valley; the corpus of research on inequality and social justice in the El Paso-Ciudad Juarez area by Josiah Heyman; and the many collaborations Richardson and Heyman have had with other social scientists.[4]

Josiah Heyman, in particular, has investigated how borderlands communities have certain flows of power, or degrees of influence, and issues of power in deciding norms, values, and national stories implicated in the phrase "studying up." As a term, "studying up" on the surface can imply that Valley leaders are always in positions of power, but to whom? For what purpose? They are a diverse group of decision-makers with varying degrees of sway, depending on the context. On the one hand, I selected people to ask to participate in my project because they were recognized as people of influence in their given community, whether

---

[4]Each of these researchers has extensive publications. Here are a few citations for Heyman (2010, 2012a, 2012b, 2012c; Heyman, Slack, & Guerra, 2018; Vélez-Ibañez & Heyman, 2017) and Richardson (1999; Richardson & Pisani, 2012, 2017; Richardson & Resendiz, 2006). There are other citations throughout the book, but I would also encourage readers to locate Heyman and Richardson's professional webpages for full references.

small town, regional, state or national, and their sector, whether education, business, health care, law enforcement, philanthropy, nonprofit social services, advocacy, or journalism. In some situations, these people do have more power. Certainly, and why I chose them, they are the Valley community members most regularly encountering and debunking border myths. Their positions in the community and their sectors, as I note throughout the book, shape how they tell a different Valley and border story. However, one's ability to influence another—their degree of power, rests largely in the relationship and the context. A city mayor has significant influence over certain civic aspects of life in her town, but unless it is a major urban hub, it is unlikely she has much power as an individual at the state level, even less at the national level.

Another way that anthropologists have talked about "studying up" is studying "elites."[5] By elites, we refer to the highest levels of status in a given community. Again, this applies to many but not all of the Valley leaders with whom I worked, and it does not take into consideration the relationships of status they have with one another and different situations that alter that relationship. A city council seat can be an important position in deciding civic matters, but rarely if the council person is newly elected or in opposition to the mayor without majority backing. I spoke with many who would definitely not define themselves as elites, but they have a voice with state and national audiences. These include activists and religious leaders who help asylum seekers and other immigrants, work with residents of *colonias*,[6] or are involved in other social justice movements that map onto national news topics. But, I also talked with elected and appointed officials in some of the state and nation's highest offices, CEOs of corporations, and journalists and editors of highly respected media outlets in the state. To most, including me, they would classify as elites, albeit with often competing political agendas. This discussion of elites and studying up highlights a point I will repeat throughout the book when I discuss the leaders: I spoke with people who

---

[5]For examples and methodological considerations on studying up with elites, see D'Alisera (1999), Ortner (2010), Heyman (2010), Souleles (2018), Gusterson (1997, 2017), and Harvey (2011).

[6]*Colonias* are unincorporated, low-income neighborhoods that historically have lacked basic infrastructure and social services.

are pro-Valley and pro-borderlands. That perspective shapes the kind of data I gathered and the analyses that resulted. For the purposes of this book, leaders, in particular, are the group of borderlanders that intentionally engage in place-making with specific, positive narratives to challenge dominant ideas about the border that are common to state and national border rhetorics. A place's identity comes into being because of its role relative to other places (Gupta & Ferguson, 1992), and leaders claim the Valley and borderlands are central, not peripheral, to the United States. Rarely studied by borderlands anthropologists,[7] leaders can be a key node in the articulation of what the border means at local, state, and national levels.

Stories Within Stories: Friday Night Lights

Over the last 20 years I've come to realize that Brownsville can't resolve its problems by itself .... McAllen can't .... Harlingen can't .... We have a lot of resources between us. We should be working together, we are one people. When one part of the Valley hurts, we all hurt.—Valley health leader

Leaders in the Rio Grande Valley significantly vary in their allegiances to Valley locales. In the Valley, your town's identity often influences your positionality. One of the truisms in Valley life is the distinct personalities and politics of Valley cities. There is sometimes fierce competition between cities and towns, which leads to the Valley's characterization of itself as having a "Friday Night Lights" mentality. Friday Night Lights refers to Friday evenings in Texas where high school football games are played outside under bright stadium lights, when what matters is your team's identity and victory above all else. Football has its own famous resonance in Texas, and it is certainly popular in the Valley. The metaphor also conveys the not infrequent and rather intense political competition over resources, such as those attached to the new University

---

[7]As mentioned earlier, the notable exception is the work by anthropologist Josiah Heyman in the El Paso-Ciudad Juarez region.

of Texas Rio Grande Valley or to transportation funds to build bridges to facilitate international commerce, and reputations, such as whose city is the most economically or socially progressive in the Valley. At the same time, leaders recognize the importance of a unified Valley as a political and economic force that could help the region.

A Friday Night Lights mentality has led to stereotypes *within* the Valley about Valley cities. People in Valley cities sometimes see more difference than similarity among them. We are not a homogenous region, even if we need to act like one sometimes in order to help our communities. The most common stereotypes in the Valley about cities refer to the three historically largest cities: McAllen, Harlingen, and Brownsville. Outside of McAllen, McAllen is "greedy" and "power-hungry." Outside of Harlingen, Harlingen is "racist" and "white and Republican." Outside of Brownsville, Brownsville is "disorganized" and "dirty." Intended as insults, the terms are not so much about accuracy as they are the legacy of drawing boundaries for resources. It is perhaps telling that Harlingen is no longer the third largest city, surpassed by Pharr, but Pharr, adjacent to McAllen, does not have a tidy stereotype that reinforces a difference from other cities.

Every established leader with whom I spoke agreed it was time to get past the Friday Night Lights mentality, even if a difficult task. Although emerging, younger leaders knew of the old insults, most saw the Valley more as one continuous urban space between Brownsville and McAllen/Edinburg, rather than distinct and bounded cities. Indeed, if one flies into any of the three airports (Brownsville, Harlingen, or McAllen) on a clear winter's night, the urban sprawl of lights spanning fifty miles could be taken for any metropolitan area in the United States with 1.4 million people, only lacking a core of glittering skyscrapers. In my work, I made every effort to talk with leaders and journalists across the Valley, from South Padre Island to Peñitas west of McAllen. In part, this was because I had spent enough time inside and outside the Valley to know that (a) people outside the Valley thought of it as one undifferentiated region, and (b) inside the Valley, there are many different experiences and perspectives, often based on where one lives. I wanted to include both shared and divergent meanings of the Valley. While my personal network is centered in Harlingen because of family, my professional networks are across the Valley, as were the leaders with whom I spoke. The majority were concentrated in Cameron County and Hidalgo County, corresponding to the urban centers of the region. I talked to leaders currently living in South Padre Island, Port Isabel, Los Fresnos, Brownsville, San Benito, Harlingen, Weslaco, San Juan, Pharr, Edinburg, McAllen, and Peñitas. Some of these leaders grew up and/or worked in other parts of the Valley, including Los Indios, Donna, Alamo, and Mission. Valley leaders today move between cities and counties with ease, and they were as likely to recommend a colleague to interview who lived in another city or county as in their own.

Conclusion

Positionality, or where one is categorized in society, shapes how we understand a place. While we will hear from leaders whose childhoods were spent in dire poverty, no leader I spoke with today lives with that level of poverty. Similarly, while I spoke with leaders born in Mexico and brought to the United States by their parents, with or without legal documentation, they all have legal documentation to be in the country now. I spoke with people who have chosen not only to make the Valley their home but to make it better. I did not speak with people with little to no choice as to where they live and what jobs are available to them or people who did not want to be in the Valley.

I want to tell a story about the U.S.–Mexico border, but there is not one story to tell. There are as many stories to tell about the borderlands as there are people, cities and towns, local and international businesses, and local political histories all along the geopolitical borderline from Brownsville, Texas, to San Diego, California. Even still, there is no more a single story about the Rio Grande Valley any more than there is one story about New York City. Instead, the story I tell in this book is about the clash of U.S.–Mexico border representations between mainstream national news media and one set of border leaders at one point in time. In the next two chapters, I turn to the national stories about the Rio Grande Valley, glossed as "the border," in the 2010s.

Works Cited

Abrajano, M., & Hajnal, Z. L. (2015). *White backlash: Immigration, race and politics*. Princeton: Princeton University Press.

Bowman, T. P. (2016). *Blood oranges: Colonialism and agriculture in the south Texas borderlands*. College Station, TX: Texas A&M University Press.

D'Alisera, J. (1999). Field of dreams: The anthropologist far away at home. *Anthropology and Humanism, 24*(1), 5–19.

De Genova, N. (2012). Border, scene and obscene. In T. M. Wilson & H. Donnan (Eds.), *A companion to border studies* (pp. 492–504). Oxford: Wiley.

DeChaine, D. R. (Ed.). (2012). *Border rhetorics: Citizenship and identity on the U.S.-Mexico border*. Tuscaloosa, AL: University of Alabama Press.

Duarte, F. (2010). What does a culture of corporate social responsibility "look" like? A glimpse into a Brazilian mining company. *International Journal of Business Anthropology, 2*(1), 106–122.

Fleuriet, K. J., & Castañeda, H. (2017). A risky place? Media and the health landscape in the (in)secure U.S.-Mexico borderlands. *North American Dialogue, 20*(2), 32–46.

Gupta, A., & Ferguson, J. (1992). Beyond "culture": Space, identity, and the politics of difference. *Cultural Anthropology, 7*(1), 1–23.

Gusterson, H. (1997). Studying up revisited. *PoLAR: Political and Legal Anthropology Review, 20*(1), 114–119.

Gusterson, H. (2017). From Brexit to Trump: Anthropology and the rise of nationalist populism. *American Ethnologist, 44*(2), 1–6.

Harvey, W. (2011). Strategies for conducting elite interviews. *Qualitative Research, 11*(4), 431–441.

Heyman, J. (2010). US-Mexico border cultures and the challenge of asymmetrical interpenetration. In H. Donnan & T. Wilson (Eds.), *US-Mexico border cultures and the challenge of asymmetrical interpenetration* (pp. 21–34). Lanham, MD: University Press of America.

Heyman, J. (2012a). A voice of the US southwestern border: The 2012 "we the border: Envisioning a narrative for our future" conference. *Journal of Migration and Human Security, 1*(2), 60–75.

Heyman, J. M. (2012b). Constructing a "perfect" wall: Race, class, and citizenship in US-Mexico border policing. In P. Barber & W. Lem (Eds.), *Migration in the 21st century: Political economy and ethnography* (pp. 153–174). New York and London: Routledge.

Heyman, J. M. (2012c). Culture theory and the U.S.-Mexico border. In T. M. Wilson & H. Donnan (Eds.), *A companion to border studies* (pp. 48–65). Oxford: Wiley.

Heyman, J., Slack, J., & Guerra, E. (2018, Winter). Bordering a "crisis": Central American asylum seekers and the reproduction of dominant border enforcement practices. *Journal of the Southwest, 60*(4), 754–786.

Ho, K. (2009). *Liquidated*. Durham, NC: Duke University Press.

Honey, L. (2013). Media, ideology, and myths of East-West difference: Constructing American ideals through images of a "Red-Hot" Russian Spy. *North American Dialogue, 16*(1), 12–28.

hooks, b. (2008). *Belonging: A culture of place*. New York, NY: Routledge.

Lincoln, M. (2014). Tainted commons, public health: The politico-moral significance of cholera in Vietnam. *Medical Anthropology Quarterly, 28*(3), 342–362.

Luque, J., Bowers, A., Kabore, A., & Stewart, R. (2013). Who will pick Georgia's Vidalia onions? A text-driven content analysis of newspaper coverage on Georgia's 2011 immigration law. *Human Organization, 72*(10), 31–43.

Maskovsky, J. (2009). Some new directions in anthropology "at home". *North American Dialogue, 12*(1), 6–9.

Moeran, B. (1996). *A Japanese advertising agency: An anthropology of media and markets*. Honolulu, HI: University of Hawaii Press.

Nader, L. (1972). *Up the anthropology: Perspectives gained from studying up*. Washington, DC: U.S. Department of Health Education & Welfare Office of Education. Retrieved from https://files.eric.ed.gov/fulltext/ED065375.pdf.

Nájera, J. R. (2015). *The borderlands of race: Mexican segregation in a South Texas town*. Austin, TX: University of Texas Press.

Narayan, K. (1993). How native is a native anthropologist? *American Anthropologist, 95*(3), 671–686.

Nevins, J. (2010 [2002]). *Operation gatekeeper and beyond: The war on "illegals" and the remaking of the U.S.-Mexico boundary*. New York: Routledge.

Nordquest, M. (2007). Of hats and switches: Doing fieldwork at home. *North American Dialogue, 10*(1), 18–20.

Ortner, S. (2010). Access: Reflections on studying up in Hollywood. *Ethnography, 11*(2), 211–233.

Peirano, M. G. (1998). When anthropology is at home: The different contexts of a single discipline. *Annual Review of Anthropology, 27,* 105–128.

Pletcher, D. M. (2010, June 15). *Treaty of Guadalupe Hidalgo*. Retrieved January 7, 2020, from Texas State Historical Commission: https://tshaonline.org/handbook/online/articles/nbt01.

Richardson, C. (1999). *Batos, bolillos, pochos and pelados: Class and culture on the south Texas border*. Austin: The University of Texas Press.

Richardson, C., & Pisani, M. (2012). *The informal and underground economy of the south Texas border*. Austin, TX: University of Texas Press.

Richardson, C., & Pisani, M. J. (2017). *Batos, bolillos, pochos, and Pelados: class and culture on the south Texas border. Revised Edition*. Austin, TX: The University of Texas Press.

Richardson, C., & Resendiz, R. (2006). *On the edge of the law: Culture, labor and deviance on the south Texas border*. Austin, TX: The University of Texas Press.

Souleles, D. (2018). How to study people who do not want to be studied: Practical reflections on studying up. *PoLAR: Political and Legal Anthropology Review, 41*(S1), 51–68.

Udupa, S. (2012). News media and contention over "the local" in urban India. *American Ethnologist, 39*(4), 819–834.

U.S. Census Bureau. (2019, May). *Annual estimates of the resident population for incorporated places of 50,000 or more*. Retrieved January 7, 2020, from United States Census Bureau: https://factfinder.census.gov/faces/tables ervices/jsf/pages/productview.xhtml?src=bkmk.

U.S. Census Bureau. (2019, July 1). *Quick facts: Starr County, Texas; Willacy County, Texas; Hidalgo County, Texas; Cameron County, Texas*. Retrieved January 7, 2020, from United States Census Bureau: https://www.census.gov/quickfacts/fact/table/starrcountytexas,willacycountytexas,hidalgocount ytexas,cameroncountytexas/PST045219.

Vélez-Ibañez, C. G., & Heyman, J. (2017). *The U.S.-Mexico transborder region: Cultural dynamics and historical interactions*. Tucson: University of Arizona Press.

Vigness, D. M., & Odintz, M. (2010, June 15). *Rio Grande Valley*. Retrieved January 7, 2020, from Texas State Historical Commission: https://tshaonline.org/handbook/online/articles/ryr01.

Wilson, T. M., & Hastings, D. (Eds.). (2012). *A companion to border studies*. Oxford: Wiley.

4

The Valley as the Border, the Border as a Dangerous, Faraway Place

By definition, borders separate. As lines on a map, they can separate nations, states, counties, school districts, or neighborhoods. Enforcement of borders can be through physical barriers and military presence, language, national laws requiring presentation of citizenship documents, state laws about record-keeping of births and deaths, maps of tax districts and collection of taxes, or a thousand other ways to demarcate difference. Borders are also social beliefs, behaviors, and actions that create and maintain social lines between people, places, and things. Beliefs about difference can become so cemented in our national imagination that they escape scrutiny. The following excerpts are from MSNBC and Fox News, two news sources that often stand in political opposition to one another. Yet, note the similar assumptions they make about the Rio Grande Valley as a place of negativity.

Transcript from MSNBC, The Rachel Maddow Show, February 28, 2014.
RACHEL MADDOW, HOST: To get this story this week, we sent some producers from the show basically to the end of the world. Technically, we just sent them to the end of the country. We sent them to the Rio Grande Valley, at the tippy toe of Texas. This is part of the

© The Author(s), under exclusive license to Springer Nature Switzerland AG 2021
K. J. Fleuriet, *Rhetoric and Reality on the U.S.—Mexico Border*,
https://doi.org/10.1007/978-3-030-63557-2_4

country that is so far south, it is south of Mexico .... And it's a really big place ... the Rio Grande Valley alone is about the size of the state of Connecticut. It's just a huge, huge place. And when you're there, you are kind of far removed from not just the rest of the country, but the rest of Texas. You're not near anything else .... It is very, very poor ... quite profoundly poor.... Along with that remoteness and poverty come health troubles, preventable, treatable diseases at rates that do not seem like they should happen in the United States.

Transcript from Fox News Network, The Sean Hannity Show, July 15, 2014.
SEAN HANNITY, HOST: And welcome to "Hannity." This is a "FOX News Alert." The influx of illegals crossing our southern border is now reaching a tipping point .... We turn to FOX's own John Roberts, who got an exclusive ride-along with the chief of the Rio Grande Valley border patrol sector -- John.
JOHN ROBERTS, FOX CORRESPONDENT: ... You know, there's all this talk in Washington about secure the borders, secure the borders, stop illegal migrants from crossing over.
Well, we got a firsthand look at just what a challenge that really is. We rode along with Chief Kevin Oaks of the Rio Grande Valley sector. It's just a small sector of the Texas border. And in that, he has 300 miles of weaving, winding river that he has to protect, hundreds of places on the Mexican side for illegal migrants to cross into the river, as many places on the American side for them to hide out until they either get caught by the border patrol or move further inland. There are some places in the river where the current runs faster, where it only takes a rubber raft eight seconds to get across .... The bottom line here is, Sean, this is almost an intractable problem, and there is no easy solution.

In this chapter, I identify the implicit and explicit rhetorical strategies in national media stories such as these as well as in political discourse that depict the U.S.–Mexico borderlands as a place in need of control, in order to prevent a perceived Mexican threat to destabilize the American status quo.

Borders and Bordering

The social processes of creating and reinforcing borders is called *bordering* and *rebordering* (Agnew, 2008; DeChaine, 2012; Heyman, Slack, & Guerra, 2018; Nevins, 2010 [2002]; Ono & Sloop, 2002). Because national borders are literally lines drawn on a map to identify different countries, their maintenance requires bordering and rebordering, a social activity. Both media and political rhetoric about the Rio Grande Valley in the 2010s build on a long-standing discourse about the Global South, including Mexico, tracing back to the doctrine of Manifest Destiny in the nineteenth century and, more recently, globalization.

Manifest Destiny was the nineteenth-century principle that divine providence led white, Christian Americans westward to conquer lands and people to promote democracy and Protestant Christianity (Stephanson, 1995). It was used to justify taking Native American lands, killing their communities, and eradicating their cultures. Manifest Destiny included a way of thinking about people that were not white, Christian Americans as "less than" in about every conceivable way: political system, economic system, gender roles, kinship, language, religion, and physical appearance. The state of Texas was a result of various political and economic incursions in the 1800s by the United States into Mexico, publicly and politically validated by the doctrine of Manifest Destiny (Gomez, 2012; Woodworth, 2010). Prior to becoming a state in 1845, Texas had a brief stint as a republic (1836–1845) but had otherwise been part of Mexico. The Mexican–American War (1846–1848) ended with the Treaty of Guadalupe Hidalgo in 1848. In addition to other land, Mexico formally ceded to the United States the south Texas region that would later become the Rio Grande Valley. Literature from that time is replete with bordering practices to validate an "us" (United States) versus "them" (Mexico) mentality to support the American war effort (Rodríguez, 2010). Most relevant for the analysis in this chapter, commonly shared American beliefs were that Mexicans were "backward, anachronistic, [and] corrupt" (Rodríguez, 2010, p. 13).

Other expansionist doctrines around the same time as the Mexican–American War were more explicitly tied to colonialism, such as in Britain and the Netherlands. Although Americans rarely used "colonialism" and its associated terms, practices and discourses to promote Manifest Destiny were quite similar to those of colonialism: expansion for land, beliefs that indigenous communities were inferior and dangerous, and a religious and moral justification to conquer and assimilate (Sabol, 2017). Colonial discourse invokes a distinction between the Global North and the Global South. These phrases are, admittedly, overly simplified shorthand for the countries that colonized and the countries that were colonized, respectively.

Decades of scholarship[1] have teased out how national, political, and everyday discourse and rhetoric privileged people or places associated with the Global North and denigrated those considered part of the Global South. "If the colonizers were deemed civilized, then the colonized were declared barbaric; if the colonizers were thought of as rational, reasonable, cultured, learned, the colonized were dismissed as illogical, awkward, naïve, ignorant" (McLeod, 2007, p. 2). The Global South was always defined in relation to the Global North, and the Global North often dominated the content and flow of discourse about one another. Stories about places and people in the Global South that circulated were generated by the Global North (Comaroff & Comaroff, 2012; Spivak, 1988). For North America, the United States and Canada are lumped into the Global North. Mexico and other Latin American countries are grouped into the Global South so that U.S.–Mexico borderline is the border between the Global North and Global South (Agnew, 2008).

The Global North/South divide does not quite so easily map onto national boundaries, though. Such is the case of borderlands and internal colonies. As I show in this chapter, the place of the south Texas borderlands accrues what could be called "courtesy stigma" (Goffman, 1963) by virtue of its Latino/a majority and its adjacency to Mexico. In effect, routine descriptors of Mexico in Global South discourse are applied to the Rio Grande Valley. An internal colony occurs when a homeland and its people are subsumed into another nation-state or adjacent empire (Chávez, 2015). Some historians recently argued for internal colonies

---

[1] Some of the early, most significant works were in postcolonial and decolonial theory (Anzaldua, 1987; Bhabha, 1994; Boone & Mignolo, 1994; Rosaldo, 1993; Said, 1978; Spivak, 1988), though it now has many theoretical articulations in multiple disciplines from literature to architecture to women's studies.

in the United States (Chávez, 2011, 2015; Sabol, 2017), including the Rio Grande Valley of Texas (Bowman, 2016). Such a classification strengthens the argument that current discourse surrounding south Texas embodies historical bordering processes to label and separate the region from the rest of the United States. That is, as an internal colony, the Valley takes on characteristics of the Global South and Mexico rather than the Global North and the United States.[2]

Just as early bordering discourse defined Mexicans and Mexico as different and inferior to white Americans using classic Global South tropes, rebordering discourse drew social lines of difference around Mexican Americans (Chávez, 2001, 2008; Flores & Villarreal, 2012; Goltz & Pérez, 2012; Nevins, 2010 [2002]; Ono, 2012), further marginalizing borderland places like the Rio Grande Valley that are majority Hispanic. From Eisenhower to Reagan to Trump, American presidents targeted immigration from Mexico as a threat to an American way of life (Nevins, 2010 [2002]). Undocumented immigration and racism toward Latinos/as conflated in the American imagination in the United States in the twentieth century, and the U.S.–Mexico border became the reference point (Abrajano & Hajnal, 2015; Nevins, 2010 [2002]). Stories about physical barriers and policing the border drew from existing ideas about Mexico and Mexican immigrants to stoke fear (Correa-Cabrera, 2012; Heyman, 2012; Payan, 2006).

Another phase of global and American rebordering is occurring with globalization,[3] or the international interdependency and flows of goods, capital, people, and ideas; national and international processes and governance that enable those flows; the international relations of power involved; and responses, including resistance, to them (Guillette, 2016). Globalization was touted as an international economic collaboration that would alleviate poverty, especially in the Global South (López, 2007). Globalization hit the U.S.–Mexico borderlands in 1965 with the Border

---

[2]It is not uncommon to hear Texans say that "Texas starts at San Antonio" and "everything south of San Antonio is Mexico." It is even more common for people across the state to say "the Valley is Mexico."

[3]This is another one of those topics in anthropology and other disciplines that has exploded in the last several decades. Two early works in anthropology and globalization are Appadurai (1996) and Kearney (1995).

Industrialization Program and the advent of transnational manufacturing companies. Later, in the 1990s, population and international trade most dramatically increased with the North American Free Trade Agreement (NAFTA), another classic globalization initiative. Globalization requires both fewer and more restrictions for transnational flows (Comaroff & Comaroff, 2012; Heyman, 2012), as international trade restrictions are lessened. Some early borderlands theorists thought that globalization would lead to the erasure of geopolitical borders, but instead, it has led to a resurgence of rebordering practices as regards social difference around national identity (Comaroff & Comaroff, 2012; Donnan & Wilson, 2010). Nationalism and xenophobia are commonplace when border flows change (Donnan & Wilson, 2010) such as during globalization. Both nationalism and xenophobia exacerbate lines of social difference, especially along geopolitical borders (Staudt, 2014) and when folded into national security discourses as they were after the terrorist attack on the United States in September of 2011 (Chavez, 2012). As a nation, we have come to treat the perceived security and maintenance of the U.S.–Mexico border as a litmus test for our economic, social, and political health.

In sum, telling stories about places such as borders can either reinforce and/or contest assumptions about differences and our national identity. For the Rio Grande Valley, national news media and political rhetoric most often border and reborder the area with various lines of social difference that are in contrast to normative, dominant values of the United States. The Rio Grande Valley is particularly susceptible to bordering and rebordering with Global South labels and stereotypes because it abuts Mexico—and *was* Mexico for a long time. The region also has characteristics of an internal colony in the United States, which further align with perceptions of the Global South. And, the U.S.–Mexico borderlands, including the Valley, is experiencing rapid industrialization and amplified international trade during a time of increasing nationalism. Below, I analyze dominant themes and plots of media stories in the 2010s about the Valley to illustrate how the region is implicitly used as an exemplar of what is presumed to be wrong with people and places that populate "the border" and, by extension, with the people and places in the Global South.

The National Story About the Valley: A Backdrop for National Problems

What does the United States really think of the Rio Grande Valley today? First and foremost, the Valley to the rest of the United States is simply the U.S.–Mexico border and a narrow version of that, too. The Valley is used to represent "the border." This use of the Valley in national news stories is a kind of synecdoche, a part that is used to refer to a whole. The Valley is the part that represents the whole of "the border" concept in national news stories. The U.S.–Mexico border means something very specific for the national imagination in the 2010s: a marginal place that is far away but a very real risk to the social and economic integrity of the United States. In many national news stories, the U.S.–Mexico border becomes shortened to "the border." As a totalizing concept, "the border" is used as a figure of speech to denote a space where undocumented immigration, poverty, and crime are defining features. In the quotations that began this chapter, it is noteworthy that opposing political viewpoints can equally reinforce these features. Below, I analyze how national news stories like these use and describe the Valley between January 2010 and August 2017 to illustrate how the Valley becomes "the border" through articles' titles, thematic content, and story elements of setting, characters, and plots. I describe the national news stories in terms of their most common setting for the Valley, major plot and subplots during this timeframe, and frames for the stories' conflict and resolution.

Detailed in the last chapter, I identified and analyzed news stories from January 2010 to August 2017 from the Nexis Uni database that referenced the Rio Grande Valley from these national news sources: ABC, CBS, CNN, Fox, MSNBC, National Public Radio (NPR), *The New York Times*, and *The Washington Post*. I also included *The Wall Street Journal* through its website archive. There were 780 articles across all news sources that mentioned the Rio Grande Valley. I present the results of the analysis of recurring ideas, or themes, and stories about the Valley. Together, they build one kind of story told about the Valley. I also consider notable exceptions that can either prove the rule or suggest alternative stories. Regular exceptions are found in two places, *The New York Times* and, though less frequently, *National Public Radio*.

The dominant national news story of the Valley is relatively straightforward. The story is that the United States has a southern border with Mexico is in need of state and federal intervention and control. The national Valley story has three recurring themes in its plots: health care shortages, corruption, and unauthorized immigration alongside human and drug smuggling. The national story implies that, without intervention and control, these phenomena will spread to the rest of our nation and destabilize national health, security, and economy. The main characters in the national Valley story are the people and organizations that can "fix" the Valley. These people and organizations are nationally recognized political forces, such as governors, presidents, congressional representatives, and heads of federal and state agencies, such as the Border Patrol. Valley residents enter the stories most often as minor characters or part of the backdrop or setting.

The lack of local characters except to provide color is not specific to Valley news stories, of course. Neither is a focus on negative stories. Plots and characters in national news stories have to appeal to a broad audience across the nation, and there is long history of negative news as a market strategy for media outlets. My interest here is to explore how settings, plots, and characters that seem logical and coherent to a diverse, national audience reveal our assumptions about a place that may be fundamentally at odds with the reality of actual daily life in that place.

Key Events and Contexts from January 2010 Through August 2017

We understand places based on our referents to that place. National news stories can make sense to a heterogeneous public only when they reference ideas, debates, or experiences that have national histories or reflect experiences people may share across the nation. We also understand stories about other places based on our personal experiences with them. For example, I grew up in the Valley, and my understanding of it is framed by my personal experience as a child. Moreover, I understand the Valley because of my experiences outside of it, where I repeatedly heard remarks such as, "How did you ever make it out of there?" and

"Is it safe?" Experiences such as these influence how I hear stories about other places that are regularly disparaged. I am suspicious about the accuracy and perspective of stories about corruption or inner city poverty in places like Detroit or Baltimore. I do not doubt the legal convictions of corruption or the poverty statistics, but I doubt their assumptions and their ability to comprehensively define life in these places. I expect there are other ways to tell the story of these cities, too, that are contextualized in larger historical and social events, such as decisions made at state and national levels about the auto industry, legacies of racism in housing and employment, and a whole host of other influences. Conversely, I know little about so many other places for which I have no personal referent, such as the urban Midwest, the Bible belt, or the Great Plains, to name a few. Instead, I make sense of these stories and places based on previous indirect exposure to them through media and peers and as illustrations of issues of national concern. This is no less true for the nation's understanding of the Valley. Five significant state and national events appeared in stories that mentioned the Rio Grande Valley between 2010 and 2017:

- the passage of the Affordable Care Act in 2010;
- the passage of Texas House Bill 2 about abortion care in 2013 and subsequent appeals of certain provisions to the United States Supreme Court through 2016;
- Drug Enforcement Administration (DEA) and Federal Bureau of Investigation (FBI) investigations into law enforcement corruption in 2013 and 2015;
- the dramatic increase of Central American families and unaccompanied children crossing into the United States at the Rio Grande Valley and claiming asylum beginning in 2010, peaking in 2014, and continuing through 2019; and
- the rise of Donald Trump and the 2016 presidential election in the United States.

Stories that include the Rio Grande Valley during this timeframe repeatedly refer to these events. I will refer back to these events in the remainder of the chapter to connect ideas about the Valley with issues of national concern.

The Frame for the National Story: The Valley *Is* "the Border"

Titles of stories suggest to readers what to expect; titles frame stories. Titles are their own kind of database to understand the connection between national ideas about the Valley and state and national events. Overall, titles of stories that include the Valley imply that the Valley is defined only through its border with Mexico and that the Texas border is somehow (and impossibly) concentrated in the Valley.

Word clouds are a way to visualize the frequency of words in a given database, such as the title database. Word clouds express the frequency based on a minimum number of occurrences. The size of the font reflects the relative frequency of the word: the bigger the word, the more frequently it occurred in the titles. The word clouds in Fig. 4.1 illustrate what words predominate in the titles of articles that reference the Valley. In turn, these dominant words act as the article frame, or the expectations and lens that a reader has for a specific story. The word clouds in Fig. 4.1 are for all news sources across the time period. Each word cloud has a different minimum number of occurrences for a word to be included. The first word cloud has the most occurrences (60 times) as the limit for inclusion, and the last word cloud has the least (10 times).

The title word clouds show us that the overwhelmingly dominant frame for stories that include the Rio Grande Valley is the "border" in "Texas." For all titles in all sources and years, the only words that occurred at least 60 times in article titles were "Texas" and "border" (Word Cloud A). With at least 50 occurrences (Word Cloud B), "immigration," and Presidents "Obama" and "Trump" appear alongside "Texas" and "border," which signals the importance of the U.S.–Mexico border in state and national political agenda setting. At 40 occurrences (Word Cloud C), "abortion" and "wall" appear, which correspond, respectively, to Texas House Bill 2 that led to the closures of dozens of abortion care clinics in Texas and the proposed extension of the U.S.–Mexico border wall by then candidate Donald Trump. At 30 occurrences, "crisis" and "immigrants" enter the word cloud (D), which related to the Central American child and family immigration increases between 2010 and 2017 and the state and national political response to them. At

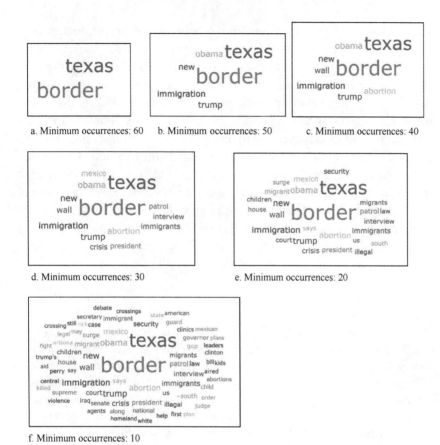

a. Minimum occurrences: 60   b. Minimum occurrences: 50   c. Minimum occurrences: 40

d. Minimum occurrences: 30   e. Minimum occurrences: 20

f. Minimum occurrences: 10

Fig. 4.1 Word clouds of article titles, all sources and years

20 occurrences (Word Cloud E), a proliferation of subthemes emerge around immigration, including "surge," "children," "patrol," "south," "security," and "Mexico." Word Clouds A and E side by side show how the Rio Grande Valley is wrapped up in stories about political and social issues surrounding immigration, abortion, and security. Within the geographical region of the U.S.–Mexico borderlands, immigration almost always refers to undocumented immigration, abortion care to shortages in health care, and security to increasing surveillance and law

enforcement presence to deter and otherwise capture undocumented immigrants and human and drug smugglers.

After the title frames the story for the reader, the opening paragraphs set the tone for the story. In national news stories that open with a description of the Valley or particular locations in the Valley, the stories use the Valley as synecdoche for "the border." This "border" has very specific meanings attached to it: perilous, impoverished, and remote, especially surrounding issues of immigration, human and drug smuggling operations, local politics, and health and health care. It is nigh impossible to find an article that does not combine these characteristics in some fashion to paint a bleak picture. In passages from a diversity of sources and across years, the Valley persists as a place you do not want to be. The descriptions below certainly do not evoke a sense of home, resilience, innovation, or resource.

The New York Times, "The Texas border draws frequent fliers," Elaine Glusac, April 11, 2010.

The Lower Rio Grande Valley is perhaps the last place where you might consider communing with nature. Where it isn't plotted into RV parks serving northern retirees who come for the warmth and proximity to cheap prescription drugs in Mexico, the valley [sic] is sectioned into shopping malls or grapefruit and onion fields. Among nonbirders, that same border is better known for illegal human migration than bird migration.

Nonetheless, this narrow green hem has become one of the nation's top spots for bird-watching ....

The United States Border Patrol is a constant presence along the river, and in light of the recent drug-related violence on the Mexican side, a welcome, if disquieting sight. An armed agent in full camouflage patrolling on foot was just one sighting on a Rio Grande canoe trip offered by the Roma birding center ...

The Associated Press, "National Guard deployment may be extended," Martha Mendoza, June 1, 2011.

A nervous man with a duffle bag of marijuana. A pack of snorting feral pigs. A woman holding a child's hand. A fluttering, rustling plastic bag. There's plenty for a National Guardsman to look at on a quiet South Texas night.

Customs and Border Protection offered a firsthand look to The Associated Press at what the troops are actually doing, around the clock, in the Rio Grande Valley in south Texas ...

The Wall Street Journal, "Affluent Mexicans flee to Texas: Violence across the border buoys housing in impoverished cities; Relocated goalie stars for school," Robbie Whelan, July 27, 2012.

MISSION, Texas—For many home buyers, the biggest motivations behind moving to a new neighborhood are a job change, rising wealth or a growing family. For Graciela Gonzalez, a private-school administrator from the nearby Mexican state of Tamaulipas, it was the constant threat of kidnapping and murder ...

The Washington Post, "Too much of too little: How the food-stamp diet is hurting the people of Hidalgo County, Tex.," Eli Saslow, November 10, 2013.

They were already running late for a doctor's appointment, but first the Salas family hurried into their kitchen for another breakfast paid for by the federal government. The 4-year-old grabbed a bag of cheddar-flavored potato chips and a granola bar. The 9-year-old filled a bowl with sugary cereal and then gulped down chocolate milk. Their mother, Blanca, arrived at the refrigerator and reached into the drawer where she stored the insulin needed to treat her diabetes. She filled a needle with fluid and injected it into her stomach with a practiced jab.

The New York Times, "Texas vote-buying case casts glare on tradition of election day goads," Manny Fernandez, January 13, 2014.

DONNA, Tex. In this Rio Grande Valley town of trailer parks and weedy lots eight miles from the Mexico border, people call them runners or *politiqueras* -- the campaign workers who use their network of relatives and friends to deliver votes for their candidates. They travel around town with binders stuffed with the names and addresses of registered voters, driving residents to and from the polls and urging those they bump into at the grocery store to support their candidates.

Despite rumors that some politiqueras went over the line in encouraging voters, the tradition continued in Donna and other border towns and cities, and campaigns for nearly every local office or seat have paid politiqueras to turn out the vote in contested races.

But in recent weeks, the suicide of the school board president here and accusations of vote buying against three politiqueras have rocked the system. The charges may threaten the existence of *politiqueras* in Donna, an impoverished community of 16,000, where politics and jobs are inseparable. The school system is the largest employer, and city government is the second largest; local politics rivals high school football as a favored pastime.

The Associated Press, "Drownings along Rio Grande spike after enforcement surge," Seth Robbins, March 29, 2015.

MISSION, Texas (AP) - A U.S. surveillance helicopter hovering over the Rio Grande spots a body floating near a muddy bank on the Mexican side of the river.

Soon another body turns up, then another. A Mexican investigator arrives and holds up his hand confirming the grim tally: four men and a woman.

The grisly discovery last month is part of a spike in drownings since October. Immigrants, desperate to avoid detection at a time of increased patrols, are choosing more dangerous and remote crossings into South Texas. The Border Patrol has responded by expanding its search-and-rescue teams to monitor the area, particularly weed-choked irrigation canals where many of the bodies are being found.

Transcript from National Public Radio, "Legal medical abortions are up in Texas, but so are DIY pills from Mexico," NPR Morning Edition, June 9, 2016.

DAVID GREENE: In Texas, it can be very difficult and very costly to get a legal abortion. This is causing more and more young women to get do-it-yourself abortions. They walk across an international bridge to a Mexican pharmacy to buy the abortion pill. As NPR's John Burnett reports, without the supervision of a doctor, the results can be troublesome.

JOHN BURNETT: Nuevo Progreso, Mexico sits across the river from Progreso, Texas. In the crowded, chaotic side-walks [sic], it's all here for the asking - dental work, eyeglasses, pirated DVDs, tequila shots, prostitutes and cheap, plentiful prescription medicine. Highly restricted drugs like Xanax, Ritalin and Valium are sold like aspirin over here …

JOHN BURNETT: Abortion is, of course, legal in the United States. In the border city of McAllen, the Whole Woman's Health clinic offers abortions. So why are Texas women going to pharmacies in Nuevo Progreso? It could be a matter of cost. A medical or surgical abortion in McAllen costs $500.

The Rio Grande Valley is one of the poorest regions in the country. In Mexico, a pack of abortion pills sells for under $50. It could be that abortions are just more trouble in Texas, with all the rules imposed by the legislature. A woman has to get an ultrasound and see the doctor three different times.

Transcript from Fox News Network, Sunday Morning Futures, February 26, 2017.

BARTIROMO: Let me -- let me ask you, Congressman, about your trip because you along with House Speaker Paul Ryan and that delegation of house lawmakers, went to the southern border and toured the Rio Grande Valley to observe border security operations. We've got some pictures here of you at the border. Tell us what you saw.

[10:04:54] MCCAUL: Well, we flew by Blackhawk and horses on the ground and patrol boats in the river, and we saw, you know, how open, wide open the Rio Grande Valley sector is in my home state, where most of the illegal crossings take place. More importantly, we got an intelligence briefing down there, the speaker and myself, about the threats south of the border from the drug cartels and potential terrorists, human trafficking, drug trafficking, violence and corruption coming into the United States.

The excerpts above emphasize certain key characteristics that tell the national audience that the Valley setting is "the border": violence from Mexico; drug smuggling; corruption spreading from Mexican law enforcement and cartels; poverty; inaccessible but adequate health care or inadequate but cheap and plentiful health care; communities with poor nutrition; development that has created landscapes inimical to nature; and unchecked undocumented immigration. Proximity to Mexico, it is implied or declared outright, heightens or causes problems.

Themes for the National Valley Story: Politics and Politicians, Undocumented Immigration, Education, Health and Health Care, Poverty, and Border Crime, Corruption, Security, and Enforcement

Titles and opening passages are readers' entry point. They set expectations for what will be read and how it will be interpreted. The story itself will revolve around themes, which can be thought of as the building blocks for stories' conflicts and resolutions. Building blocks for national Valley stories revolve around the major events and issues of national concern, as described above. They are set within enduring ideas about "the border." For example, stories about unauthorized migration into the United States from Mexico and Central America often open with Valley scenes that suggest the border is exclusively poor, unruly, and remote. Most articles weave together multiple themes. For example, articles on the 2014 Central American children and family immigration (theme: Central American child and family immigrants) regularly discussed competing political solutions by Texas Governor Perry and President Obama (theme: politics and politicians) for the immediate humanitarian issue of processing the immigrants in the Valley and the comprehensive immigration reform plans both favored (theme: immigration, broadly), which included increased law enforcement at the border as a deterrent (theme: border security). These articles frequently opened with an immigrant apprehension scene in a rural part of the Valley or in a very poor Valley community (theme: poverty).

Recurring themes in the national news stories that reference the Valley (Chart 4.1) point toward relevant current events and persistent characterizations about the Valley. Some themes need careful contextualization. On first glance, the themes in Chart 4.1 may seem to overlap, but they do not in terms of article content and for coding purposes. For example, if I coded an article with "border" and "border violence," that meant that the article dealt with specific events tied to a concept of border violence, and it discussed other issues associated with being a national border. "Border" and "border violence" are different themes, because

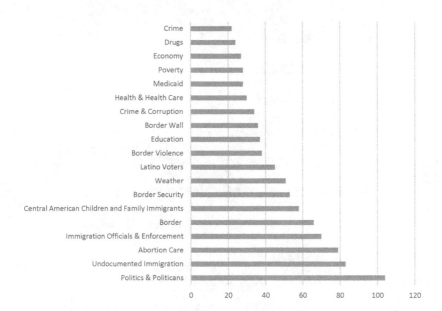

Chart 4.1   2010–2017 Article theme counts, *N* = 780 (More than one theme can be present in one article. Most common themes shown)

not all stories about the border are about violence, and not all border violence stories incorporate other aspects of life in a borderlands region. Crime and corruption were also themes used in very specific ways in stories. Crime and corruption were associated with smuggling operations that could include human smuggling, but crime and corruption rarely appeared in stories about immigrants themselves. Crime was most often associated with Mexican drug cartels that have diversified in the last decade by expanding their human smuggling operations. Corruption was most often associated with drug cartels bribing local and state law enforcement as a strategy for drug smuggling.

Once I had identified themes in each article, I then grouped themes based on how article content constructed their relationships (Chart 4.2). For example, border wall, border violence, and border security references appeared in stories that could logically fall under the umbrella theme of border. Border violence is its own umbrella theme for stories about crime and drugs, as well. Stories about border violence and crime most often targeted human and drug smuggling operations. Similarly, I grouped

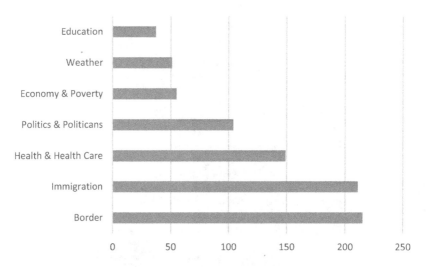

Chart 4.2 2010–2017 Primary article themes, $N = 780$

themes of Central American children and family immigrants and also immigration officials and enforcement under immigration. Abortion care and Medicaid fit under health and health care, although health and health care also included other issues, such as diabetes and health care access. Poverty and economy were themes that were related but neither one subsumed the other. The economy theme emerged in articles related to international trade with Mexico, SpaceX and a rocket launch site outside of Brownsville, and development and construction, whereas the poverty theme focused on enduring economic struggles in Valley communities. The education theme was perhaps the most internally consistent, whether discussing Valley educational outcomes, the impact of poverty on education, or new educational institutions such as The University of Texas Rio Grande Valley.

The thematic analysis makes it clear. Themes of border, immigration, health and health care, and politics and politicians dominate national news stories that reference the Valley (see Chart 4.2). Economy and poverty, weather, and education are the next most frequent themes. Very often, primary themes were interrelated in stories, except for weather. The theme of weather did not regularly evoke other themes or reproduce any common Valley story. The national news stories about these weather events are short summaries of major weather patterns that could impact large swaths of the state or nation or severe weather events, such as a Category 5 hurricane. The Rio Grande Valley is in a hurricane and tropical storm path due to its coastal location on the Gulf of Mexico. It is often a geographical reference point for landfall or flooding associated with these storms. I will not include weather in the remainder of the analysis due to its independence from other themes and its lack of a Valley story. The remaining primary themes are used to craft stories that support the impression that the Valley is in desperate need of state and federal intervention to survive as a region and to protect the rest of the United States. In effect, the Valley becomes the exemplar to illustrate national debates regarding immigration, health care, and poverty.

Even in the small minority of articles about other topics, such as birding or cuisine, the images of the Valley persist. In a 2016 article in *The New York Times* about the popularity of Mexican Topo Chico carbonated water, for example, the first sentence is "Bottles of Topo Chico are tabletop everywhere in Texas this time of year, including tatty taquerias in the Rio Grande Valley and reservations-only restaurants in Houston" (Murphy, 2016). These shabby Valley settings are reminiscent of those that open articles with titles about roiling debates around immigration, health care and economy, reinforcing a national understanding of "the border" in need of intervention to help the region and secure the state and nation. That is the major story about the Valley in national news. Stories about corruption, insecure borders, and poor health and health care work with assumptions about "the border" as a place to reproduce, rather than challenge, such a shallow, incomplete, and negative rendering of the Valley. These stories reborder the region as distinct from the rest of the United States in ways that make it problematic to the nation's well-being.

Three Variations on a Theme: Story Plots

Variation #1: Poverty and politics cause health challenges and health care shortages, especially in remote borderlands.

To begin an analysis of health and health care stories about the Valley from January 2010 through August 2017, we need to go back one year to 2009. In 2009, Atul Gawande published an article in *The New Yorker* that propelled the Rio Grande Valley into the national spotlight with accusations of gross overuse of health care to increase profit for individual doctors. Below is an excerpt.

The New Yorker, "The cost conundrum: What a Texas town can teach us about health care," Atul Gawande, June 1, 2009.
It is spring in McAllen, Texas. The morning sun is warm. The streets are lined with palm trees and pickup trucks. McAllen is in Hidalgo County, which has the lowest household income in the country, but it's a border town, and a thriving foreign-trade zone has kept the unemployment rate below ten per cent. McAllen calls itself the Square Dance Capital of the World. "Lonesome Dove" was set around here.
McAllen has another distinction, too: it is one of the most expensive health-care markets in the country ... along the banks of the Rio Grande, in the Square Dance Capital of the World, a medical community came to treat patients the way subprime-mortgage lenders treated home buyers: as profit centers.
... As America struggles to extend health-care coverage while curbing health-care costs, we face a decision that is more important than whether we have a public-insurance option, more important than whether we will have a single-payer system in the long run or a mixture of public and private insurance, as we do now. The decision is whether we are going to reward the leaders who are trying to build a new generation ... [like the Mayo Clinic and the Grand Junction medical community]. If we don't, McAllen won't be an outlier. It will be our future.

President Obama had promised on the 2008 campaign trail to address the American healthcare system, and Gawande's article became one of the touchstones for his staff as they waded into healthcare reform (Redden, 2009). Gawande's in-depth analysis explored why health care costs were skyrocketing in the United States. He travelled to a city with one of the most expensive health care markets in the country: McAllen, Texas. Its Medicare costs were particularly unexplainable after controlling for the costs of available medical technology, the health profile of the community, and the quality of health care provided. Gawande attributed the problem to deep flaws in the American healthcare system. He argued that our healthcare system allowed, even encouraged, professional cultures of doctors to have an "entrepreneurial spirit" and seek profit in ways that are not in the patient's best interest. When such a professional culture runs amok as it had in McAllen, he wrote, the problems are many. Patient outcomes worsen. Unethical business practices flourish, such as kickbacks to doctors for admitting patients to hospitals or contracting with home health agencies. Gawande implied that only a few Valley physicians had the self-awareness to recognize the problem and grapple with its moral implications and impact on their patients' well-being. Gawande's article established the Valley as the exemplar for health and health care problems facing the nation, especially as they related to poverty, health care expense, and access to health care. The politicization of healthcare reform kept the Valley example buoyant in national news stories. With the passage of the Affordable Care Act in 2010 and Texas' subsequent refusal to expand Medicaid, the Valley continued to be an illustration of problems gone wrong in the healthcare system of the United States.

In 2010, President Barack Obama signed the United States' Patient Protection and Affordable Care Act (ACA) into law. ACA had three goals: increase availability of health insurance, expand the Medicaid program to cover all adults below a certain income level, and lower health costs through innovative health care delivery models (Silvers, 2013). The second provision, expansion of the Medicaid program, was successfully challenged in court (*National Federation of Independent Business (NFIB) v. Sebelius*, 2012), which made adoption optional for states. Texas chose not to expand its Medicaid program under ACA.

Transcript from NPR's Morning Edition, "Texas Medicaid debate complicated by politics and poverty," Sarah Varney, March 22, 2013.
    When the sun rises over the Rio Grande Valley, the cries of the *urracas* — black birds — perched on the tops of palm trees swell to a noisy, unavoidable cacophony. That is also the strategy, it could be said, that local officials, health care providers and frustrated valley [sic] residents are trying to use to persuade Gov. Rick Perry and state Republican lawmakers

to set aside their opposition and expand Medicaid, a key provision of the federal health law.

The Rio Grande Valley has a load of troubles: high unemployment, low-paying jobs, warring Mexican cartels, a meager tax base and legions of people without health insurance. While many of those woes seem incurable, expanding Medicaid to the region's uninsured is, to Paula Gomez, who runs several local health clinics, a no-brainer.

In the above 2013 NPR story, the description of the Valley includes the usual setting: poverty, violence, and "legions" of people without health insurance. The statistics on the Valley uninsured population are truly troubling. Between 22.3% and 31.2% of people in every Valley county was uninsured according to 2019 estimates (U.S. Census Bureau, 2019). Uninsured people are many working poor who are American citizens, but also any unauthorized immigrant, regardless of income, as unauthorized immigrants are not eligible for health insurance in the United States. Adequate health care coverage is a very real need in the Valley; I do not argue that point. Lack of insurance is a desperate problem for many Valley residents. My interest is in uncovering the assumptions about the Rio Grande Valley as a place in these stories.

Paula Gomez, the woman cited in this article, is a tremendous advocate for community health care centers, and her success in improving Valley health care is nationally lauded. Ms. Gomez has served as the Executive Director of Brownsville Community Health Center since 1984. She has been appointed to positions in numerous influential national policy-making and advocacy organizations, including the United States Surgeon General Committee on Hispanic Health, the Advisory Board of the National Health Service Corps, the Advisory Board of the National Environment Justice Advisory Council, and the executive board of the Gorgas Science Foundation. Ms. Gomez's national work and recognition are due to her local achievements in improving community health in the Valley (The White House President Barack Obama, n.d.). Although news stories often use her expert commentary about challenges in Valley health and health care, her own work in improving Valley health and health care is rarely noted in national news. As a result of these and similar characterizations, the enduring image of Valley health and health care is that it needs state or federal intervention, rather than state and federal support for ongoing, local and regional work improving health and health care in Valley communities.

Not all articles about health and health care that use the illustration of the Valley fail to cite ongoing efforts, but the frames even for those articles imply local efforts will be to little effect. For example, in a 2014 article in *The New York Times* about Texas' refusal to expand Medicaid under the Affordable Care Act provision, the dire situation for the Valley's uninsured is first established through the article setting:

The New York Times, "Trying to help thousands in colonias obtain health coverage," Alexa Ura, February 23, 2014.

EDINBURG -- Sitting at an old picnic table in front of a dilapidated house, María Díaz, a hotel housekeeper, tells stories of the rejection that comes with living in impoverished Texas *colonias*.

The trash on her street is not picked up regularly, so she is used to a wretched smell at night when her neighbors burn their garbage. There is no drainage system on her block, so Ms. Díaz, a 44-year-old single mother of four, is accustomed to heavy flooding on her street when it rains.

As she looks into buying private health insurance under the federal Affordable Care Act, which requires most people to obtain coverage in 2014, Ms. Díaz is facing a new type of rejection. She probably does not make enough money to qualify for tax credits to afford coverage through the federal health insurance marketplace ...

To increase awareness, organizations like La Unión del Pueblo Entero, a nonprofit community union, hold public seminars and enrollment events, where staff members provide *colonia* residents information about the federal health reform law and navigator referrals.

Ann Carol Cass, executive director of Proyecto Azteca, a nonprofit affordable-housing organization in the Rio Grande Valley, said the organization referred residents to navigators and helped with enrollment efforts but added that being uninsured was a situation to which *colonia* residents were accustomed.

The story mentions two Valley nonprofit organizations: LUPE (La Unión del Pueblo Entero) and Proyecto Azteca but does not elaborate on their work or their missions. Located side by side in San Juan,

Texas, LUPE and Proyecto Azteca have advocated for the Valley poor for decades with some significant successes. LUPE was started by César Chávez and Dolores Huerta, labor rights activists, in order to build "stronger, healthier communities where *colonia* residents use the power of civic engagement for social change. From fighting deportation, to providing social services and English classes, to organizing for street-lights and drainage, LUPE responds to the needs of the community" (LUPE, 2016). LUPE's advocacy is multi-pronged, coordinated, and aimed at immediate help for individual members and long-term social change from labor laws to immigration reform to health care coverage. Proyecto Azteca traces its origins back to a collaboration in 1991 between United Farm Workers, Texas Rural Legal Aid, and the Texas Low Income Housing Information Service. Proyecto Azteca finances and trains families in "self-help construction" of homes in *colonias* and rural areas to improve living conditions (Proyecto Azteca, 2019). In 2012, Proyecto Azteca began construction of the first Silver-LEED (Leadership in Energy and Environmental Design) neighborhood south of Austin with homes built with and for low-income families at 0% interest. The extent of LUPE and Proyecto Azteca's impact on the community is rarely, if ever, noted in national news articles. Similar to the example above of Paula Gomez, representatives from the organizations are asked to speak about the problems, not about how ongoing, local efforts could be supported and expanded to help craft long-term solutions.

National news stories about the Valley and other topics of health and health care continue the impression of the Valley as a place where our national problems are most acute. Sometimes, this is accurate, as when Texas and the Valley re-entered the national dialogue about abortion in 2013. National news covered multiple Texas legislative actions to restrict funding for family-planning clinics and impose new restrictions on abor-tion care. The legal battles reached the Supreme Court of the United States, which increased both the press coverage and demonstrated the relevance of the state's actions to the rest of the nation. Texas' laws on abortion often herald legal trends for the nation, which is one reason why national news stories follow them. In these national stories, the Valley is a region where there is little or no abortion care access. The Valley became the test case as to whether an abortion law creates "undue burden" on a woman's ability to seek an abortion, as mandated by the landmark 1992 Supreme Court case (*Planned Parenthood of Southeastern Pa v. Casey*, 1992: 845–846).

The national lead-in to the 2013 abortion law stories was the effective dismantling of Planned Parenthood by the Texas legislature in 2011, which led to a reduction of preventive, non-abortion care services for thousands of Valley residents. The state legislature approved a 66% reduction in family planning grants, and the remaining funding was diverted from family-planning clinics to prioritize comprehensive care clinics. Eighty-two family planning clinics closed, one-third of which were affiliated with Planned Parenthood (Stevenson, Flores-Vazque, Allgeyer, Schenkkan, & Potter, 2016). Subsequently, the state legislature excluded Planned Parenthood from its Medicaid-funded women's health program and the later 2013 Texas Women's Health Program, even though the participating Planned Parenthoods did not perform abortions (White, Hopkins, Grossman, & Potter, 2018). Planned Parenthood was a primary provider of health care, including preventive health care, for men, women and adolescents in the Valley. Notably, Planned Parenthood did not offer abortion care in the Valley. A 2011 piece in *The New York Times* explains the situation in Hidalgo County:

> *The New York Times, "Planned Parenthood struggles after state budget cuts," Thanh Tan, October 16, 2011.*
>
> Hidalgo County, situated along the border that separates Texas and Mexico, is home to one of the country's fastest-growing but poorest populations. Largely Hispanic and Catholic, the county also has one of the highest birth rates in a state where Medicaid finances more than half of all deliveries ...
>
> In 2010, the Hidalgo County network's eight clinics provided family-planning services to 23,000 patients, many of whom are uninsured and cannot afford to pay. The services include contraception, breast and cervical cancer screenings, testing for sexually transmitted diseases, and wellness exams for both men and women -- but not abortions ...
>
> Operating in a region with a limited donor base and high need for health services, Mr. Gonzales said, the clinics have relied heavily on government financing. So when state cuts to family planning took effect in September, the Hidalgo County network lost a $3.1 million contract

and was forced to lay off half its staff and shut down four of its facilities. (Another five clinics have closed around the state since the beginning of September.) ...

What is happening in Texas is emblematic of a national trend. Unable to overturn Roe v. Wade, anti-abortion campaigners have worked in recent years within Congress and state legislatures, many of which have become increasingly conservative, to make gaining access to the procedure as difficult as possible ...

Family planning services declined as a result of the shifting of funds and funding priorities in state health care delivery, and in 2013, House Bill 2 (H.B. 2) passed. H.B. 2 included provisions requiring doctors performing abortions to have admitting privileges with a hospital within 30 miles and abortion care clinics to have the same specifications and technical standards as ambulatory surgery centers. The Valley became the "undue burden" test case due its relative and absolute lack of abortion care facilities. Prior to 2014, there were two facilities that offered abortion services, one in McAllen and one in Harlingen. Both McAllen and Harlingen clinics closed their doors in 2014 as a result of H.B. 2 provisions. The closest abortion care facility became Corpus Christi, approximately 155 miles away. It closed later in 2014, leaving the closest clinic in San Antonio, approximately 240 miles from McAllen. Traveling to both required passing through an immigration checkpoint to affirm legal presence in the United States. The national news stories followed H.B. 2 as it went to and fro in the state and federal appeals processes, and the Valley's situation was noted for its potential undue burden due to various combinations of distance, citizenship, and poverty.

In the following 2013 and 2014 transcripts and article, particular characteristics about the Valley make it the test case for H.B. 2 and undue burden:

Transcript from All Things Considered, NPR, "A doctor who performed abortions in south Texas makes his case," Wade Goodwyn, September 11, 2014.

And for women on the state's border with Mexico, there's another barrier — an inland Border Patrol checkpoint on the highway to San

Antonio. Women whose visas confine them to the border, or who are completely undocumented, can't get past the checkpoint to San Antonio.

For [Democratic State Senator] Lucio that's a plus. "I'm OK with that," he says. "Because all they're looking for is putting an end to a life. And I'm not for that."

Transcript from The Rachel Maddow Show, MSNBC, October 31, 2013.

MADDOW: When you described McAllen, for example, as one of the places with your facility closing, that means there'll be no facility in the area that provides abortion services or the related services, can you describe what McAllen is like, what kind of population you'd serve at a clinic like that and what's going to happen to those women?

HAGSTROM MILLER: Yes, we serve a population -- it's a border community. So, there's a lot of people both from Mexico and from the Rio Grande Valley. The majority of our patients don't have health insurance, they don't have Medicaid. Most of the women we serve there are mothers, they're working mothers.

And they can't travel 300 or 400 miles up to San Antonio and get their, you know, get off of work and get child care covered or whatever.

So when people say, oh, they'll be able to just go to San Antonio -- well, the procedure itself is going to take a few days and most of these women are needing to have an abortion because they can't make the ends meet with their family already.

The Associated Press, "Reinstatement of abortion law leaves few options," Christopher Sherman and Chris Tomlinson, November 1, 2013.

If this clinic and one in nearby McAllen are forced to close, women seeking abortions would be faced with taking days off work, finding childcare and paying for hotels in cities such as San Antonio, Austin or Houston.

That's more than many can afford, including a 39-year-old woman from Willacy County who was waiting Friday to see [Dr.] Minto. She spoke on condition of anonymity because she was fearful of the judgment she would face in her small, rural community.

The woman said she and her husband are happily married but already have several children. They're just getting back on their feet financially after her husband recently found work. The pregnancy was not planned.

"I just can't afford to have another one," she said, crying. But the money to travel north for an abortion isn't there either.

"It's so unfair. It's just politics," she said. "It's my decision. It's not anybody else's."

Asked what she would do if the clinic were not allowed to perform her abortion, she said: "I think I will have to go through with the pregnancy. I don't have the finances to travel."

In each of these excerpts, recurring themes about the Valley are distance from adequate health care, a constituency that includes Mexican women living in south Texas with limited visas or undocumented, and poverty. Several lawsuits and cycles of appeals and three years later, H.B. 2 was in front of the United States Supreme Court (*Whole Woman's Health v. Hellerstedt*, 2016) with the argument that a 240-mile drive for abortion care presented an undue burden on women seeking an abortion, especially for low-income women. The Supreme Court overturned the two provisions requiring admitting privileges at a hospital within 30 miles of the abortion care clinic and ambulatory surgical standards for abortion care clinics. The McAllen clinic has reopened; it remains the only clinic with abortion services in the Rio Grande Valley. National news closely followed the two lawsuits as they traveled through the federal appeals process, and the Valley figured as the perfect storm. Valley poverty and state politics colluded to prevent women from their constitutional right to seek abortion.

Variation #2: Proximity to Mexico causes corruption.

Transcript from NPR's Morning Edition, "Corruption on the border: Dismantling misconduct in the Rio Grande Valley," John Burnett and Marisa Peñaloza, July 6, 2015.

This week, NPR examines public corruption in South Texas. The FBI has launched a task force to clean up pervasive misconduct by public servants in the Rio Grande Valley. But as NPR's John Burnett and Marisa Penaloza report, the problems are entrenched …

The second variation of the national news story about the Valley is all about corruption: corruption in law enforcement, corruption in education, and corruption in politics. The assumptions are threefold. First, corruption stems from the influence of Mexico. The second assumption is that corruption is deeply rooted in local culture. Third, local efforts to combat corruption are insufficient or compromised. These assumptions play out in news stories about several FBI investigations, including drug running and extortion in Hidalgo County law enforcement (the Panama Unit case), vote-buying (*politiqueros*), extortion among Donna School Board members, and racketeering, extortion, and fraud in Cameron County's legal system and judiciary. It is important to note that I am not challenging the court rulings on any of these events. Each has multiple legal decisions based on years of investigation and trials that prove the corruption existed. Instead, I am challenging the assumptions about the prevalence and exclusivity of corruption that these stories lay bare, and I am suggesting that corruption stories overwhelm the narrative and reinforce and validate certain ideas about the region.

Valley corruption stories bubble up to the national news often due to the role of the FBI. Stories chart the FBI investigations. The FBI is charged, along with state law enforcement agencies, with investigating and combatting public corruption. Public corruption is "the FBI's top criminal investigative priority," and its Public Corruption program has four areas of emphases: federal law violation by local, state, and federal public officials; fraud involving federal programs and contracts; public corruption along United States' border in order to combat drug, human, and weapons smuggling, espionage, and terrorism; and election fraud and environmental crime related to federal procurement, programs and contracts (Federal Bureau of Investigation, n.d.). Note the third area of emphasis, the border. This includes the northern and southern land borders and the shorelines of the United States, but rarely are northern borders noted in stories about American borderlands corruption in law enforcement. In fact, FBI investigations in the Rio Grande Valley are often part of larger initiatives. In 2016, the FBI corruption task force in the Valley was one of 22 such investigations at various points on the southern and northern borders and its shorelines (Federal Bureau of Investigation, 2016).

Stories on Valley corruption begin with the assumption that the region is corrupt, and the implication (or direct assertion) is that the Valley is more corrupt than other places because of its proximity to Mexico. For example, in the 2012 article in *The Wall Street Journal*, the author takes it for granted that corruption "plagues" a border region, which is parlayed into a comment by a local professor that "a culture down here" accepts corruption as a "part of life."

The Wall Street Journal, "Fraud probe hits Texas prosecutor," Nathan Koppel, May 8, 2012.

A district attorney in South Texas was indicted Monday on federal fraud charges in a mushrooming case unusual even in a border region plagued by public corruption …

But in recent years, criminal charges have been leveled against judges, police officers and even school officials in the Rio Grande Valley, a four-county region along the Mexican border that is one of the fastest-growing areas in the state, with a population of more than a million. High-profile corruption cases have led to a perception that Valley officials too often enter public office to enrich themselves or do favors for friends, many in the area complain.

"There is a culture down here that seems to accept corruption as a part of life," said Anthony Knopp, a longtime Valley resident and professor at the University of Texas at Brownsville. He said it is common in Mexico to bribe public officials in hopes of favorable treatment—a tradition, he fears, that has crept across the border.

In the NPR series, one of the articles is entitled "With Corruption Rampant, Good Cops Go Bad in Texas' Rio Grande Valley." The title frames the article's content with the assumption that corruption permeates the region. Its opening lines reinforce this idea: "In the Rio Grande Valley of Texas, where people are accustomed to seeing public officials led away in handcuffs, the case of the Panama Unit shocked everyone" (Burnett & Peñaloza, 2015b). The Panama Unit case was indeed shocking. A Hidalgo County sheriff's unit created to combat drug dealing ended in arrests of the entire unit for drug dealing. The scope of the corruption was far larger than individual law enforcement members from county sheriffs to Border Patrol officers charged with corruption in the past. A piece in *The Associate Press* called the Panama Unit debacle "the Rio Grande Valley's latest corruption scandal" (Sherman, 2014).

There are a few exceptions to how the Valley is portrayed in corruption stories. More precisely, of the stories my search yielded, there was one. In a story in *The New York Times* about the Panama Unit, the Valley is contextualized as part of the larger "high temptation environment" that is the U.S.–Mexico border:

> *The New York Times, "In Drug Fight on Texas Border, Some Officers Play Both Sides," Manny Fernandez, January 2, 2013.*
>
> The four men [in the Panama Unit] were the latest in a long line of officers accused of escorting, stealing or distributing drug loads near the 1,254-mile border that Texas shares with Mexico. Since 2007, more than 40 police officers, sheriff's deputies, Border Patrol agents and other law enforcement personnel have been arrested and accused of using their positions to profit from the drug trade along or near the border, from El Paso to the Rio Grande Valley …
>
> Will Glaspy, an official with the Drug Enforcement Administration in Houston who is in charge of the agency's operations in the Rio Grande Valley, said he believed law enforcement corruption was happening in the region at the same rate as in other parts of the country …

Fernandez frames the Panama Unit in three ways in these excerpts: as evidence of continuing corruption in the Rio Grande Valley, as part of borderlands corruption more broadly, and with a key caveat that even with these two frames, corruption may very well *not* happen more frequently in the Rio Grande Valley. Even the article's title is less accusatory than others: "In Drug Fight on Texas Border, Some Officers Play Both Sides."

The NPR three-article series in 2015 by Burnett and Peñaloza (2015a, 2015b, 2015c) is particularly interesting for three reasons. The series includes the only story I found that actually attempted to provide support for the claim that the Valley is steeped in corruption. One co-author is John Burnett, a journalist who regularly reports on the Valley and more often than not portrays the Valley in more complex, realistic ways than other national journalists do. Also, if you searched for "Rio Grande Valley corruption" on any search engine in 2018, these stories are the reference point for most other stories. They have become the benchmark. Yet, the articles are problematic in several ways. The titles and opening lines claim a level of corruption that is "entrenched" and all-encompassing to the region. In addition to the titles and opening lines discussed above, a NPR *Morning Edition* story entitled "In Rio Grande Valley, Some Campaign Workers are Paid to Harvest Votes" opens with these paragraphs:

> This week, NPR examines public corruption in South Texas. The FBI has launched a task force to clean up entrenched wrongdoing by public servants in the Rio Grande Valley. In the final part of this series, we examine vote-stealing and election fraud.
>
> A new FBI anti-corruption task force is trying to clean up the Rio Grande Valley of Texas. According to the Justice Department, in 2013, more public officials were convicted for corruption in South Texas than in any other region of the country. (Burnett & Peñaloza, 2015c)

This is the only national news article on Valley corruption in my dataset that presented any support for the claim of pervasive corruption in the Valley. There are issues with the statistic presented, however. Burnett and Peñaloza (2015c) cite a report that has an appended chart listing federal corruption convictions in the last decade (U.S. Department of Justice, 2014). Burnett and Peñaloza are correct. In 2013, the United States Attorney's office for the Southern Texas District did have the most federal convictions for public corruption. I do not dispute that figure. But, it does not tell the whole story. First, the Southern District of Texas is not limited to the Rio Grande Valley. It comprises seven divisions, two of which are in the Rio Grande Valley (McAllen Division and Brownsville Division). Other divisions in the Southern District include Laredo, Corpus Christi and Houston, Texas. The 2013 figure includes all seven divisions. There is no information on location of public corruption by division. Second, while the 2013 number (87) of federal conviction cases was very high as compared to other districts, it was also high in comparison to annual conviction numbers in the Southern District before and after 2014 (see Table 4.1 [U.S. Department of Justice, 2017]). Burnett and Peñaloza's (2015c) article cites the high 2013 number but

Table 4.1 Federal Districts with highest number of public corruption convictions by year, compared to the Southern Texas District (U.S. Department of Justice, 2017)

Year	Three Districts with Highest Number of Public Corruption Convictions		Southern Texas District
2004	Florida, Southern	78	11
	New Jersey	44	
	California, Eastern	39	
2005	Illinois, Northern	51	25
	Arizona	48	
	California, Central	42	
2006	New Jersey	47	21
	Florida, Middle	39	
	Virginia, Eastern	38	
2007	New Jersey	62	34
	California, Central	55	
	Alabama, Northern	39	
2008	Virginia, Eastern	72	64
	District of Columbia	66	
	Texas, Southern	64	
2009	Virginia, Eastern	57	26
	Ohio, Northern	49	
	Illinois, Northern	47	
2010	Ohio, Northern	65	23
	Virginia, Eastern	50	
	New Jersey	47	
2011	Puerto Rico	130	43
	Maryland	58	
	Virginia, Eastern	57	
2012	District of Columbia	47	26
	Texas, Western	47	
	Virginia, Eastern	41	
2013	Texas, Southern	83	83
	Maryland	47	
	Illinois, Northern	45	
2014	California, Central	66	29
	Puerto Rico	47	
	Texas, Northern	39	
2015	California, Central	53	11
	Texas, Northern	48	

(continued)

Table 4.1 (continued)

Year	Three Districts with Highest Number of Public Corruption Convictions		Southern Texas District
2016	Florida, Southern	42	3
	Georgia, Northern	67	
	Texas, Northern	49	
	Puerto Rico	41	

not the lower 2014 number of convictions in the Southern District: 29. Finally, data for these reports are based on survey recall responses, and survey completion rates are not given (Cordis & Milyo, 2016). An outlier year like 2013 in the Southern Texas District, then, could be a result of more corruption or just more convictions, and the bulk of those convictions could have been in the divisions other than the Rio Grande Valley. News articles such as the NPR story leave an indelible impression of embedded, inescapable corruption in the Valley. A review of data such as Table 4.1 suggests a different interpretation.

Corruption does exist in the Rio Grande Valley, as it does elsewhere. The convicted cases reported in the news attest to its presence in the Valley. There is corruption in local, state and federal officials and their offices, from school boards to elected state officials to federal law enforcement. But, is Valley corruption really more prevalent or pervasive than in other areas? That is, is there something inherently "Valley" about corruption? The impression is the Rio Grande Valley must be corrupt. The corruption must stem from its citizens and its proximity to Mexico. There are, of course, other possibilities. Convictions of local officials are on the rise throughout the country (Cordis & Milyo, 2016), which could suggest more scrutiny of local officials, an increase in corruption, or both. Might it be due to a higher proportion of what the FBI calls "high temptation environments," such as New York City or Chicago, in which law enforcement is regularly exposed to illegal economies, such as drug running or racketeering? Except for two years of conviction data pulled from recall surveys in a federal judicial district that includes one of America's largest cities as well as the Rio Grande Valley, there is scant evidence to suggest that Valley corruption is more extensive than in other parts of the nation.

Variation #3: Unauthorized migration and human and drug smuggling into the United States threaten the wellbeing of American communities and the security of the United States.

The Washington Post, "Competing border security plans in works," David Nakamura and Ed O'Keefe, July 23, 2014.

The Senate and House are poised to act on separate emergency border security plans, likely setting up a protracted debate in Washington as the Obama administration warns that it is running out of money to address the child-migrant crisis at the southern border …

Administration officials warned Tuesday that federal border control agencies are running out of money, even as they hailed progress in slowing the flow of undocumented immigrants entering the country through the southern Texas border …

"We're seeing the numbers of illegal migrants into the Rio Grande Valley drop over the last four to six weeks," Johnson said at a news conference in Washington. "We're not declaring victory …

Johnson's announcement came a day after Texas Gov. Rick Perry (R) announced that he is sending 1,000 of his National Guard troops to the border to help state law enforcement agents combat Mexican drug cartel activity inside Texas. Perry accused the Obama administration of not keeping the state secure while dealing with the crisis involving the minors.

But Johnson said DHS has increased resources since June under Operation Coyote, which has arrested and charged 192 human smugglers and their associates over the past month. Johnson said the administration had not received details from Perry's office detailing the role of the National Guard troops. Perry said Monday in Austin that the Guard would not have the power to apprehend people at the border but would work alongside state troopers at observation posts …

In the third common variation on the plot for news stories that refer to the Rio Grande Valley, unauthorized migration and human and drug smuggling into the United States threaten the well-being of the American community and the security of the nation. I spend more time on this variation of the national news story of the Valley, because it was by far the most prevalent variation. The Valley became synonymous with immigration in national news in the 2010's for two reasons: (1) an increase in the number of unaccompanied minors and family units from Central America crossing into the United States in the Valley and (2) immigration as a defining and polarizing element in election platforms in gubernatorial and presidential races during this time.

The significant increase in Central American children and families entering the United States without authorization in the early and mid-2010s was a flashpoint for American political debates over immigration, which increasingly became about national security (Pew Research Center, 2014). Prior to the 2010s, unauthorized migration into the United States historically was associated with Mexico and the American southern border, including crossings near El Paso, Texas, Tucson, Arizona, and San Diego, California (Chávez, 2001, 2008). In the 2010s, the overwhelming majority of Central Americans crossed in one Border Patrol region, the Rio Grande Valley.

The characterization of the Valley region as overburdened with migrants[4] and a region unable to police its borders became central to a state and national, largely Republican narrative of insecure, unsafe

---

[4]An important note about terminology: There was swirling debate in 2018 whether Central Americans crossing the border into the United States were refugees or unauthorized immigrants. Since the early 2010s, Central Americans are more likely to claim asylum when they cross into the United States. The term *refugee* is a state-recognized term that affords international legal protection, whereas *asylum seeker* applies to anyone who claims asylum upon entry and is awaiting determination of refugee status. Public opinion can influence whether the state recognizes certain categories of people as *refugees*, so use of the term prior to state designation also occurs. In essence, there is not one umbrella term than can capture all reasons, possible legal statuses, and perspectives for people who leave their home country and move to a new country. The term *immigrant* is ambiguous to the point that it elides or complicates humanitarian, legal, and political aspects of moving to a new country. More often than not, adjectives are placed in front of *immigrant* to differentiate. For example, *unauthorized, undocumented,* or *illegal immigrants* refer to people without official permission to enter or remain in a country and do not claim asylum; they have few legal protections. Each of these three adjectives is used in specific immigration rhetoric attached to certain political platforms and policies, and they are used differently by immigrants themselves (Merolla, Ramakrishnan, & Haynes, 2013). The term *illegal immigrant* is no longer an academic convention, as it implies criminality. In academic circles, *migrant* is preferred over *immigrant* as a general term (Castañeda, 2018; De Genova, 2002). Finally, there is often not a distinction between *migrant* and *immigrant* in popular usage, though some use *migrant* to indicate movement for work or education or to indicate some kind of temporality, such as seasonal movement for work. Because of the political stakes for migrants and politicians, terms applied to people who move from one country to another are often points of serious contention that have critical legal implications.

borders and understaffed immigration and law enforcement. It was countered with a mostly Democratic narrative that our southern borders were safer and more secure than ever but in the midst of a humanitarian crisis. Both sides called for immigration reform but with different priorities and strategies. The Valley became Ground Zero for the debate.

The New York Times, "G.O.P. pushes back on approving border funds," Ashley Parker, July 11, 2014.
WASHINGTON -- Congressional Republicans pushed back Thursday at President Obama's request for nearly $4 billion to help stem the surge of young migrants from Central America to Texas and to deal with the humanitarian crisis there, signaling that they expected concessions for their legislative approval.

The Republicans said that at the very least they planned to amend a 2008 law that affords migrant children from Central American countries extra legal protections when they cross the border. That measure, signed by President George W. Bush, has inadvertently made it more difficult to quickly return these children home.

"We're not giving the president a blank check," Speaker John A. Boehner said. "This is a problem of the president's own making. He's been president for five and a half years. When's he going to take responsibility for something?" …

Jeh Johnson, secretary of the Department of Homeland Security, told the committee that "we can and we will stem this recent tide of illegal migration into the Rio Grande Valley sector." …

USA Today, "Sen. Ron Johnson: Border agents report more violence since Obama immigration order," February 9, 2015.
WASHINGTON: Sen. Ron Johnson, fresh from a tour of the U.S.-Mexican border, said Monday agents told him they are seeing "an uptick in more violent behavior" among immigrants trying to cross into the United States illegally since President Barack Obama issued an executive order in November deferring deportation for millions of undocumented immigrants …

The Wisconsin Republican spent the weekend visiting Corpus Christi, Hidalgo and McAllen, Texas, where he met with ranchers, business owners, and local, state and federal law enforcement officials. He was joined by Delaware Sen. Tom Carper, the highest ranking Democrat on the Homeland Security Committee. They surveyed border areas in the Rio Grande Valley by helicopter, visited the U.S. Customs and Border Protection station in McAllen, took a boat tour and got a briefing on drone surveillance operations.

Johnson said he was struck by just how close and easy it is for immigrants to cross over illegally from Mexico and to get into American cities and towns where they blend in with Americans ...

Transcript from Fox News Network, HANNITY, August 24, 2016.

SEAN HANNITY, FOX NEWS HOST: And welcome to "Hannity." And we are broadcasting live from the ACL Theater in the Moody Theater in Austin, Texas, part two of our exclusive event with Republican presidential nominee Donald Trump. (CHEERS AND APPLAUSE)

HANNITY: Last night, you heard the heartbreaking stories of family members whose loved ones were killed by illegal immigrants. And we also showed you a lot of statistics on the impact that illegal immigration is having on you, the American people, and we'll be putting those slides and the information up on the screen all night.

DONALD TRUMP (R), PRESIDENTIAL CANDIDATE: Illegal immigrants are pouring into our country. They are being released by the tens of thousands into our communities with no regard for the impact on public safety or resources.

UNIDENTIFIED MALE: Anything that comes across, whether it's human beings, whether it's narcotics -- what people don't realize is that it takes a human being to bring something across.

TRUMP: By ending catch and release on the border, we will end the cycle of human smuggling and violence.

UNIDENTIFIED MALE: These are business ventures by criminal organizations.

TRUMP: We are going to build a great border wall to stop illegal immigration, to stop the gangs and the violence, and to stop the drugs from pouring into our communities!

The Rio Grande Valley was the epicenter of the border crossings by Central American families and children in 2014, 2015 and 2016. As a result, the Valley eclipsed San Diego, California, and Tucson, Arizona, in the national imagination as "the border." Stories in these years built on earlier narratives that pitched the region as littered with corruption in law enforcement. The corruption story bled into the undocumented immigration and border security stories to suggest an insecure and dangerous borderline in south Texas that could not be managed by local communities. Much of the political wrangling over the Valley's border was whether the Valley had the resources to keep unauthorized immigrants from crossing the geopolitical borderline, to apprehend them if they did cross, and to process them humanely and efficiently if they claimed asylum, as indicated in the excerpts below.

Fox News Network, YOUR WORLD WITH NEIL CAVUTO, "Interview with Texas Lieutenant Governor David Dewhurst," August 15, 2014.

ERIC BOLLING, GUEST HOST: A new report shows another 30,000 illegal immigration kids will cross the border in September and October, as the weather cools. And most of them will end up in the state of Texas.

David Dewhurst is the Republican lieutenant governor of that state. Thank you for joining us, sir. Tell us a little bit about the concerns Texas has with all these influx - this flooding of illegal children?

LT. GOV. DAVID DEWHURST (R), TEXAS: Well, this is a huge problem, Eric.

Obviously, we have had over 50,000 unaccompanied children come into Texas already. And using your number, if another 30,000 come in, that's a huge, huge number. Each 5,000 children, if we have to educate them, is going to cost the state of Texas some $50 million[5].

That's a huge amount of money. But, more importantly, this is -- to pick up something you just said, this is Barack Obama doing an end-around the Constitution. All he has to do is enforce his obligation, the federal government's obligation to secure the border.

But the federal government has failed miserably. That's why the state of Texas -- I started seven years ago, Eric, appropriating money to secure our border. We have appropriated $800 million. We have got high-altitude spotter aircraft, helicopters. We have got armor-plated gunboats. We have got people in the brush ...

---

[5]This number is disputed by financial analysts who work for public school districts in the Rio Grande Valley. According to a number of education leaders in the Valley, it is approximately half that figure.

The Washington Post, "National Roundup," December 16, 2015.
Gov. Greg Abbott (R) ordered Texas National Guard troops on Tuesday to remain at the Mexico border, extending once again a mission that began in 2014 when unaccompanied children started pouring into the country and that will continue because of another wave of arrivals.

As many as 1,000 armed troops patrolled the Rio Grande Valley at the height of what the White House once called a "humanitarian crisis" of children showing up at the Texas border. Military officials who previously refused to publicly state an end date on the deployment said after Abbott's announcement that December was supposed to have been the end of a nearly 18-month mission.

Neither Abbott nor the Texas National Guard would say when troops would now go home. Lt. Col. Travis Walters also would not disclose how many troops would remain, but he said no new troops would be deployed.

Abbott issued the order in response to U.S. Border Patrol figures showing that more than 10,000 unaccompanied children crossed into the United States in October and November, double the number of crossings in the same two months of 2014. The increase has already prompted federal officials to open two shelters in Texas and one in California.

The Associated Press, "2nd immigrant holding facility opening at Texas border," Frank Bajak, November 30, 2016.
HOUSTON (AP) - Federal immigration officials will set up a second temporary holding facility on the Texas border to deal with a surge in arrivals of families and unaccompanied children fleeing violence and poverty in Central America.

The temporary shelters at the Donna-Rio Bravo International Bridge in the Rio Grande Valley city of Donna will hold up to 500 people, U.S. Customs and Border Protection said Wednesday.

Earlier this month, officials opened a similar tent facility in Tornillo, outside El Paso, another busy port of entry.

CBP spokesman Richard Pauza said he did not yet have a date on when the Donna facility would open.

Donna bridge director Josue Garcia said federal officials contacted his office Monday about the plan, asking that arrangements be made for electricity.

The federal government has struggled to manage a surge in immigrants from the troubled nations of El Salvador, Honduras and Guatemala that began in 2014 ...

Republican and Democratic engagements with immigration in the Valley differed in terms of their scope, too. For the largely Republican narrative that arose in 2014, emphasis was on a purported recent (2012–2014) increase in unauthorized immigration numbers. For the largely Democratic narrative, emphasis was on a longer comparison (mid-1980s or mid-1990s to 2014).

There are four essential facts about immigration along the Southwest United States border from Texas to California to keep in mind at this point. First, proper use of terms is critical for correct interpretation of statistics about border crossings reported by U.S. Customs and Border Protection (CBP). CBP presents its statistics on undocumented immigration by two categories of immigrants, by fiscal year or month, and by geographic sector. The two CBP categories of immigrants are "apprehensions" and "inadmissibles." CBP uses specific definitions for each category:

Inadmissibles refers to individuals encountered at ports of entry who are seeking lawful admission into the United States but are determined to be inadmissible, individuals presenting themselves to seek humanitarian protection under our laws, and individuals who withdraw an application for admission and return to their countries of origin within a short timeframe.

Apprehensions refers to the physical control or temporary detainment of a person who is not lawfully in the U.S. which may or may not result in an arrest. (U.S. Customs and Border Enforcement, 2019)

Anyone who is detained crossing the border and does not have "inadmissibility" status will be arrested; however, inadmissibility status is often determined after detention, or legally defined *apprehension*. In a legal sense according to the CBP, then, *apprehension* is the action of arrest only for "removable" immigrants, which would not include people seeking asylum. Yet, clear distinctions in the number of immigrants who claim asylum and those who do not are not easy to come by. *Inadmissibles* is rarely used in publicly available data tables until 2016 or in public discussions in media or political platforms. *Apprehensions* is used almost exclusively. Seldom does *apprehension* refer only to the definition above: someone who is detained for crossing the border without documentation but prior to determination of arrest. Instead, *apprehension* in common parlance includes inadmissibles. *Apprehension* may be used to indicate a person detained by law enforcement under suspicion of being in the United States unlawfully but who may be seeking asylum.

It gets more confusing. Another formal, federal definition of *apprehension* does not include arrest of inadmissibles. The Glossary for U.S. Citizenship and Immigration Services (ICE) limits *apprehension* to "The arrest of a removable alien by U.S. Immigration and Customs Enforcement (ICE)" (U.S. Citizenship and Immigration Services, 2019). But, CBP data reports apprehensions that do and do not include those with inadmissibility status. Moreover, journalists, politicians, and CBP alike use *apprehensions* as an overarching category to report both detentions and arrests, and arrests in colloquial usage could include people seeking asylum as well as persons who are deemed "removable aliens." In sum, the use of *apprehension* to mean one of several kinds of detention, arrest, or motivations for immigration to the United States makes data interpretation difficult, at best, and easily coopted, at worst.

There are other layers, too, to understanding reported numbers of apprehensions. Each apprehension does not represent an individual detained for crossing the border. One individual may be apprehended more than once, but the numbers reported are frequently assumed to represent distinct individuals detained. Apprehensions also include people who have overstayed visas in addition to people who entered without authorization (Sapp, 2011). Annual statistics include processing not only at border offices but also at interior offices, such as Spokane, Washington; Buffalo, New York; and Grand Forks, North Dakota. They include people who may have been living and working in the United States for years who are picked up in immigration raids by Immigration and Customs Enforcement (ICE), whose frequency is influenced by national political action. *Apprehensions*, therefore, do not exclusively refer to people at the point of crossing the United States–Mexico border, and

Table 4.2 Apprehension numbers for select fiscal years (U.S. Border Patrol, 2018, 2019)[a]

Fiscal year	All sectors	Southwest border sectors	Rio Grande Valley sector
1986	1,693,000	1,615,844	121,783
1996	1,507,020	1,507,020	210,553
2000	1,676,438	1,643,679	133,243
2010	463,382	447,731	59,766
2014	486,651	479,371	256,393
2017	310,531	303,916	137,562

[a]For some years, different CBP reports cite different apprehension numbers, though the difference is rarely more than a few hundred

their counts reflect number of occurrences, not the number of individuals detained. Finally, apprehension and inadmissible numbers are not representations of border activity alone.

Second, overall undocumented immigration across the Southwest border as measured by "apprehensions" (in the general use of the word) has peaked three times, all before 2010 (see Table 4.2). That is, the impression that the overall number of people unlawfully entering the United States at the southern border since 2010 has increased is incorrect, according to CBP records. Moreover, the percentage of apprehensions of people from Mexico has remained the same or decreased. Mexican immigrants constitute less than half of all undocumented immigrants detained—that is, apprehensions, each year (Passell & Cohn, 2017). Third, while the number of apprehensions has decreased overall in the United States, the percentage of those apprehensions occurring in the Rio Grande Valley has significantly increased. In 1986, Rio Grande Valley sector apprehensions accounted for only 7.5% of total apprehensions whereas they accounted for 53.5% in 2014 and 45.3% in 2017 (see Table 4.2).

Fourth, the Valley made the news in 2014 not for its number of apprehensions in general but because of the rapid increase in the number of unaccompanied children and families from Central America entering the United States to seek asylum. Again, these people are not ultimately categorized as apprehensions-as-arrests. The peaks of "inadmissibles" have a different pattern and timeline than "apprehensions" (that result in deportation without consideration of asylum). The absolute numbers of inadmissible immigrants increased in the 2010s with a noticeable jump in 2014, so that a larger proportion of apprehensions consisted of people seeking asylum. They were more likely to cross the border in the Rio Grande Valley in the 2010s than another crossing point, although there was also an increase in crossings at El Paso, Texas, in 2019 (Gramlich & Noe-Bustamante, 2019). In sum, while more families and unaccompanied minor children were crossing the border to seek asylum in the mid-2010s, the overall number of unauthorized immigrants decreased or remained about the same from 2010 until 2018 (Biailik, 2019).

These dates and terms reframe the national news stories about the Valley, border security, and immigration. Their slippage in media, CBP, and political statements helps explain the political discourse around immigration in gubernatorial and presidential campaigns in the mid-2010s. The public debate over immigration quickly turned into a debate about national security and identity, perhaps in large part because of misunderstandings about immigration terms and patterns and assumptions about migrants themselves, but also because the 2014 peak coincided with state and national election cycles. It then stayed higher than normal in 2015 and 2016, right in the middle and end of the presidential election cycle when potential candidates built and executed their political platforms. Indeed, five state and national political leaders were often the subject of stories about immigration and treatment of Central American children in the Rio Grande Valley: Rick Perry, Barack Obama, Gregg Abbott, Hillary Rodham Clinton, and Donald Trump.

The 2014 Texas Gubernatorial and 2016 Presidential Election Cycles

The year 2014 was a gubernatorial election year in Texas. In 2013, Texas Governor Rick Perry announced he would not seek another term as governor, and then Texas Attorney General Greg Abbott announced his bid for the seat. Abbott was elected Texas governor in 2014. In 2014, Abbott launched his Bicentennial Blueprint (https://www.gregab bott.com/issues/, accessed August 13, 2018), his political action plan as governor. After economic growth and protection of individual liberties comes "Secure our Communities: Making sure Texans are safe." The first priority under Secure our Communities is "Securing the border."

In 2014, the sitting president was a two-term Democrat, Barack Obama. Hillary Rodham Clinton became the Democratic presidential candidate in 2016. President Obama's approach to immigration emphasized border enforcement, pathways to citizenship for unauthorized immigrants, and increased deportations of immigrants convicted of crimes. In a 2013 immigration speech, Obama characterized unauthorized immigrants as having "been here for years. And the overwhelming majority of these individuals aren't looking for any trouble. They're contributing members of the community. They're looking out for their families. They're looking out for their neighbors. They're woven into the fabric of our lives." He talked about how to "fix the system" to improve communities' lives and economies, not just those of immigrants. His approach entailed the following: "continuing to strengthen security at the border," to enforce laws for criminals, and to have a clear "pathway to citizenship" for others (Obama, Remarks by the President on Comprehensive Immigration Reform, 2013).

Political differences over approaches to immigration begin to play out in the national news during 2014, when the number of unaccompanied minor children crossing into the United States peaked during the summer months. Texas Governor Perry blamed President Obama for not securing the border. President Obama focused on a more comprehensive approach to reducing unaccompanied minor crossings. The Valley is the example for stories about the political drama as well as the actual crossings and conditions of the detained children, as illustrated by the following excerpts.

The Wall Street Journal, "*Obama urges lawmakers to pass border measures,*" *Colleen McCain Nelson, July 9, 2014.*

After the meeting [with President Obama], Gov. Perry said in a statement that he had urged the president to take steps to secure the border and ease the crisis.

"Five hundred miles south of here in the Rio Grande Valley, there is a humanitarian crisis unfolding that has been created by bad public policy, in particular the failure to secure the border," Mr. Perry said. "Securing the border is attainable, and the president needs to commit the resources necessary to get this done."

The Associated Press, "Perry sending National Guard troops to border," Christopher Sherman and Will Weissart, July 22, 2014.

Gov. Rick Perry is deploying up to 1,000 National Guard troops to the Texas-Mexico border over the next month to combat what he said Monday were criminals exploiting a surge of children pouring into the U.S. illegally.

Perry, a vocal critic of the White House's response to the border crisis who is himself mulling a second presidential run, said the state has a responsibility to act after "lip service and empty promises" from Washington.

"I will not stand idly by while our citizens are under assault and little children from Central America are detained in squalor," the governor said …

President Obama also responded with calls for more extensive immigration reform. He placed the unaccompanied minor crossings within the larger problem of a broken immigration system, not an insecure border. In his rebuttal to Gov. Perry after meeting with him in Texas, Obama made a public statement, saying,

Now, right now, there are more Border Patrol agents and surveillance resources on the ground than at any time in our history, and we deport almost 400,000 migrants each year. But as soon as it became clear that this year's migration to the border was different than in past years, and I directed FEMA to coordinate the response to the border, members of my Cabinet and my staff have made multiple trips to facilities there.

And we're also addressing the root of the problem. I sent Vice President Biden and Secretary Kerry and Secretary Johnson to meet with Central American leaders, as well as working with our international partners to go after smugglers who are putting their kids' lives at risk.

The challenge is, is Congress prepared to act to put the resources in place to get this done? Another way of putting it, and I said this directly to the governor, is, are folks more interested in politics or are they more interested in solving the problem? (as quoted in CNN, 2014)

In a 2014 immigration speech (Obama, 2014), Obama began by claiming problems in the immigration system in the United States were due to people who "flout the rules" by immigrating without authorization but also due to policies that force those who are unauthorized to "remain in the shadows, or risk their families being torn apart." Obama went on to say how his first action as President was "doing what I could to secure our borders" even though "the number of people trying to cross our border illegally is at its lowest level since the 1970s." The remainder of his speech focused on "comprehensive immigration reform" from increased border security to improved retention of high-skilled immigrants to focusing deportations on immigrants convicted of crimes.

As the political debates over immigration matured during this time, in news coverage the Valley remained a place out of control. There were stories about smugglers who took advantage of an overtaxed Border Patrol and increased shipments. Other stories focused on increasing numbers, "waves" and "surges" of children and adults crossing the border. Stories told of militias appearing with weapons in the dead of night, dressed in camouflage, ostensibly to aid an understaffed border enforcement team of Border Patrol, National Guard, and Texas Department of Public Safety officers. Some stories talked about the existing border wall as little more than nuisance to smugglers, rather than an impediment. Below are but a few examples.

The Associated Press, "Militias complicate situation on Texas border," Christopher Sherman, August 18, 2014.
MISSION, Texas (AP). – On a recent moonlit night, Border Patrol agents began rounding up with immigrants hiding in and around a canal near the Rio Grande. A state trooper soon arrived to help. Then out of the darkness emerged seven more men in fatigues.
Agents assumed the camouflaged crew that joined in pulling the immigrants from the canal's milky green waters was a tactical unit from the Texas Department of Public Safety .... These men belonged to the Texas Militia, a group that dresses like a SWAT team and carries weapons but has no law enforcement training or authority of any kind.

Transcript from Fox News Network, HANNITY, July 11, 2014.

HANNITY: Welcome back to HANNITY. And we are broadcasting tonight from the southern border. The Rio Grande is right behind me in Texas, where the invasion of illegals is now spiraling out of control ...

USA Today, "Fence along the border is not enough," Rick Jervis, May 13, 2014.

The drive between Brownsville and McAllen on U.S. Highway 281 is a pastoral stretch studded with cornfields, palm groves, taquerías and small, well-kept homes.

The border with Mexico sits a stone's throw away. Every dozen yards or so, the massive, rust-colored border fence emerges from a cornfield and winds its way toward the highway. It's an imposing sight: an 18-foot-high steel-and-concrete structure stretching for miles and seemingly impenetrable.

But the barricade belies the rising influx of humans and drugs passing through the Rio Grande Valley each day. Smugglers in recent years have shifted their efforts away from Arizona to this stretch of land in South Texas.

In 2015, both former Texas Governor Rick Perry and Donald Trump publicly announced bids for the Republican candidate for President. Perry's run was short; he pulled out of the race later that year. Perry had often said during his gubernatorial years, including at the 2015 Conservative Political Action Conference, that he would not consider comprehensive immigration reform until the border was "secure" (Price, 2015; Ramshaw & Aguilar, 2011). Donald Trump won the American presidential election in November of 2016 on a Republican platform that centered on immigration reform markedly different in tone than that of opponent Hillary Rodham Clinton and outgoing President Obama. In his Republican National Convention speech, Trump opened with a picture of an unsafe, chaotic, and violent America, and he placed blame squarely on "illegal immigrants with criminal records." He later returned to the theme of violent, unauthorized immigrants whose work lowers wages for American citizens. Trump claimed, "We are going to build a great border wall to stop illegal immigration, to stop the gangs and the violence, and to stop the drugs from pouring into our communities .... By ending catch-and-release on the border, we will stop the cycle of human smuggling and violence. Illegal border crossings will go down. Peace will be restored" (Trump, 2016).

Trump's immigration reform almost exclusively focused on border enforcement and deportation. He promised to end the DACA (Deferred Action for Childhood Arrivals) program, instituted through an Executive Branch policy memorandum by President Obama. In Trump's vision, the Rio Grande Valley was the place where the United States would stop all undocumented immigrants through the construction of a continuous wall and increased militarization. By contrast, the Democratic nominee for president, Hillary Rodham Clinton, advocated for comprehensive immigration reform, which typically indicates a simultaneous push for pathways to citizenship, more efficient processing of immigration applications and deportations, and increased border enforcement. Clinton went further than Obama to include health care for all families, regardless of immigration status, enhanced naturalization procedures and immigrant integration programs, ending family detention, and closing private immigration detention centers (Office of Hillary Rodham Clinton, 2019). Donald Trump won the 2016 American presidency, and his vision of the border, typified by the Valley image in the news, began to dominate:

Transcript from NPR's Weekend Edition, "The Call-In: Crossing the U.S.-Mexico border," Sunday, March 5, 2017.
MARY LOUISE KELLY: And this is the Call In, our segment where you tell us what you are thinking. As you'll have noticed, Lulu Garcia-Navarro is away this week. That's because she's been reporting from Texas along the U.S.-Mexico border. Securing that border has been one of President Trump's signature agenda items. He reiterated the point during his first joint address to Congress this past week.

The Associated Press, "House speaker gets firsthand look at US-Mexico Border," February 22, 2017.
MCALLEN, Texas (AP) - U.S. House Speaker Paul Ryan visited the Rio Grande valley [sic] on Wednesday for a firsthand look at the

U.S.-Mexico border as the Trump administration steps up immigration enforcement and prepares to ask Congress to pay for a border wall.

It was the first time the Wisconsin Republican had visited the border, and protesters gathered to meet his arrival in McAllen, Texas, with hand-painted signs protesting Trump policies. Ryan led a small group of fellow Republicans on the trip, including Rep. Michael McCaul of Texas, who chairs the Homeland Security Committee in the House.

In McAllen, Ryan came face to face with some of the challenges that arise in building a wall along the entire 2,000-mile border, which includes much remote and inhospitable terrain as well as the Rio Grande, the river between Texas and Mexico. He met with local officials and toured the area by boat and helicopter, and even briefly rode on a horse.

"When you see with your own eyes the many challenges facing our law enforcement professionals along the border, it gives you even greater respect for the work that they do day-in and day-out. But more tools and more support are needed for them to do their jobs effectively," Ryan said in a statement after the visit. "Congress is committed to securing the border and enforcing our laws, and together with the Trump administration, we will get this done."

Transcript from CNN LIVE, "Before the wall, a journey on the border," February 11, 2017.

ED LAVANDERA, CNN CORRESPONDENT: So this is the Rio Grande valley [sic]?

ROBERT CAMERON, TEXAS BORDER TOURS: This is the Rio Grande valley [sic].

LAVANDERA: And this is a common sight?

CAMERON: This is a very common sight. So this is a wall that George Bush built us, the fence.

LAVANDERA: This journey across the U.S./Mexico border begins in south Texas where the Rio Grande empties into the Gulf of Mexico and on a rugged ride in an all-terrain vehicle with Robert Cameron. He runs an ATV border tour business in the small town of Progresso. Do you think people have that impression of the border as this scary dangerous place?

CAMERON: A scary, dangerous place, absolutely. It's not as bad as people make it seem to be.

LAVANDERA: Cameron was born in Mexico, is now a U.S. citizen, was a long time Democrat until Donald Trump came along and made him Republican. He supports the idea of Trump's wall, but he sees holes in the plan.

The Washington Post, "Trump's 'big, beautiful wall' will be much smaller than billed," by Tracy Jan and David Nakamura, April 25, 2017.

Despite more than a year of campaign rhetoric about a "big, beautiful wall" spanning the entirety of the border with Mexico, the Trump administration plans to start with a much less ambitious footprint focusing only on the most highly trafficked corridors, according to a Department of Homeland Security planning document.

Identified as "high priority" in the document are the border sectors of the Rio Grande Valley in the southern tip of Texas - encompassing Rio Grande City, McAllen and Weslaco - as well as El Paso, Tucson and San Diego.

The areas were selected because of their proximity to urban centers and roads, allowing those who cross illegally to vanish quickly, according to the document, which was made public by congressional committee staffers ...

President Trump's depictions of the border were not the only ones represented in national news stories. To be sure, the majority of the stories that referenced the Valley in 2015 through August 2017 focused on immigration and political debate or policy. However, a few stories with descriptions of the Valley and its residents emphasized the diversity of landscape and viewpoints. A small but noticeable shift occurred to include depictions of a significantly more differentiated Valley in some national news stories. Common tropes and stereotypes were recognized, and a few alternative storylines were proposed. Valley characters in the stories became less predictable. Economic development directors were quoted, and local politicians were cited as having differing viewpoints.

For example, the same NPR journalist, John Burnett, who wrote the stories about corruption in the Valley in 2015 wrote a story earlier that same year about enduring impacts of negative stereotypes of the Valley in national political discussions about national security, framed around the ultimately unsuccessful Secure Our Borders First Act (H.R. 399):

Transcript from All Things Considered, "Beefed-up border security proposal unsettles Texas business leaders," John Burnett, January 27, 2015.

A bill proposing tighter security on the southern border has provoked a backlash from some South Texas leaders. They say the measures may hurt trade with Mexico, the state's largest trading partner ...

BURNETT: If it passes, the Secure Our Border First Act of 2015 would effectively put the Department of Homeland Security on a wartime footing in regard to the southern border, deploy more spy blimps, drones and ground sensors, build more fences, roads, boat ramps and forward operating bases, call in more National Guard, borrow air assets from the Department of Defense, divert military equipment headed home from Afghanistan. And if the Homeland Security secretary can't stop illegal crossers in five years, he cannot fly on government aircraft or get a raise. When Keith Patridge heard about it, he blanched. Once again, Washington doesn't get the border.

KEITH PATRIDGE: And what they're proposing with more walls and more military equipment is not what we would prefer to see .... We deal with it every day. When people call, they say - they maybe have an interest in locating here - they'll say, is it safe for us to come to McAllen? Well, that's absolutely ridiculous. You know, every day there are over 800,000 people that get up in the morning, go to work, come home at night, have dinner, go to a ballgame, and nothing happens.

BURNETT: Keith Patridge says FBI statistics consistently show that Texas border cities have among the lowest crime rates in the country ...

In the NPR story above and the article in *The Associated Press* quoted below, the counterargument is that the border is safer, not more violent, than other areas of the United States. Keith Patridge, president and CEO of the McAllen Economic Development Corporation, was a central figure in efforts to rescript the border story to one of thriving binational trade and economic potential in rapid response manufacturing. In the *Associated Press* story, international trade is described as "booming" in the Rio Grande Valley, benefitting not only the region but also the state and nation. In the excerpt below, even the landscape is hospitable and "fertile":

The Associated Press, "Americans who live near border say Trump's wall is unwelcome," Frank Bajak, November 22, 2016.

LOS EBANOS, Texas (AP) - Forget Donald Trump's Great Wall.

The people who live in the bustling, fertile Rio Grande Valley, where the U.S. border meets the Gulf of Mexico, think a "virtual wall" of surveillance technology makes a lot more sense. It's already in wide use and expanding.

Erecting a 40-foot concrete barrier across the entire 1,954-mile frontier with Mexico, as Trump promised during the presidential campaign, collides head-on with multiple realities: geology, fierce local resistance and the question of who pays the bill ...

The U.S. side of the border is quite safe, Weisberg-Stewart [chair, Committee on Immigration and Border Security, Texas Border Coalition] said. "We are not in a war zone."

In fact, cross-border trade has been booming. In 2014, more than $246 billion worth of goods and 3.7 million trucks crossed the Texas-Mexico border, according to the coalition.

While much of the border's Mexican side has been afflicted by drug cartel-related violence, crime in the Rio Grande Valley, home to 1.3 million people, has been consistently lower than other Texas cities ...

A few stories considered the environmental impact of additional physical barriers on the U.S.–Mexico border. In 2017, a NPR story, again by John Burnett, emphasized the biodiversity of the Valley region, connecting it to critiques of Trump's planned wall extension:

Transcript from NPR's Morning Edition, "Specs for border wall show it would divide Texas wildlife refuge," David Greene and John Burnett, August 24, 2017.

DAVID GREENE: The South Texas borderlands get a lot of bad press as the site of illegal immigration, drug smuggling, occasional cartel mayhem. That's how the president sells the border wall. What many people don't realize is the southernmost tip of Texas is also home to many butterflies and other rare animals, native grasses and herbaceous plants. They're one-of-a-kind nature preserves. And as NPR's John Burnett reports, residents are furious that the border wall could destroy the refuges.

JOHN BURNETT: To see another view of the Rio Grande Valley, climb up the metal steps to the top of the hawk tower in the Santa Ana National Wildlife Refuge. The rest of the valley [sic] may be awash with trailer parks and great fruit orchards and Home Depots, but from up here, you look down on a dense emerald canopy of original subtropical forest.

JIM CHAPMAN: It is so primeval.

JOHN BURNETT: Within this 2,000-acre federal sanctuary dwells an ark of biodiversity - 400 species of birds, half of the nation's butterfly species and the shy, endangered ocelot …

JOHN BURNETT: The chief of the Rio Grande Valley sector of the Border Patrol is adamant that an 18-foot iron fence through the reserve is necessary because smugglers like the dense brush, too.

MANNY PADILLA: The refuge is a huge refuge for smuggling activity as well.

Despite these few exceptions, the overwhelming majority of national news stories that included mention of the Rio Grande Valley from 2010 through August 2017 were about poor health care access, corruption and drug smuggling, and undocumented immigration. Excluding weather (see beginning of chapter), a minority of stories focused on other topics in the Valley that were of interest to national audiences. In fact, less than 15% of stories were about something other than the dominant themes discussed in this chapter.

My experience reading the hundreds of articles is telling. Each day of coding, I would become increasingly depressed as story after story characterized my home as something wrong with our nation. If I came upon an article that took a different approach, I found myself sitting up straighter with hands poised over my keyboard to take notes. I would slow my reading speed to catch any suggestion of something other than the negative. I wanted to privilege the positive but did not want to ignore the very real challenges our region faces. The solution, to me, seemed apparent. Let Valley residents tell their own stories and define their own home.

Conclusion

The single story creates stereotypes, and the problem with stereotypes is not that they are untrue, but that they are incomplete. They make one story become the only story. (Adichie, 2009)

In all cases, it seems to me, the moral of the stories is that things are and are not what they seem. (Abu-Lughod, 2008, p. 19)

In the summer of 2016, I was on my way back to my parents' home after spending several wonderful hours with a group of community leaders and nuns in a *colonia* up the Valley ('up the Valley' means following the Rio Grande River as it meanders northwest from Brownsville). Through collaboration and long years of political and physical work, the *colonia* had plumbing, electricity, a community center with a health care clinic, a resale store, an exercise room, and a workforce development area where community members decided what to make and how to sell their items. Hopping back onto Highway 83/Interstate 2, I picked up some El Pato *queso* and chips in La Joya. I detoured a half mile south for a walk with the locusts and grackles in Bentsen State Park, tucked up against the Rio Grande River. After I parked, I walked around a roadblock by Border Patrol. I thought about news stories about border security. On my way to the picnic tables, I ran into birders from other parts of the United States, locals taking a lunch break, and several dozen butterflies. The locusts were loud that day, overshadowing the noisy grackles in the trees. It was humid but the ground was dry and cracked with scraggly grey-green grass around the picnic tables—summer in the Valley. As I watched the people and animals in the park, I thought about other people I know who are unauthorized immigrants and the restrictions on their movements. They could not have "gone around" the Border Patrol. Then I checked myself. I was thinking of a group of people exclusively by their citizenship status rather than all of their other identities that also matter, including family member, community member, student, worker, person of faith, and others. Certainly, the surveillance in the Valley can be overwhelming, and citizenship status directly impacts well-being. But, surveillance does not exclusively define who people are.

My point is this. There are many truths to what the Valley is. One truth we share in the Valley is that the Rio Grande Valley is located on the border of Mexico. We are what is known as a borderlands, a mixing of two places that produces something distinct and unto itself. Another truth is that the Valley is militarized and surveilled compared to other parts of the nation. Border surveillance is a daily part of life here, but militarization is not the extent of Valley life. This is perhaps the most important truth for us in the Valley as it is for anyone anywhere else: we define our lives by our relationships and our communities. These relationships and communities make the Valley "home" to us, even for some of us who no longer live in the Valley. National news stories are incomplete pictures of our home. The enduring single story of the Valley is one of negativity, rooted in a very old idea that Mexico is not as good as the United States. The region's descriptors—corrupt, poor, sick, and a threat to the rest of the United States by virtue of its porosity and proximity Mexico, are classic tropes in the Global North's discourse about the Global South.

Creative writers, e.g., Anzaldua (1987) and artists, e.g., Guillermo Gómez-Peña (2001, 1996), have been challenging the incomplete borderlands image for decades. Academics really began to understand the borderlands and, though to a lesser extent, the Valley in the 1990s as a complex, hard to pin down and rapidly changing place. I distinctly remember being in graduate school in the mid-1990s and watching the U.S.–Mexico borderlands literature develop in Anthropology. I was both elated and disgruntled. It was high time the region was recognized as significant and powerful. But, it was also as if anthropologists felt they were "discovering" a foreign place.

Borderlands writers and artists do not have one story of the Valley, nor do Valley leaders. They do, however, share a few ideas about our region. We are a place of variation and difference that is productive and emergent as a result of living in a bicultural, bilingual, and binational region. Languages, ideas, and cultural norms mix, match, conflict, and bump up against one another. Most see the Valley as a distinct social sphere that can produce new and better solutions to national problems of poor health outcomes, economic opportunities, and education. Stories from activists, creative writers, and academics have so much in common, even though they acknowledge and respect the different ways people come to understand and experience the borderlands. Just as there should be no single story about the Valley in the national news, there is not a single story of the Valley among its leaders, artists, writers or scholars. We would not expect there to be. Rather, our national understanding of a region should be rooted in the voices and experiences of the people who live there. It is also a matter of thinking differently about a place.

Works Cited

Abrajano, M., & Hajnal, Z. L. (2015). *White backlash: Immigration, race and politics*. Princeton: Princeton University Press.

Abu-Lughod, L. (2008). *Writing women's worlds: Bedouin stories* (2nd ed.). Berkeley: University of California Press.

Adichie, C. N. (2009, July 10). The danger of a single story. *TEDGlobal*. TED.

Agnew, J. (2008). Border on the mind: Re-framing border thinking. *Ethics & Global Politics, 1*(4), 175–181.

Anzaldua, G. (1987). *Borderlands: The new Mestiza = La Frontera*. San Francisco: Spinsters/Aunt Lute.

Appadurai, A. (1996). *Modernity at large: Cultural dimensions of globalization*. Minneapolis, MN: University of Minneapolis Press.

Bhabha, H. (1994). *The location of culture*. London: Routledge.

Biailik, K. (2019, January 16). *Border apprehensions increased in 2018—Especially for migrant families*. Pew Research Center. Retrieved May 5, 2019, from https://www.pewresearch.org/fact-tank/2019/01/16/border-apprehensions-of-migrant-families-have-risen-substantially-so-far-in-2018/.

Boone, E. H., & Mignolo, W. D. (Eds.). (1994). *Writing without words: Alternative literacies in Mesoamerica and the Andes*. Durham, NC: Duke University Press.

Bowman, T. P. (2016). *Blood oranges: Colonialism and agriculture in the south Texas borderlands*. College Station, TX: Texas A&M University Press.

Burnett, J., & Peñaloza, M. (2015a, July 6). Corruption on the border: Dismantling misconduct in the Rio Grande Valley. *All Things Considered*.

Burnett, J., & Peñaloza, M. (2015b, July 6). With corruption rampant, good cops go bad in Texas' Rio Grande Valley. *All Things Considered.*

Burnett, J., & Peñaloza, M. (2015c, July 7). In Rio Grande Valley, some campaign workers are paid to harvest votes. *Morning Edition.*

Castañeda, H. (2018, August 10). Personal communication.

Chávez, J. R. (2011). Aliens in their native lands: The persistence of internal colonial theory. *Journal of World History, 22*(4), 785–809.

Chávez, J. R. (2015). *Beyond domestic empire: Internal- and post-colonial New Mexico* (pp. 1–31). History Faculty Publications. Retrieved November 4, 2019, from http://scholar.smu.edu/hum_sci_history_research/3.

Chávez, L. R. (2001). *Covering immigration: Popular images and the politics of the nation.* Berkeley: University of California Press.

Chávez, L. R. (2008). *The Latino threat: Constructing immigrants, citizens, and the nation.* Stanford: Stanford University Press.

Chavez, M. (2012). Border theories and the realities of daily public exchanges in North America. *Eurasia Border Review, 3*(1), 201–214.

CNN. (2014, July 9). Transcript. *360 Degrees.* CNN.

Comaroff, J., & Comaroff, J. L. (2012). *Theory from the south or, how Euro-America is evolving toward Africa.* Boulder: Paradigm Publishers.

Cordis, A. S., & Milyo, J. (2016, January 6). Measuring public corruption in the United States: Evidence from administrative records of federal prosecutions. *Public Integrity, 18*(2), 127–148.

Correa-Cabrera, G. (2012). The spectacle of drug violence: American public discourse, media, and border enforcement in the Texas-Tamaulipas border region during drug-war times. *Norteamérica, 7*(2), 199–220.

DeChaine, D. R. (Ed.). (2012). *Border rhetorics: Citizenship and identity on the U.S.-Mexico border.* Tuscaloosa, AL: University of Alabama Press.

De Genova, N. P. (2002). Migrant "illegality" and deportability in everyday life. *Annual Review of Anthropology, 31,* 419–447.

Donnan, H., & Wilson, T. M. (Eds.). (2010). *Borderlands: Ethnographic approaches to security, power, and identity.* Lanham, MD: University Press of America.

Federal Bureau of Investigation. (2016, December 22). *Corruption on the border: New campaign enlists the public's help.* FBI. Retrieved January 7, 2020, from https://www.fbi.gov/news/stories/border-corruption-campaign-enlists-publics-help.

Federal Bureau of Investigation. (n.d.). *What we investigate: Public corruption.* FBI. Retrieved January 7, 2020, from https://www.fbi.gov/investigate/public-corruption.

Flores, L. A., & Villarreal, M. (2012). Mobilizing for national inclusion: The discursivity of whiteness among Texas Mexicans' arguments for desegregation. In D. R. DeChaine (Ed.), *Border rhetorics: Citizenship and identity on the US-Mexico frontier* (pp. 86–102). Tuscaloosa, AL: The University of Alabama Press.

Gawande, A. (2009, June 1). The cost conundrum: What a Texas town can teach us about health care. *The New Yorker.* https://www.newyorker.com/magazine/2009/06/01/the-cost-conundrum.

Goffman, E. (1963). *Stigma: Notes on the management of spoiled identity.* New York, NY: Simon & Schuster.

Goltz, D. B., & Pérez, K. (2012). Borders without bodies: Affect, proximity, and utopian imaginaries through "lines in the sand". In D. R. DeChaine (Ed.), *Border rhetorics: Citizenship and identity on the US-Mexico frontier* (pp. 163–180). Tuscaloosa, AL: The University of Alabama Press.

Gomez, A. (2012). Deus Vult: John L. O'Sullivan, manifest destiny, and American democratic messianism. *American Political Thought,* 236–262.

Gómez-Peña, G. (1996). *The new world border: Prophecies, poems & locuras for the end of the century.* San Francisco, CA: City Lights.

Gómez-Peña, G. (2001). *Dangerous border crossers.* New York: Routledge.

Gramlich, J., & Noe-Bustamante, L. (2019). *What's happening at the U.S.-Mexico border in 6 charts.* Pew Research Center. Retrieved May 2, 2019, from https://www.pewresearch.org/fact-tank/2019/04/10/whats-happening-at-the-u-s-mexico-border-in-6-charts/.

Guillette, G. S. (2016, May 6). *Globalization.* Oxford Bibliographies in Anthropology. Retrieved January 5, 2020, from https://www.oxfordbibliographies.com/view/document/obo-9780199766567/obo-9780199766567-0010.xml#firstMatch.

Heyman, J. M. (2012). Constructing a "perfect" wall: Race, class, and citizenship in US-Mexico border policing. In P. Barber & W. Lem (Eds.), *Migration in the 21st century: Political economy and ethnography* (pp. 153–174). New York and London: Routledge.

Heyman, J., Slack, J., & Guerra, E. (2018). Bordering a "crisis": central American asylum seekers and the reproduction of dominant border enforcement practices. *Journal of the Southwest, Winter,* 754–786.

Kearney, M. (1995). The local and the global: The anthropology of globalization and transnationalism. *Annual Review of Anthropology, 24,* 547–565.

López, A. J. (2007). Introduction: The (post)global south. *The Global South, 1*(1), 1–11.

LUPE. (2016). *About us*. LUPE. Retrieved January 7, 2020, from https://lup enet.org/about-us/.

McLeod, J. (2007). Introduction. In J. McLeod (Ed.), *The Routledge companion to postcolonial studies* (pp. 1–18). London: Routledge.

Merolla, J., Ramakrishnan, S. K., & Haynes, C. (2013). "Illegal", "undocumented", or "unauthorized": equivalency frames, issue frames, and public opinion on immigration. *Perspectives on Politics, 11*(3), 789–807.

Murphy, K. (2016, August 10). Texans beat the heat with water from Mexico. *The New York Times*, p. (digital).

National Federation of Independent Business v. Sebelius. 567 US 519 (2012).

Nevins, J. (2010 [2002]). *Operation gatekeeper and beyond: The war on "illegals" and the remaking of the U.S.-Mexico boundary*. New York: Routledge.

Obama, B. (2013, January 29). *Remarks by the president on comprehensive immigration reform*. The White House President Barack Obama. Retrieved January 2, 2020, from https://obamawhitehouse.archives.gov/the-press-off ice/2013/01/29/remarks-president-comprehensive-immigration-reform.

Obama, B. (2014, November 20). Transcript: Obama's immigration speech. *The Washington Post*. Retrieved January 7, 2020, from https://www.washin gtonpost.com/politics/transcript-obamas-immigration-speech/2014/11/20/ 14ba8042-7117-11e4-893f-86bd390a3340_story.html.

Office of Hillary Rodham Clinton. (2019). *Immigration reform*. Office of Hillary Rodham Clinton. Retrieved January 7, 2020, from https://www.hil laryclinton.com/issues/immigration-reform/.

Ono, K. A. (2012). Borders that travel: Matters of the figural border. In D. R. DeChaine (Ed.), *Border rhetorics: Citizenship and identity on the US-Mexico frontier* (pp. 19–32). Tuscaloosa, AL: The University of Alabama Press.

Ono, K. A., & Sloop, J. M. (2002). *Shifting borders: Rhetoric, immigration, and california's proposition 187*. Philadelphia, PA: Temple University Press.

Passell, J. S., & Cohn, D. (2017). *As Mexican share declined, U.S. unauthorized immigrant population fell in 2015 below recession level*. Pew Research Center. Retrieved May 2, 2019, from https://www.pewresearch.org/fact-tank/2017/ 04/25/as-mexican-share-declined-u-s-unauthorized-immigrant-population-fell-in-2015-below-recession-level/.

Payan, T. (2006). *The three U.S.-Mexico border wars: Drugs, immigration, and homeland security*. Westport, CT: Praeger.

Pew Research Center. (2014, July 16). *Surge of central American children roils U.S. immigration debate*. Pew Research Center. Retrieved January 7, 2020, from https://www.people-press.org/2014/07/16/surge-of-central-ame rican-children-roils-u-s-immigration-debate/.

Planned Parenthood v. Casey. 505 US 833 (1992).

Price, B. (2015, February 27). Perry at CPAC: No immigration reform without border security. *Breitbart*.

Proyecto Azteca. (2019). *About us*. Proyecto Azteca. Retrieved January 7, 2020, from https://www.proyectoazteca.org/.

Ramshaw, E., & Aguilar, J. (2011, September 11). Is Perry tough enough on immigration—For republicans? *The Texas Tribune*.

Redden, M. (2009, June 9). Obama's favorite New Yorker article. *The New Yorker*. Retrieved March 21, 2019, from https://www.newyorker.com/news/news-desk/obamas-favorite-new-yorker-article.

Rodríguez, J. J. (2010). *The literatures of the U.S.-Mexican war: Narrative, time, and identity*. Austin, TX: University of Texas Press.

Rosaldo, R. (1993). *Culture & truth: The remaking of social analysis*. Boston, MA: Beacon Press.

Sabol, S. (2017). *The touch of civilization: Comparing American and Russian internal colonization*. Boulder, CO: University of Colorado Press.

Said, E. (1978). *Orientalism*. London: Routledge & Kegan Paul Ltd.

Sapp, L. (2011). *Apprehensions by U.S. border patrol: 2005–2010*. Department of Homeland Security. Retrieved May 6, 2019, from https://www.dhs.gov/xlibrary/assets/statistics/publications/ois-apprehensions-fs-2005-2010.pdf.

Sherman, C. (2014, April 30). *South Texas officers sentenced on drug charges*. The Associated Press.

Silvers, J. (2013). The affordable care act: Objectives and likely results in an imperfect world. *Annals of Family Medicine, 11*(5), 402–405.

Spivak, G. C. (1988). Can the subaltern speak? In C. Nelson & L. Grossberg (Eds.), *Marxism and the interpretation of culture* (pp. 271–313). Basingstoke: Macmillan Education.

Staudt, K. (2014). The border, performed in films: Produced in both Mexico and the US to "bring out the worst in a country". *Journal of Borderland Studies, 29*(4), 465–479.

Stephanson, A. (1995). *Manifest destiny: American expansion and empire of the right*. New York, NY: Hill and Wang.

Stevenson, A. J., Flores-Vazque, I. M., Allgeyer, R. L., Schenkkan, P., & Potter, J. E. (2016, March 3). Effect of removal of planned parenthood from the Texas women's health program. *New England Journal of Medicine, 374*, 853–860.

The White House President Barack Obama. (n.d.). *Paula S. Gómez and David G. Hall*. Champions of Change: Winning the Future Across America. Retrieved January 7, 2020, from https://obamawhitehouse.archives.gov/

champions/leaders-in-closing-the-justice-gap/paula-s.-g%C3%B3mez-and-david-g.-hall.

Trump, D. (2016, July 21). *Address accepting the presidential nomination at the republican national convention in Cleveland* (U. o. Barbara, Ed.) Cleveland, OH: The American Presidency Project. Retrieved July 12, 2018, from http://www.presidency.ucsb.edu/ws/index.php?pid=117935.

U.S. Border Patrol. (2018). *United States Border Patrol: Southwest border sectors, total illegal alien apprehensions by fiscal year (Oct 1 through Sept. 30th).* U.S. Border Patrol. Retrieved May 2, 2019, from https://www.cbp.gov/sites/def ault/files/assets/documents/2019-Mar/bp-southwest-border-sector-apps-fy1 960-fy2018.pdf.

U.S. Border Patrol. (2019). *United States Border Patrol: Total illegal alien apprehensions by fiscal year (Oct. 1st through Sept. 30th).* U.S. Border Patrol. Retrieved May 2, 2019, from https://www.cbp.gov/sites/default/files/ass ets/documents/2019-Mar/BP%20Total%20Apps%2C%20Mexico%2C% 20OTM%20FY2000-FY2018%20REV.pdf.

U.S. Census Bureau. (2019, July 1). *Quick facts: Starr County, Texas; Willacy County, Texas; Hidalgo County, Texas; Cameron County, Texas.* United States Census Bureau. Retrieved January 7, 2020, from https://www.census.gov/ quickfacts/fact/table/starrcountytexas,willacycountytexas,hidalgocountyte xas,cameroncountytexas/PST045219.

U.S. Citizenship and Immigration Services. (2019, May 5). *Glossary: Apprehension.* Retrieved from U.S. Citizenship and Immigration Services: https:// www.uscis.gov/tools/glossary/apprehension.

U.S. Customs and Border Enforcement. (2019, May 2). *CBP enforcement statistics FY 2019.* Retrieved from U.S. Customs and Border Enforcement: https://www.cbp.gov/newsroom/stats/cbp-enforcement-statistics.

U.S. Department of Justice. (2014). *Report to Congress on the activities and operations of the public integrity section for 2013.* United States Department of Justice, Public Integrity Section, Criminal Division. Washington: Public Integrity Section, Criminal Division, United States Department of Justice. Retrieved January 7, 2020, from https://www.justice.gov/sites/default/files/ criminal/legacy/2014/09/09/2013-Annual-Report.pdf.

U.S. Department of Justice. (2017). *Report to Congress on activities and operations of the public integrity division for 2016.* United States Department of Justice, Public Integrity Division. Washington: Public Integrity Division Criminal Division United States Department of Justice. Retrieved January 7, 2020, from https://www.justice.gov/criminal/file/1015521/download.

White, K., Hopkins, K., Grossman, D., & Potter, J. E. (2018). Providing family planning services at primary care organizations after the exclusion of planned parenthood from publicly funded programs in Texas: Early qualitative evidence. *Health Services Research, 53*(S1), 2770–2786.

Whole Woman's Health v. Hellerstadt. 579 US (2016).

Woodworth, S. E. (2010). *Manifest destinies: America's westward expansion and the road to the civil war*. New York, NY: Knopf.

5

The Valley in the Time of Trump, or Why the Border Stereotype is So Durable

Imagine for a moment that you are the mayor of a Texas city just shy of 200,000 people. It is February of 2014. This year, your city will win national awards from the Robert Wood Johnson Foundation and the National Civic League for its community health initiatives and downtown revitalization, such as bike trails and farmers' markets. Your city has two national award-winning community health centers, one of which pioneered the Community Health Worker model to improve preventive health and access to health care and the other is a national leader in preventive health care and clinical quality improvement. Your city's public school system has chess programs in which student groups have won six national titles, and that is not counting the national and international wins for the university's chess team. This year, 2014, your city will be recognized as the Chess City of the Year by the US Chess Federation. Your city's brand new university has just recruited one of the most successful diabetes and obesity research groups in the southern United States with technology for genetic sequencing that outpaces similar technology at many established research universities. Your unemployment rate has steadily decreased since 2011 (United States Department of Labor, 2018). Elon Musk, architect of Tesla, co-founder of PayPal,

K. J. Fleuriet, *Rhetoric and Reality on the U.S.—Mexico Border*, https://doi.org/10.1007/978-3-030-63557-2_5

among many other business enterprises, and easily considered one of the most creative people in global business, decided to put his SpaceX launch site and spaceport for commercial space travel on the outskirts of your city. Next day, you are reading the news. Greg Abbott, the Republican candidate for Texas governor, unveiled a border security plan in Dallas, five hundred miles to the north. He called out your border county, not for its achievements but for its corruption. He likened it to the Third World: "This creeping corruption [in Cameron, Hidalgo and Starr counties] resembles Third World country practices that erode the social fabric of our communities and destroys Texans' trust and confidence in government" (Abbott quoted Santella, 2014).

I just described Brownsville, Texas, in Cameron County. Brownsville sits on the Rio Grande River across from its sister city, Matamoros, Mexico. Brownsville and Matamoros are inextricably linked by kinship, social networks, economy, education, and health care extending over 150 years. In the last chapter, I traced what the national news says about border places like Brownsville, which is a kind of bordering, or producing ideas of difference about places and people. In this chapter,[1] I showcase the importance of national political movements in rebordering the U.S.–Mexico borderlands region, or reinscribing and reproducing assumed differences. I suggest here that the durability of misunderstandings about the Valley and U.S.–Mexico border arises from a particular cultural phenomenon, the concept-metaphor. I use the rise of Donald Trump to the American presidency and his intentional rhetorical framing of "the border" to illustrate how and why national representations of the borderlands can be so fundamentally different than the lived realities of residents and leaders of the Rio Grande Valley and how the old, incorrect ideas of the borderlands persist. I continue to emphasize the inherently political nature of "the border" by highlighting attempts to control the message about the border for political purposes during the rise of Donald Trump in 2015, 2016, and August 2017.

---

[1]Much of this chapter benefitted from the collaboration of Mari Castellano who helped me think through the media analysis for this chapter and co-authored the analysis published in the academic journal, *Culture, Media and Society* in 2020 (Fleuriet & Castellano, 2020).

Concept-Metaphors

A concept-metaphor is a fundamental concept or idea that is widely recognized, regularly used to understand other issues, and defined slightly differently depending on one's perspective (Moore, 2004). In order to be used by a large community or society, a concept-metaphor has to have fuzzy boundaries and some flexibility. *The border* as a concept-metaphor has to be both instantly recognizable as a concept of place and also a flexible metaphor, in order for a society to talk about issues such as immigration. "The border" becomes a rhetorical shortcut to reference a wide variety of phenomena which, in the 2010s, were largely perceptions of long-standing problems with immigration policy, the economy, and Mexico.

Concept-metaphors allow conversations about shared ideas that structure our individual lives but with which we may not have much direct or individual experience (Moore, 2004). *The border* as a concept-metaphor is less a real place than an idea about a place in American news media and political discourse. In these discourses, *the border* becomes a metaphor for insecurity and lawlessness. When "culture" gets folded into a concept-metaphor like *the border*, it can effectively create perceptions of people who are very different (Abu-Lughod, 2008). Trump's use of the concept-metaphor of *the border* was a rebordering process, resignifying the region as un-American and inherently dangerous to the nation of the United States.

Once recognized, concept-metaphors become sources of combinations of existing ideas as well as new ideas. Academic inquiry routinely identifies and interrogates concept-metaphors, e.g., *the global* or *the market*, for their assumptions, uses, and implications on society. There are moments in time when popular concept-metaphors come under public scrutiny, too. *Gender* and *race* are two concept-metaphors perhaps most often critically analyzed in popular discourse. For national conversations and political dialogue, concept-metaphors can be powerful in creating spaces for action, such as public debate and subsequent civil rights laws related to equality across sexual, gender, and racial identities.

There is also a danger in concept-metaphors. Unquestioned concept-metaphors can be misunderstood as realistic renderings of daily lives. A kind of naïve realism can emerge, whereby there is a tendency to operate as if everyone thinks about and acts upon a concept in similar ways. Assumptions remain hidden. Diversity of experience and opinion go unacknowledged and excluded from policy conversations. *Race, gender,* and *citizen* are several telling examples in American history of concept-metaphors reproducing inequality through institutional and attitudinal discrimination. Once concept-metaphors are recognized as assumptions about the way people understand and see the world, they can become a site of "reformulation and resistance" (Moore, 2004, p. 72). The concept-metaphor is therefore a critical device to analyze how the idea of *the border* operates in American popular understanding during increasing xenophobia toward immigrants, nationalism, and populism (Gusterson, 2017).

By tracing how *the border* was used as concept-metaphor in national news and political discourse during the rise of Donald Trump, we can see how the idea of "*the border*" was a bit like an accordion, narrowing to a few ideas and then expanding. It is not surprising that Donald Trump's campaign presented a very limited view of life in the U.S.–Mexico borderlands. The U.S.–Mexico borderlands often figure into political discourse about immigration in the United States. What is particularly interesting in the story of the Valley is how the national news started to reflect a slightly more nuanced telling of the Valley story because of the overly restrictive border story in Trump's political discourse. In effect, in the mid-2010s, the inherent intangibility of *the border* as a concept-metaphor facilitated Donald Trump's political agenda on immigration. While a narrow telling of *the border* was crucial to Trump's success, it also inadvertently provoked a small but significant, more expansive array of border representations in national news stories. These broader, more nuanced national conceptualizations of *the border* remained rooted in how we as Americans think about "others," sovereignty, immigration, and, broadly, the Global South, but they also suggest room for a different way to tell the Valley and U.S.–Mexico border stories.

Who Gets to Define *the Border*?

The border has been a cornerstone in domestic and international policy and public discourse about immigration, national security, and societal security since the 1970s and even more so in the post 9/11 world (Ackleson, 2005; DeChaine, 2012b; Weibel, 2010). Politicians, news media, academics, activists, artists, and people from the borderlands all have attempted to define *the border*. Historians and social scientists place the U.S.–Mexico borderlands within temporal histories of indigenous occupation, Spanish colonialism, internal American colonialism, and waves of migration from Mexican and American interiors in response to international and national economic policies (Alvarez, 2012a, 2012b). Prior to Spanish colonialism of the sixteenth century, dozens of indigenous groups moved seasonally through the region (Valerio-Jiménez, 2013). The 1848 Treaty of Guadalupe Hidalgo established the current borderline, and subsequent land development through agriculture and industry in the twentieth and twenty-first centuries have led to dramatic population increases in border cities (Bowman, 2016; Nájera, 2015). The region itself lacks definable borders, although 100 miles to the north and south are considered geopolitical boundaries for the purposes of enforcement (Plascencia, 2017).

Notions of race and class, difference writ large, are central to historical and current discursive treatment of the U.S.–Mexico borderlands by the American body politic. Racist ideologies about Hispanics and, specifically, low-income Mexicans, permeate border discourse (DeChaine, 2012a; Nájera, 2015; Nevins, 2010 [2002]; Valerio-Jiménez, 2013). Artists, scholars, and people living in the U.S.–Mexico borderlands have challenged stereotypical, racialized renderings of the region (e.g., Anzaldua, 1987). They argue that the border is so much more. It is a metaphorical place of non-normative belonging, social disruption, and identity-making that can sometimes result in new forms of creative expression. For people who live in the U.S.–Mexico border region, their communities and landscape are blended, bi/multicultural spaces rooted in deep histories of cultural and economic exchange, albeit with significant economic and social inequality as well (Heyman, 2012c; Heyman & Symons, 2012; Vélez-Ibañez & Heyman, 2017; Wilson &

Hastings, 2012). These lived realities and creative understandings of the U.S.–Mexico borderlands contrast sharply with popular, political understandings of *the border*: us/them racial dichotomies and peripheral geographical areas in need of state control. The inaccuracy of portrayals of the U.S.–Mexico border in news media and political discourse is essential to the national imaginary of *the border* (Alvarez, 2012a, 2012b; Chávez, 2001, 2008; Fleuriet & Castañeda, 2017; Vila, 2000, 2005).

The difference between national, popular renderings of *the border* and those of borderlanders, academics, and artists is due to the intensely political nature of borders and their metaphorical value of delineating concepts of citizenship and belonging (Lucaites, 2012). A border must be regularly enacted and materialized by governments, citizens, and other actors— the rebordering process (Johnson, 2012; Salter, 2011). Formal and practical claims of the border include definitions, defenses, and politics of enforcing a border, while the popular claims are the ways in which ideas of particular borders are shared, contested, and, sometimes, redefined (Salter, 2011). Donald Trump's political rhetoric tried hard to bind the popular claim of *the border* to unauthorized immigration that spurred violence and crime, all ostensibly fixable by a wall. National news media, however, reacted by engaging a broader, deeper concept-metaphor of *the border* in their reporting.

Concept-metaphors and attempts to define and use them can shape practice and policy, and the distance between daily life in borderlands and popular claims of the border is profoundly shaped by statecraft (Johnson, Jones, Paasi, & Amoore, 2011; Nevins, 2010 [2002]). United States' political and public discourse has deployed the phrase *the border* with increasing frequency since the reemergence of a national security discourse after the terrorist attacks of 9/11 and in debates about international economic relationships as well as migration and citizenship. *The border* in current American narratives of security and immigration is a concept-metaphor with the following key elements: next to Mexico, corrupt, poor, overrun with unchecked and unauthorized immigration, dangerous due to overflow drug cartel violence, and most often, rural (Dorsey & Diáz-Barriga, 2010; Fleuriet & Castañeda, 2017; Heyman, 2012b; Vélez-Ibañez & Heyman, 2017).

2015 The Border Encounters Donald Trump

Through early 2015, *the border* concept-metaphor had a suite of attributes: unauthorized immigration, health care shortage, Hispanic voters, Central America and Mexico, and the region as a security risk for the rest of the United States (exemplar stories: Harris-Perry [2015]; Meckler [2015]; Markon & Partlow [2015]; O'Reilly et al. [2015]; Sherman [2015a]; Soffen [2015]; Weber [2015]). As the year began, national news about the U.S.–Mexico border region largely focused on increased National Guard and Texas Department of Public Safety presence in the Valley. These were state responses to the 2014 Central American children immigration phenomenon—in eight months, more than 50,000 migrant children were detained (Dewhurst cited in Cavuto, 2014), a 100% increase from the year before. The Valley was the primary crossing site for the children. Stories about increased border securitization, immigration reform, and children's detention centers were common (exemplar stories: Bustillo & Koppel [2015]; O'Reilly et al. [2015]; Weber [2015]). For example, Robbins and Weber (2015) wrote about the Texas legislature's approval of an $800 million budget for ramping up border security through 2017, including gunboats, a high-altitude plane, a crime data center, grants for year-round helicopter patrols, a training center for local law enforcement agencies, a dozen Texas Rangers to investigate corruption, and new state troopers assigned to the area. The subject of children crossing the U.S.–Mexico border in the Valley became enmeshed in state-level political discourse about Mexican drug cartel violence and criticisms of the Obama administration (e.g., Robbins & Weber [2015]; Weber [2015]).

Health care shortage stories lingered about the closure of reproductive services clinics due to Texas House Bill 2 in 2013 and its United States Supreme Court challenge (exemplar stories: [Bravin, 2015; Fernandez & Eckholm, 2015; Sherman, 2015b; Soffen, 2015]). As noted in the last chapter, the Valley was underserved in terms of women's health care, including abortion care, with high rates of women without medical insurance, and Mexican pharmacies a short drive away sold medications that could induce abortion. In these news stories, *the border* became a gloss for unauthorized immigration and poverty contributing to health care shortages. For example, in June of 2015, Bravin discussed the Supreme Court's temporary block on certain House Bill 2 provisions due to the possible "undue burden" impact on West Texas and the Rio Grande Valley. Amy Hagstrom, president of Whole Woman's Health in the Valley, argued that the law was designed to "make abortion unavailable and unaffordable by closing down clinics," especially in the Rio Grande Valley (Bravin, 2015). This would disproportionately impact unauthorized immigrant women, because regular border patrol checkpoints interrupt all outgoing highways from the Valley. At checkpoints, members of each car must disclose their citizenship status to Border Patrol agents.

Donald Trump launched his campaign in August of 2015, and his campaign increasingly gained traction throughout the latter part of 2015. From this point on, news stories about *the border* were almost uniformly politicized in the context of the presidential election. As presidential contenders and Republican political discourse emerged to challenge the Obama Administration, *the border* raised the specter of communities dominated by unauthorized immigration, violence, and drugs. Stories about the increase to the state budget for border security, the addition of more state troopers to the Texas–Mexico border, and the extension of the deployment of the National Guard troops predominated (exemplar stories: Burnett [2015a, 2015b]; Markon & Parlow [2015]; Preston [2015]; Robbins [2015]).

By the fall of 2015, presidential campaigns were in full swing, and another, albeit smaller, influx of unauthorized immigration occurred, though these included adults as well as unaccompanied minors, migrants from Mexico, and asylum seekers from Central America. The November Paris terrorist attack happened, and the news about more immigrants in the Valley often referenced the increasing national fear that terrorists would enter the United States from Mexico. For example, Preston (2015) emphasized that most people attempting to cross were still Central American families and unaccompanied minors fleeing gang violence, poverty, and sexual and domestic abuse, but noted three Syrian families also presented themselves at the Laredo checkpoint for asylum and five Pakistanis and one Afghan individual were apprehended in Arizona.

In this and other stories, the Valley became the focal point for political debates over national security.

The year 2015, then, continued to populate a concept-metaphor of *the border* with attributes of unauthorized immigration, health care shortages, Mexico, and a security threat to the rest of the United States but increasingly narrowed to an articulation of unauthorized immigration that necessitated securitization and militarization. Articles about immigration were not about the human cost of crossing the U.S.–Mexico geopolitical borderline, the daily lives of Valley people as they are or are not impacted by the increased immigration, or ongoing, non-law enforcement responses to immigrants and asylum seekers. Instead, the immigration articles largely focused on issues of legality, numbers, danger, and law enforcement responses— that is, securitization and militarization, both part of political discourses building up to the 2016 presidential election.

2016: The Border as a Threat to the United States

The Rio Grande Valley and *the border* first appeared in national news media in 2016 with Super Tuesday coverage and Hispanic voters (exemplar story: Goodwyn, 2016). For a short time, *the border* as a threat to the United States was parlayed into a potential influence on national politics by virtue of the region as central to immigration reform and wooing Hispanic voters. NPR covered the Clintons' visit to Texas, in which Bill Clinton mocked Donald Trump's "make America great again" slogan, stating that America was "already great," due to the contributions that immigrants made to America (Goodwyn, 2016). The Clintons attempted to cement their alliance with Hispanic voters by referencing their "forty years of history with the black and Hispanic communities," including Hillary Clinton's time in the Valley as a Yale law student working in voter registration (Goodwyn, 2016).

News media about the Valley, abortion care, and national security followed for a brief period (exemplar stories: Barnes [2016]; Burnett

[2016]; Kendall & Bravin [2016]; Thomas [2016]). Health care short-ages momentarily made headlines again in June 2016 as the Supreme Court heard the case against House Bill 2. Burnett (2016) wrote about the inaccessibility to abortions in Texas, specifically in the Rio Grande Valley due to its poverty and its proximity to Mexico with the so-called abortion pills. After that, however, national security articles quickly eclipsed them, returning to Donald Trump's claims about unauthorized immigration, such as "Illegal immigration is going to stop. It's dangerous. It's terrible. We either have a border or we don't. And if we don't have a border, we don't have a country. Remember that" (quoted in Burnett, 2016).

With the election of Trump in 2016, the concept-metaphor of *the border* became increasingly restricted to "the wall," *the border* repre-senting generalized danger from outside the United States, especially from Mexico and Central America (exemplar stories: Galvan [2016]; Lemon [2016]). Trump had started talking about building "a wall" early in 2015, but the presidential rallies and debates in 2016 generated a specific news focus on "the wall" as a serious element of Trump's political strategy.

Restricting *the border* to a place of foreign threats and foreign people as a political strategy appears to have worked to rally a political base. In November of 2016, newly elected President Trump used "*the border*" to reference new national policies about immigration, national security, and militarization of borderlands regions. National news reported on another "surge" of Central Americans, ostensibly immigrating before Trump's actions to increase surveillance and deportations and to build more barriers along the U.S.–Mexico border (exemplar stories: Jordan [2016]; Whelan [2016]). Then small but significant modifications to the threat-based concept-metaphor of *the border* appeared, taking the form of local voices from south Texas borderland communities and referencing bina-tional linkages between the United States and Mexico, whether family, environment, or economy (exemplar stories: Jervis 2016a, 2016b).

For example, Frank Bajak (2016) introduced local voices of dissent against the border wall. The Rio Grande Valley, which was previously documented as one of the poorest regions in the United States, became the "bustling, fertile Rio Grande Valley." Local residents were more in favor of the existing "'virtual wall' of surveillance technology," including tower-mounted surveillance cameras and "blimp-like" aerostats that monitor the borderlands region via remote-controlled cameras. The region remained framed as an area in need of securitization, just not the kind President Trump proposed.

News media began to cover the numerous challenges to building additional sections of a border wall, lending *the border* breadth that had been missing in the preceding 12 months. For example, Valley residents lost land when the previous wall sections were constructed during the George W. Bush administration, and some residents were still waiting for government payouts (Jervis, 2016a). Other residents experienced the proposed wall as a challenge to their cultural and land heritage (Jervis, 2016b). Areas of existing wall were dubbed "breaks of privilege," such as the area near a golf club and resort (Bajak, 2016). Valley political leaders disagreed with additional wall construction, though had varying opinions on the utility or need for other barriers (e.g., Chozick & Fernandez, 2016). Geological and financial considerations were raised. Many areas along the south Texas–Mexico borderline have erosion-prone soil, which can decrease the integrity of wall construction (e.g., TK, 2016). These new angles to "the wall" story presented a region, landscapes, and communities with complex challenges to additional barrier construction rather than a regional, violent, uncontrolled threat to the United States that should be kept at bay with physical barriers such as fences and walls.

2017: The Border Returns to Its Original Contours

From January to August 2017, national news stories about the borderlands region of south Texas still trended toward a narrow emphasis on securitization and militarization, yet with attention to local lives and environments and international relations with Mexico impacted by the proposed wall (exemplar stories: Fears [2017]; Jan [2017]; Lavandera [2017]). An Associated Press news story about House Speaker Paul Ryan's visit to the Rio Grande Valley (The Associated Press, 2017a; also see

Flegenheimer, 2017; Rein, 2017) included a sidebar with Ryan's tweet about how *the border* is a risky, menacing place that needs more law enforcement. To be sure, themes of securitization and militarization persisted in 2017, and notably, the picture in the story about Ryan's visit was not of the urban Valley with 1.4 million people but the rural, brush country parts with a river snaking through it. The national news surrounding Ryan's visit reinforced that there was still the rhetoric of *the border* as the place where the United States keeps bad people out and *the border* as unruly and in need of more law enforcement (e.g., Guilfoyle, Watters, Gutfield, Perina, & Williams, 2017).

But there was also the sense in 2017 articles that *the border* may be a place with people living there long-term with vested interests and diverse points of view (exemplar stories: Ahmed, Fernandez, & Villegas [2017]; Fernandez [2017]; Lavandera [2017]). For example, Nixon (2017) wrote about the residents of Los Ebanos, Texas, gearing up for legal battle against the federal government for the right to retain their property. Nixon discussed how many residents in this small border town had already lost land, or had land bisected by the wall erected a decade ago. Ninety cases remained open against the federal seizure of privately owned land since 2008. Many residents were confident they could wait out President Trump's tenure by using the courts to stall.

Also during 2017, there was an explicit recognition of the environment, particularly water resources and access, endangered animals, and migratory flyways potentially impacted by the wall. Stories began to reflect the complexity of building a wall, drawing in other border attributes (e.g., Caldwell, 2017). Any wall construction must adhere to the 1970 Water Treaty with Mexico (Burnett, 2017a), which prohibits building a wall or levee in the Rio Grande flood plain that cuts through private and federal land. Another story focused on the executive director of the National Butterfly Center Texas, presenting the perspective of Texas naturalists on the proposed border wall (Hardy, 2017) and possible legal challenges to it. Hardy (2017) and others (Burnett, 2017b; Fears, 2017; The Associated Press, 2017b) wrote about the Valley's Santa Ana Wildlife Refuge, an essential area for endangered species and one of the most popular bird-watching destinations in the United States. A wall through the refuge would destroy habitat and cause a significant decrease in ecotourism dollars, a major part of the local economy. Each of these stories resisted an overly simplistic rendering of *the border*, although they remained within the primary theme of border security (e.g., Bajak, 2017).

In 2017, there was also some reference to the binational economy; *the border* might include reference to its productive economy, rarely, if ever, remarked upon before (exemplar story: Carlton [2017]). The Valley as *the border* continued in national news almost always in reference to Trump's comments about "the Wall" and "the Border," but *the border* as a concept-metaphor now allowed for other attributes not entirely scripted by national politicians. For example, Carlton (2017) discussed the economic decline among border businesses due to loss of revenue from Mexican nationals who stopped shopping in American border cities in protest after the presidential election or in fear of increased delays by border law enforcement.

Trump's oft-repeated claim that Mexico would pay for the future construction of the border wall pulled international relations into *the border* concept-metaphor in a new way as well. The focus on international politics within *the border* concept-metaphor was primarily on relations between the United States and Mexico. Previously Mexico was a backdrop for the threat; now, it was a source of funds for additional wall construction as part of Trump's political blaming. Trump held Mexico responsible for what he viewed as unchecked immigration into the United States, and he repeatedly publicly claimed Mexico would "pay for the wall" (e.g., CNBC Live TV, 2016; Pirro, 2015). In 2017, Mexican President Peña Nieto pushed back, canceling meetings with President Trump and publicly calling him to task. *The border* became part of a larger, public debate between the two presidents. Estepa (2017) wrote about a series of President Trump's tweets that detailed his reasons why Mexico would have to pay for the border wall, such as "Tremendous drugs are pouring into the United Sates, at levels no one has ever seen before" and "The wall will stop much of the drugs from pouring into this country and poisoning our youth." The Mexican government responded: "on the basis of the principles of shared responsibility, teamwork and mutual trust," they could solve the problems that the drug trade had caused. They would not negotiate public policy on social media platforms—and notably, not pay for a wall (Estepa, 2017). Elements of the earlier, broader concept-metaphor contributed to the story: immigration, violence, drug-related crime, economics, environment, and international politics.

To further illustrate the dominance of securitization and militarization, it is noteworthy that despite the Valley as the site of the first case of local transmission of the Zika virus in the United States in 2016 and Zika's reappearance in the Valley in 2017, Zika did not become part of *the border* concept-metaphor. In May and July 2017, CBS (Pelley & Lapook) and The Associated Press (2017c), respectively, reported on the first instance of the Zika virus in Texas. These were the only two mentions of Zika in the Rio Grande Valley in 2017 articles in search results. In 2017 through August, *the border* concept-metaphor continued to revolve around Mexico and immigration with some modifications, noted above, around the fringes.

The Border According to Donald Trump

Donald Trump's presidential bid and campaign in 2015 and 2016 included very specific political framing of the U.S.–Mexico border. He talked about a place where violent criminals from Mexico and drug and human smugglers cross into the United States with relative impunity (Gravelle, 2018), and he asserted the U.S.–Mexico border was a primary threat to the national security of the United States. Trump's virulent public statements against Mexican immigrants (Hill & Marion, 2017; Hooghe & Dassonneville, 2018) similarly positioned *the border* as perilously open. Trump's solution was a wall that would extend from the Gulf Coast of Texas to the shore of San Diego, California, immediate deportation of unauthorized immigrants, and deterrents such as parent–child separation for families upon unauthorized entry into the United States (for additional detail, https://www.whitehouse.gov/issues/immigration/, access date: 7 December 2018; Hill & Marion, 2017; Stringer, 2018).

Trump's tweets, interviews, and comments during rallies, debates, and the Republican National Convention in 2015 and 2016 evidenced his rhetorical strategy to restrict *the border* to an idea of a place that endangered American security and an American way of life. The primary crossing site on the U.S.–Mexico border in 2016 was the Rio Grande Valley. The majority of immigrants were from Central America and, secondly, Mexico. In his acceptance speech at the Republican National Convention on July 21, 2016, Trump said of unauthorized immigrants and *the border*,

> The number of new illegal immigrant families who have crossed the border so far this year already exceeds the entire total from 2015. They are being released by the tens of thousands into our communities with no regard for the impact on public safety or resources .... We are going to build a great border wall to stop illegal immigration, to stop the gangs and the violence, and to stop the drugs from pouring into our communities. (Trump, 2016)

Trump's construction of *the border* soon thereafter became a powerful concept-metaphor dominated by an exclusionary wall. In an August 24, 2016, appearance on the Hannity Show (Hannity, 2016) on Fox Network, he fashioned *the border* thusly:

> It's not a question of wanting [to build the wall]. We have no choice. We have no choice .... And it'll be a real wall. It'll be a real wall. It won't be one of these little toys that you see every once in a while, our government throws up a little wall like this. Do you ever see the picture in the magazines where a ramp goes up and down? I don't know why they don't just push it over, it would have been cheaper, but .... The drugs, the drugs come over, and the cash goes back .... I think the height could be 35 to 45 feet. That's a good height.

Donald Trump's meteoric rise in national politics in 2015 and 2016 in part was based on a political agenda that consciously crafted an imaginary U.S.–Mexico border to generate fear through a blending of national security concerns, xenophobia toward Mexicans, criminalization of immigration, and an idea of the U.S.–Mexico border as porous.

The solution proposed by the Trump nationalist campaign was additional securitization and militarization in U.S.–Mexico borderland regions and faster deportations. Trump's restrictive vision of *the border* was a deliberate strategy for political success. As a concept-metaphor, *the border* has resisted Trump's vision to some degree, especially within the workings of the national news media. In large part, the very narrowing of *the border* concept-metaphor in Trump's discursive framing provoked more and varied attention to the region.

Why Identifying *the Border* as a Concept-Metaphor Matters

The enduring qualities of *the border* concept-metaphor are easy to identify as largely manufactured when one lives and works in the Valley. In the Valley, leaders and other residents often talk about American assumptions about life in the U.S.–Mexico borderlands. During my research, I regularly encountered local Valley leaders disgruntled or disgusted with the continual portrayal of *the border* as unmanageable, corrupt, and dangerous. Donald Trump's campaign took those assumptions, made the racism in them explicit, and wove them into his political strategy. Trump's use of *the border* augmented the American notion that the border is different than the rest of the United States. His claims rebordered the region as a place of negative influence on the rest of the nation and thus different from the rest of the nation. In his words before and after the presidential election of 2016, the borderlands were a place paradoxically very far away and imminently threatening to U.S. social fabric. Presidential Tweets such as, "If you don't have Borders, you don't have a Country!" (Trump, 2018), reinforce such long-standing elements of *the border* concept-metaphor.

Political strategies and their discursive regimes such as these can become backgrounds for tragedies. In August 2019, a white supremacist orchestrated a mass shooting of Hispanics in El Paso, Texas, and his manifesto used the same language as President Trump when referring to Mexican immigrants (Ura, 2019). *The border* as a concept-metaphor of the United States in Trump's political discourse was a story about people from other countries that weaken the nation, and the story preyed upon pre-existing biases. Trump's use of *the border* concept-metaphor in the late 2010s directly influenced events such as the El Paso shooting, the 2018 mid-term elections, the government shutdown of 2018–2019, and the enduring fallout of family separation policies. President Trump's border encapsulated a particular politico-moral logic that supported deployment of thousands of additional military troops to the U.S.–Mexico border, additional wall construction, and xenophobic immigration and citizenship policies, such as the proposed revocation of the Fourteenth Amendment of the U.S. Constitution that guarantees birthright citizenship. To say that the attributes of *the border* promulgated during 2015, 2016, and 2017 determined the balance of power in U.S. politics and thus affect the rest of the world would be an over-statement. Yet the influence of *the border* concept-metaphor in American political life is indisputable, acting as a rebordering process to reinforce difference and division between the United States and Mexico established as a typical Global North–South relationship over 150 years ago.

In his book, *God Save Texas*, author Lawrence Wright quotes Texan Fernando Garcia, "There are two narratives about what the border is .... The farther away you are, the more chaotic and violent it appears, but when you live at the border, there is a different reality" (2018, p. 218). Leaders in the Rio Grande Valley tell a vastly different story than the national U.S.–Mexico border story, in order to challenge the dominant discourse about the U.S.–Mexico border. They, too, have the power to reborder and deborder. Theirs is not the story told by American presidents or borderlands creative writers and artists. The leaders' story blends and bridges the national and political rhetoric and the alternative story from creative genres that the borderlands are something unique. We turn now to that story.

Works Cited

Abu-Lughod, L. (2008). *Writing women's worlds: Bedouin stories* (2nd ed.). Berkeley: University of California Press.

Ackleson, J. (2005). Constructing security on the U.S.-Mexico border. *Political Geography, 24,* 165–184.

Ahmed, A., Fernandez, M., & Villegas, P. (2017, February 9). Life along the U.S.-Mexico border. *The New York Times.*

Alvarez, R. (2012a). Borders and bridges: Exploring a new conceptual architecture for (U.S.-Mexico) border studies. *Journal of Latin American and Caribbean Anthropology, 17*(1), 24–40.

Alvarez, R. R. (2012b). Reconceptualizing the space of the Mexico-US borderline. In T. M. Donnan (Ed.), *A companion to border studies* (pp. 538–556). Malden: Wiley Blackwell.

Anzaldua, G. (1987). *Borderlands: The new Mestiza = La Frontera.* San Francisco: Spinsters/Aunt Lute.

Bajak, F. (2016, November 22). Americans who live near border say Trump's wall is unwelcome. *The Associated Press.*

Bajak, F. (2017, January 26). A look at border security, fencing as Trump announces wall. *The Associated Press.*

Barnes, R. (2016, February 29). All eyes on Kennedy for fate of Texas abortion law. *The Washington Post.*

Bowman, T. P. (2016). *Blood oranges: Colonialism and agriculture in the south Texas borderlands.* College Station, TX: Texas A&M University Press.

Bravin, J. (2015, June 29). Supreme court temporarily blocks Texas abortion restrictions. *The Wall Street Journal.*

Burnett, J. (2015a, October 20). Texas created its own border patrol police, but is it necessary? *NPR Morning Edition.*

Burnett, J. (2015b, September 5). In Texas, complaints of too many troopers with too little to do. *NPR Weekend Edition Saturday.*

Burnett, J. (2016, June 9). Legal medical abortions are up in Texas, But so are DIY pills from Mexico. *NPR Morning Edition.*

Burnett, J. (2017a, April 25). Mexico worries that a new border wall will worsen funding. *NPR Morning Edition.*

Burnett, J. (2017b, August 25). Specs for border wall show it would divide Texas wildlife refuge. *NPR Morning Edition.*

Bustillo, M., & Koppel, N. (2015, April 3). Texas grapples with how to continue border surge. *The Wall Street Journal.*

Caldwell, A. A. (2017, March 26). Trump's border-wall proposal faces many obstacles. *The Associated Press.*

Carlton, J. (2017, June 4). On the U.S. Side of Mexico border, retailers say Trump's tough talk hurts business. *The Wall Street Journal.*

Cavuto, Neil. (2014, August 15). Interview with Texas lieutenant governor David Dewhurst. *Fox Your World with Neil Cavuto.*

Chávez, L. R. (2001). *Covering immigration: Popular images and the politics of the nation.* Berkeley: University of California Press.

Chávez, L. R. (2008). *The Latino threat: Constructing immigrants, citizens, and the nation.* Stanford: Stanford University Press.

Chozick, A., & Fernandez, M. (2016, December 23). Seeking a path for a Mexico barrier. *The New York Times.*

CNBC Live TV. (2016, March 3). Trump: I guarantee Mexico will pay for the wall. *CNBC.* Retrieved November 26, 2018, from cnbc.co: https://www.cnbc.com/video/2016/03/03/trump-i-guarantee-mexico-will-pay-for-the-wall.html.

DeChaine, D. R. (Ed.). (2012a). *Border rhetorics: Citizenship and identity on the U.S.-Mexico border.* Tuscaloosa, AL: University of Alabama Press.

DeChaine, D. R. (2012b). Introduction: For rhetorical border studies. In D. R. DeChaine, *Border rhetorics: Citizenship and identity on the U.S.-Mexico frontier* (pp. 1–18). Tuscaloosa: The University of Alabama Press.

Dorsey, M., & Diáz-Barriga, M. (2010). Beyond surveillance and moonscapes: An alternative imaginary of the US-Mexico border wall. *Visual Anthropology, 26*(2), 128–135.

Estepa, J. (2017, August 3). Trump presses Mexico's Peña Nieto to stop openly opposing border wall. *USA Today.*

Fears, D. (2017, August 8). Border wall would slice through wildlife refuges. *The Washington Post.*

Fernandez, M. (2017, January 26). Rejecting the wall 'is too emotional,' and other voices From the border. *The New York Times.*

Fernandez, M., & Eckholm, E. (2015, June 10). Court upholds Texas' limits on abortions. *The New York Times.*

Flegenheimer, M. (2017, February 22). Paul ryan Tours Texas border area where Trump wants a wall. *The New York Times.*

Fleuriet, K. J., & Castañeda, H. (2017). A risky place? media and the health landscape in the (In)secure U.S.-Mexico borderlands. *North American Dialogue, 20*(2), 32–46.

Fleuriet, K. J., & Castellano, M. (2020). Media, place-making, and concept-metaphors: The US-Mexico border during the rise of Donald Trump. *Culture, Media & Society.* https://doi.org/10.1177/0163443719890539.

Galvan, A. (2016, December 7). Customs and border chief: Migrant surge not letting up. *The Associated Press.*

Goodwyn, W. (2016, February 29). Hillary Clinton counts on Texas ties to bring in a super tuesday win. *NPR Morning Edition.*

Gravelle, T. B. (2018). Politics, time, space and attitudes toward US-Mexico border security. *Political Geography, 65,* 107–118.

Guilfoyle, K., Watters, J., Gutfield, G., Perina, D., & Williams, J. (2017, August 1). Transcript. *Fox The Five.*

Gusterson, H. (2017). From Brexit to Trump: Anthropology and the rise of nationalist populism. *American Ethnologist, 44*(2), 1–6.

Hannity, S. (2016, August 24). Donald Trump on Immigration, the wall and the Southern border; Donald Trump holds town hall in Austin, Texas. *Fox Hannity.*

Hardy, M. (2017, August 13). In South Texas, threat of border wall unites naturalists and politicians. *The New York Times.*

Harris-Perry, M. (2015, January 24). Transcript. *MSNBC Melissa Harris-Perry.*

Heyman, J. M. (2012a). Constructing a "perfect" wall: Race, class, and citizenship in US-Mexico border policing. In P. Barber & W. Lem (Eds.), *Migration in the 21st century: Political economy and ethnography* (pp. 153–174). New York and London: Routledge.

Heyman, J. M. (2012c). Culture theory and the U.S.-Mexico border. In T. M. Wilson, & H. Donnan (Eds.), *A companion to border studies* (pp. 48–65). Oxford: John Wiley & Sons, Ltd.

Heyman, J., & Symons, J. (2012). Borders. *A companion to moral anthropology* (pp. 540–557). Hoboken: John Wiley & Sons Inc.

Hill, J. B., & Marion, N. E. (2017). Crime in the 2016 presidential election: A new era? *American Journal of Criminal Justice, 43,* 222–246.

Hooghe, M., & Dassonneville, R. (2018). Explaining the Trump vote: The effect of racist resentment and anti-immigrant sentiments. *Political Sciences & Politics, 51*(3), 528–534.

Jan, T. (2017, March 22). Speed bumps for Trump's wall. *The Washington Post.*

Jervis, R. (2016a, September 19). Texas border residents bristle at Trump's talk of wall to block Mexicans; Proposal is not feasible, and a fence now in place has never worked, they say. *USA Today.*

Jervis, R. (2016b, September 21). Wall would split land owner's heritage. *USA Today.*

Johnson, J. (2012). Bordering as social practice: Intersectional identifications and coalitional possibilities. In D. R. DeChaine (Ed.), *Border rhetorics: Citizenship and identity on the US-Mexico frontier* (pp. 33–47). Tuscaloosa, AL: The University of Alabama Press.

Johnson, C., Jones, R., Paasi, A., & Amoore, L. (2011). Interventions on rethinking 'the border' in border studies. *Political Geography, 30*(2), 61–69.

Jordan, M. (2016, November 14). U.S. detention facilities struggle With new migrant surge. *The Wall Street Journal.*

Kendall, B., & Bravin, J. (2016, March 2). Deeply divided supreme court wrestles with Texas abortion case. *The Wall Street Journal.*

Lavandera, E. (2017, February 11). Before the wall, a journey on the border. *CNN Live Event.*

Lemon, D. (2016, August 25). Donald Trump doubling down on charges against Hillary Clinton; Trump flip-floping on immigration; difficulty of building a wall across the border. *CNN Tonight.*

Lucaites, J. L. (2012). Afterword: Border Optics. In D. R. DeChaine (Ed.), *Border rhetorics: Citizenship and identity on the US-Mexico frontier* (pp. 227–230). Tuscaloosa, AL: The University of Alabama Press.

Markon, J., & Partlow, J. (2015, December 17). Unaccompanied children surging anew across Southwest U.S. border. *The Washington Post.*

Meckler, L. (2015, April 17). Republican party wrestles with immigration stance as it courts hispanics. *The Wall Street Journal.*

Moore, H. (2004). Global anxieties: Concept-metaphors and pre-theoretical commitments in anthropoology. *Anthropological Theory, 4*(1), 71–88.

Nájera, J. R. (2015). *The borderlands of race: Mexican segregation in a South Texas town.* Austin, TX: University of Texas Press.

Nevins, J. (2010 [2002]). *Operation gatekeeper and beyond: The war on "illegals" and the remaking of the U.S.-Mexico boundary.* New York: Routledge.

Nixon, R. (2017, May 7). Trump's border wall faces a barrier in Texas: Lawsuits by landowners. *The New York Times.*

O'Reilly, B., Comes, A., Tantaros, A., Bream, S., Shawn, E., MacCallum, M., & Miller, D. (2015, February 25). Hating President Obama; where do our rights come from? *Fox the O'Reilly Factor.*

O'Reilly, B., Tantaros, A., Williams, J., Roberts, J., & Stossel, J. (2015, July 22). Human life and the left in America; Chattanooga shooting; Nation of immigrants. *Fox The O'Reilly Factor.*

Pelley, S., & Lapook, J. (2017, May 5). Spring is here. *CBS Evening News.*

Pirro, J. (2015, August 23). Trump: I will get Mexico to pay for the border wall. *Justice with Judge Jeanine.* Retrieved November 26, 2018, from https://video.foxnews.com/v/4440053359001/?#sp=show-clips.

Plascencia, L. F. (2017). Where is "the border"? The fourth amendment, boundary enforcement, and the making of an inherently suspect class. In C. Velez-Ibañez, & J. Heyman, *The U.S.-Mexico transborder region: Cultural dynamics and historical interactions* (pp. 244–280). Tucson, AZ: University of Arizona Press.

Preston, J. (2015, November 26). Number of migrants illegally crossing Rio Grande rises sharply. *The New York Times*.

Rein, L. (2017, February 23). Ryan makes his first trip to border. *The Washington Post*.

Robbins, S. (2015, November 25). Thousands of children crossed US-Mexico border in October. *The Associated Press*.

Robbins, S., & Weber, P. (2015, June 16). Is Texas spending $800 M to create its own border patrol? *The Associated Press*.

Salter, M. (2011). Places everyone! Studying the performativity of the border. *Political Geography, 30*(2), 66–67.

Santella, D. (2014, February 12). Valley officials blast Abbott's 'third-world' talk. *Brownsville Herald*.

Sherman, M. (2015a, November 14). Texas abortion law draws hearing from Supreme Court. *The Associated Presss*.

Sherman, M. (2015b, November 13). Justices agree to hear first abortion case since 2007. *The Associated Press*.

Soffen, K. (2015, August 20). Texas could be a template for reducing abortion access. *The New York Times*.

Stringer, A. (2018). Crossing the border: Latino attitudes toward immigration policy. *Journal of International Migration and Integration, 19*(3), 701–715.

The Associated Press. (2017a, February 22). House speaker gets firsthand look at US-Mexico border. *The Associated Press*.

The Associated Press. (2017b, August 5). Congressmen oppose Texas wildlife refuge as border wall site. *The Associated Press*.

The Associated Press. (2017c, July 26). Texas case of local Zika transmission reported. *The Associated Press*.

Thomas, K. (2016, Spril 23). For Clinton, plenty of homecomings on the campaign trail. *The Associated Press*.

TK. (2016, October 16). U.S.-Mexico border area is complex mix of culture, terrain, politics. *The Washington Post*.

Trump, D. (2016, July 21). Address accepting the presidential nomination at the republican national convention in Cleveland, Ohio. July 21, 2016. (U. o. Barbara, Ed.) Cleveland, Ohio: The American Presidency Project. Retrieved July 12, 2018, from http://www.presidency.ucsb.edu/ws/index.php?pid=117935.

Trump, D. (2018, June 19). If you don't have Borders, you don't have a Country! *Twitter*, 6:52 am.

United States Department of Labor. (2018, November 26). *Databases, tables & calculators by subject*. Retrieved from Bureau of Labor Management: https://

data.bls.gov/timeseries/LAUMT481518000000003?amp%253bdata_tool= XGtable&output_view=data&include_graphs=true.

Ura, A. (2019, August 5). *A racist manifesto and a shooter terroizes Hispanics in El Paso and beyond.* Retrieved January 7, 2020, from Texas Tribune: https://www.texastribune.org/2019/08/05/hispanics-terror ized-after-el-paso-shooting-and-racist-manifesto.

Valerio-Jiménez, O. S. (2013). *River of hope: Forging identity and nation in the Rio Grande borderlands.* Durham, NC: Duke University Press.

Vélez-Ibáñez, C. G., & Heyman, J. (2017). *The U.S.-Mexico transborder region: Cultural dynamics and historical interactions.* Tucson: University of Arizona Press.

Vila, P. (2000). *Crossing borders, reinforcing Borders: Social categories, metaphors and narrative identities on the US-Mexico frontier.* Austin: University of Texas Press.

Vila, P. (2005). *Border identifications: Narratives of religion, gender, and class on the U.S. Mexico border.* Austin: University of Texas Press.

Weber, P. J. (2015, December 16). Texas extends national guard order amid new border crossings. *The Associated Press.*

Weibel, J. C. (2010). Beyond the border: On rhetoric, U.S. immigration, and governmentality. *Dissertation.* University of Iowa.

Whelan, R. (2016, December 23). Central Americans surge at border before Trump takes over. *The Wall Street Journal.*

Wilson, T. M., & Hastings, D. (Eds.). (2012). *A companion to border studies.* Oxford: John Wiley & Sons LTD.

Wright, L. (2018). *God save Texas: A journey into the soul of the Lone Star State.* New York: Alfred A. Knopf.

6

The Border and the Valley as Home

How we understand a place depends on our associations with it. Without associations other than national news stories, most people would understand the Rio Grande Valley of south Texas as only "the border," and the border as only threatening, faraway, corrupt, unhealthy, and poor. In Chapters Four and Five, I detailed how these understandings played out in national politics and news in the 2010s. The stories we tell as a nation about the Rio Grande Valley are not so much about an actual place as about American cultural ideas of Mexico and the United States and the concomitant Global South and Global North. National media and politicians reinforce, or reborder, social, ethnic, economic, and political differences often associated with Mexico and those who live closest to it. Rebordering these differences undergirds political platforms and policies for fortified, militarized boundaries along the U.S.–Mexico border; more immigrant detention centers and harsher penalties for unauthorized immigrants, including family separation policies; and declines in public services. Our national assumptions about the U.S.–Mexico borderlands regions derive from a centuries-old, colonial legacy of thinking about Mexico and those living closest to it as less hardworking, honest, or moral as United States citizens living in the nation's interior. In turn,

© The Author(s), under exclusive license to Springer Nature Switzerland AG 2021
K. J. Fleuriet, *Rhetoric and Reality on the U.S.—Mexico Border*,
https://doi.org/10.1007/978-3-030-63557-2_6

these assumptions influence our presidential elections, our policies, and state and federal spending on immigration, health care, education, and law enforcement (Nevins, 2010 [2002]).

What would these policies look like if we instead thought of the border region as longtime Valley education leader Dr. Juliet García does? In a book about the Valley's ecologies, García writes,

> [I]t is when we are away from this very special place that we most appreciate it. When we visit other cities, we miss the *ambiente* of the Rio Grande Delta. We miss the smiles we share with strangers in our cafés, the shocking splashes of color blooming on our trees, and the call of the parrots at dusk .... [O]ur "Pride of Place" is evident when we try to describe the magnificence to someone in New York or Washington D.C. We talk about how little the river separates us from our neighbors, and how instead, it nourishes the land, the wildlife, and the history we share .... With my family gathered around me and purposeful work to be done, there is no place I would rather live than right here in *el Valle*. (García in Patterson & Lof, 2010, p. 19)

In this chapter, I turn to García's kind of border story, one that asks the nation to think in another way about the U.S.–Mexico border. This border story is commonly told by a diverse group of leaders of the Rio Grande Valley of south Texas, from CEOs and law enforcement officials to immigrant rights activists and congressmen. These leaders attempt to remake the borderlands as central to the United States, expressly its ideals and its futures. Their border stories are a strategic effort to deborder, or erase social differences between the borderlands and the rest of the United States. As a group, Valley leaders make three claims. The first claim, explored in this chapter, is that the Valley is more, not less, American because of its proximity to Mexico. The second claim is that problems in the Valley and other borderlands regions result from poor policy decisions due to national and state misunderstandings, not from inherent regional difference between the borderlands and the rest of the nation (Chapter 7). The third claim in the leaders' border story is that the Valley's successful efforts to address educational, health care, and economic challenges arise from intentional collaboration and partnership across historical social differences, providing a model for the nation (Chapter 8).

The border stories told by Valley leaders are of home, family, and opportunity. For leaders, the Valley is home, and home is a symbol of resilience, potential, and the success of binational economic and cultural relationships. Below, I examine the frames of home and culture for leaders' stories of the Valley. Leaders frame the Valley with a common understanding of home as a place of safety, family and ties to the land directly connected to Mexico and Mexican heritage—and as such, decidedly American. Their Valley stories are replete with descriptions of the natural beauty of the area and its attendant outdoor recreational opportunities, such as fishing, visiting the beach, birding, and hunting, once again, a very different backdrop than that of national political rhetoric and media. Leaders describe a culture strongly influenced by Mexico that emphasizes and maintains traditional American values of family, community, hard work, and respect for education, with a commitment to economic growth and an entrepreneurial spirit.

Home as a Political Project

Above all else, the Valley is home for those who love it and for those who lead its communities, whether through activism, business, health care, law enforcement, education or philanthropy. For these Valley leaders, *home* means a place of heritage of land and labor, a place to raise a family, and a place to do good work. How each of us understands home is complex, mutable, personal, and political (Andits, 2015; Buch, 2018; Kapchan, 2006; Vélez-Ibañez, 1997 [1996]). When I think of the Valley, for example, I have a simultaneously visceral and intellectual reaction based on my own associations. I can almost feel the heavy, humid breeze that comes off the Gulf Coast in the late afternoons and hear the Southern (now Union) Pacific train whistle as the train approaches the switching yard. In my mind, I see and hear the throaty *cha-cha-lac-a* of the pheasant-like Plain Chachalaca bird, squeaky vocalizations of grackles, and loud Mexican green parrots zooming around in noisome flocks over my parents' backyard. Bamboo knocks against itself along the back fence. Wild olives sprinkle my parents' back patio. In my late 40s now, I still squish them with my feet as I did when I was a child. Banana trees, red hibiscus, pink bougainvillea, and yellow lantana border their yard. A lime tree sits in one corner. Nearby is a tangerine tree that I would plunder each December and January. Four forty-foot Washingtonia palms stand sentinel along the back fence, guarding the graves of childhood pets. Those palm trees have survived more than one hurricane. My mind's eye shifts to both sets of grandparents' houses as if I were walking up their sidewalks. Then I am inside them, going room by room, seeing each grandparent in their favorite chair, watching a younger version of myself talk, eat, and play with them.

A cascade of memories follows of childhood, school, adulthood, work, family, friends, happy times, and sad times. I do not think of drugs, cartels, or violence because those things were not part of my childhood. I do think about the class and ethnic segregation that ordered our lives in the 1970s and 1980s. It was apparent then and with years of anthropological training under my belt, even more so now. Because of my personal networks and previous research, I also think of some themes from the national news stories, especially the experiences and struggles of unauthorized immigrants, limited health care access, and poverty reinforced by decades of segregation by ethnicity and citizenship. Even still, what I know of these Valley themes is fundamentally different than if I had experienced them personally or what I read in the national news. Just like those national news stories, my experiences alone cannot tell the story of the Valley.

Our sense of home cannot be separated from our identities forged there. For many, home is associated with a sense of belonging, but it can also be, at the same, a place beset with problems (hooks, 2008). In a contested, fluid, and transnational space such as international borderlands, the idea of home can be particularly thorny. There are geographical hierarchies and linkages to contend with (Appadurai, 2000; Escobar, 2001; Gupta & Ferguson, 1992). In the highly militarized and surveilled U.S.–Mexico borderlands with checkpoints at the geopolitical borderline and 100 miles inland from it, home can be a place of stressful policing, marginal opportunity, and restriction for people who are unauthorized immigrants (Dorsey & Díaz-Barriga, 2017; Richardson & Pisani, 2017). Economic inequalities and poverty are notably widespread within and across border communities, largely referencing pernicious effects of de facto and legal ethnic/racial segregation in the twentieth century (Heyman, 2010; Nájera, 2015; Richardson & Pisani, 2017; Ruíz, 1998). These variables are but a few that impact how people who live in the Valley think of home. There are many others. But Valley leaders, even though different in political orientations, citizenship and economic backgrounds, and gender, ethnic, age, and religious identities, project a shared, coherent idea of home that is uniformly positive, albeit not without recognition of challenges. How are their stories so internally consistent and why?

Valley leaders incorporate an idea of home and its associated values of family, community, hard work, and public service in their border stories as a specific strategy to demystify and deborder the region. By so doing, leaders assert these borderlands are the American embodiment of home. Despite very different Valley origin stories and current professions, Valley leaders share a profound conviction that the Valley is *home*, which indexes a place of commitment to family, community, and education. Home is a place to do work that benefits family and the larger community, working collaboratively through the close ties that permeate Valley life. For example, for a non-Hispanic white activist, home refers to a sense of belonging predicated on American values of local responsibility to solving community problems:

Home. The Valley is home. The Valley, it really is, I think, that the people that are here, they live in a situation where there is suffering, but they have so much hope. It's a place where even though it's from the outside, it may seem a very negative place. I think that what we see is the endurance of the people but also the persistence that things can be better. And they can have a role in making the place better. And we've shown throughout the years that this is the case.

Her words are similar to those of a Hispanic health care leader with whom she has had several contentious public debates about health care

provisioning and access in the Valley. He, too, projects an idea of home
that is rooted in community service and also family:

> What is the Valley? Home. It's home. When you're young, you think "I
> want to move to New York and do such and such" ... but really, the
> Valley is home. [When] I really look at the Valley, it's my home. My
> family is here. I've [worked with] many people who know my dad, know
> my grandfather. "I know you. You're [dad's name]'s son." And it does play
> out in how you take care of your community. My mom would come back
> [from Heaven] and scare the heck out of me if I didn't take care of our
> community.

These statements hint at the power of the leaders' Valley stories. Valley
leaders' simple yet radical idea is that the U.S.–Mexico borderlands are
more, not less, American, than the interior of the United States, precisely
because of its proximity to Mexico. While their stories of home and
family emerge from an array of shifting social, political, and racial/ethnic
orders since the 1800s, they are remarkably consistent in their posi-
tioning of the region as embodying American values. In effect, Valley
leaders deborder the region through their framing of home in the Valley.
They try to eliminate historical and assumed social differences between
the borderlands and the rest of the United States. As a group, they argue
that these borderlands are fundamentally—but also uniquely, American.
Specifically, American ideals of family, hard work, ties to the land, and
entrepreneurialism are central to life in the region, because of the influence from, history with, and geographical closeness to Mexico. The
setting of heritage, family, community, and cultural and physical landscapes for these border stories suggests something entirely different than
that of the national story.

Home: Heritage, Land, Work, Family, Community

> I knew I was coming home. It would take six teams of horses to keep me from coming home. This is where I wanted to have a family, be with my family. Everything that is who I am is here. So, I came home. – Valley leader, health care

It is October 2016. I am back in the Valley for participant observation and interviews. Fall in the Valley means low 90s. My dog, Sunshine, and I are up early with the doves and *chachalacas* to avoid the heat during our walk. I drive the seven minutes from my childhood home to McKelvey Park, one of a dozen parks in our city of about 75,000. The drive parallels my old walk to elementary school. I was the kid who walked to school with her nose in a book. My parents each attended the same Austin Elementary. My grandmother taught there. I take a right onto Business 77, or "77 Sunshine Strip," the drag in high school. On the right is the shuttered Blockbuster Video where my mom and I would walk during high school and, later, during Christmas holidays in my college and early graduate school days. Up a bit is the refurbished old grocery store building, now the Administration Building of Harlingen Consolidated Independent School District (HCISD). Across the railroad tracks is my old junior high school, of which there were two in the 1980s. Now, there are six.

Next to my old junior high sits Harlingen's football stadium. That has not changed, the importance of Friday night high school football for community building and bonding. Across the street stand two restaurants and a 30-year-old argument. I think Pepe's has the best Mexican food in town, and a dear friend from high school says El Pato does. Whenever he visits the Valley, he still stops for a meal of Pato's handmade, soft flour tortilla tacos filled with chicken *guisado*. McKelvey Park is a few blocks ahead on the left. I see the new ADA accessible, shaded playscape where I took my daughter a few years back to swing. My mother helped make that playscape happen. Harlingen now has three accessible playgrounds, a joint venture of the school district and the city. Partnerships are important to the Valley.

I smell freshly cut grass, and the automatic sprinklers turn on as I attach Sunshine's leash. The parking lot borders an apartment complex where my brother lived and fell in love with a woman who later passed away from cancer in the hospital a few miles away. He went on to law school. He and my sister-in-law, also from Harlingen, now live and work near Washington, D.C., and Paris, France, returning each year to visit family in the Valley and hunt on their ranch up near Laredo. Sunshine and I walk down the path to "the Arroyo," a section of the Arroyo Colorado that meanders through Harlingen.[1]

The Arroyo cuts through town. Sunshine and I follow it. Joggers pass us regularly, calling out good morning. A couple of people fish, and someone else throws a cast net into the Arroyo, probably for shiners to use as baitfish. Further along the path, I see the telltale roll of an alligator gar, an edible fish with seriously sharp teeth, just below the surface. I walk under the 77 Sunshine Strip overpass that has new graffiti art, and I see the Chinese food restaurant on the edge of the steeply sloped bank where we would sometimes go with my grandparents after church on Sundays. We would leave straight away after the benediction to "beat the Baptists" to the line there or at Luby's Cafeteria. To the right is the path to the field where in high school I used to walk dogs for the pound, a sad, underfunded place then but now relocated, better funded, and improving. The weather is already steamy, headed toward hot and humid. And one more time I think, *this is home*. It is changed, changing, but I can see my memories, myself, and my family and friends everywhere.

---

[1]Geologically speaking, an arroyo can be dry or filled with water. When filled with water, an arroyo can be narrow and shallow or wide and relatively deep. Arroyos are common features across the southwestern U.S. landscape. In the Valley, "the Arroyo" refers to the Arroyo Colorado, a distributary of the Rio Grande River that feeds into the Laguna Madre. The Arroyo is 52 miles long (McWhorter, 2010) with a width varying between 40 and 200 feet and depth between two and 13 feet (Arroyo Colorado Watershed, n.d.). The Arroyo Colorado is economically, ecologically, and socially significant to the Rio Grande Valley (Patterson & Lof, 2010; Texas Commission on Environmental Quality, 2019).

In this section, I bring together personal stories of the Valley as told by its leaders, a group committed to improving Valley border communities and changing the national narrative. Regularly, they tell their border stories as a way to deborder by confronting misperceptions and stereotypes. Like my border story, their stories are rooted in long-standing, intensely personal associations with the Valley as a place. Their stories are embedded in the work they do to improve Valley communities. Valley leaders are so accustomed to combatting negative stereotypes about their home that their ways of talking about the Valley are at once personalized, explanatory, and protective or defensive. *Place* matters to each of them very much. This is in contrast to the many Valley friends and family members with whom I spoke about my research project. Friends and family who were not leaders could easily talk about Valley stereotypes but their personal identities were not wrapped up in the Valley as a *place*. Their sense of self was less likely to be woven into stories about the Valley, except in reference to family. For leaders, the *place* of the Valley is essential to their identities, professional decisions, and philosophical reflections about the future of the region. In leaders' stories, the Valley is a main character with definable features and personality, best expressed through cultural references, metaphors, and insider jokes about city and Valley stereotypes.

Many Valley leaders perceive the Valley as inextricable from their heritage. For them, heritage is a specific family connection to land or work that signifies perseverance and commitment to the region despite hardship. These claims resonate with the American ideals associated with land: working the land for prosperity and owning land (Isenberg, 2016). Leaders with far-reaching ties to the land uniformly identified as having at least some Hispanic or Mexican descent. This is particularly noteworthy. Those borderlanders with the longest attachments to land and labor, two American values, are of Mexican descent. This is the first act of debordering in the Valley story, that Mexican Americans embody the American ideal of land tenure and working the land.

Connection to place for Valley leaders is most often in terms of land ownership or literal physical engagement with the land through work. The two most frequent references by leaders to heritage through land were Spanish land grants prior to the 1848 Treaty of Guadalupe Hidalgo and twentieth-century family histories of farm work. Some family land histories extend back over 300 years. Other leaders detail working as children in desperate conditions in twentieth-century agricultural fields. Both connections to the land are essential to Valley history, understanding the Texas–Mexico border region today and challenging implicit ideas about Mexican immigrants and Mexican Americans. Neither is represented in the national renderings of the Valley. In telling what locals call "our Valley stories," leaders framed their discussion of the Valley as a place of potential and strength through their ties to family and the land. For example, one Hispanic physician and state leader in health care began his Valley story with his family legacy in the region:

> I come at [the Valley] from a deep perspective. My perspective is similar to other leaders down here who are descendants of the original pioneer families that settled this area. So, my perspective is different than a lot of other folks but very similar to other folks, many of whom are my relatives …. You have to understand where I come from. I am the product of two very wonderful individuals who are very active in the community and both come from old families …. My family goes back on this side and the other side …. We go back 250 years …. Our family has been here in northern Mexico and southern Texas for a very long time. I'm fourth generation born in [this Valley county].

Understanding the intertwined story of land and heritage in the Rio Grande Valley requires a bit of borderlands history. Spanish colonists arrived in what is today the Valley in the middle of the sixteenth century, ultimately displacing approximately four dozen indigenous groups through conflict, forced assimilation and new political, economic, social and religious orders (Miller & Almaráz, Jr., 1998; Valerio-Jiménez, 2013). Spanish landowners were at the top of the hierarchies. River settlements protected and facilitated trade, first within Mexico and then between Mexico and the United States (Amberson, McAllen, & McAllen, 2003). Mexican and non-Mexican settlers and more conflict followed in the seventeenth century. By the late nineteenth century, another race- and citizenship-based social order emerged, in which non-Hispanic white Americans were at the top of the hierarchy, but wealthy Hispanic American ranching families also had major political and economic influence. Descendants of those early Spanish landowning families still wield significant economic and political power today, and they connect their land ownership and Mexican culture with their Valley stories. As one Hispanic business and political leader said,

[Many families] have experienced the culture as they were growing up – the Hispanic culture, absolutely predominant down here, the Mexican culture as they brought it over, when those individuals came over. There's a lot of history going back hundreds of years. My last name is [*redacted for anonymity*] and you do a little history on your name. [My family] settled here in this part in 1600s, south Texas and northern Mexico. There are a lot of [family name] here in this area ...

In each of the Spanish colonial (1749–1821), Mexican national (1821–1848), and American national (1848–1900) periods in the Valley, land was taken and given according to political regimes that encouraged economic development through their respective ethnic, socioeconomic, national, and citizenship hierarchies (Valerio-Jiménez, 2013). The Spanish colonial period established primarily defensive settlements, first with common land grants and later individual land grants along and to the south of today's Mexican side of the Rio Grande River (Miller & Almaráz, Jr., 1998). Ranching and livestock were primary industries, heavily influential in the wider North American cattle trade. After the Mexican–American War (1846–1848), Brownsville was one of the first cities established on the northern side of the Rio Grande River, with the notable earlier exception of what today is Laredo, Texas. Spanish and Mexican land grant titles were ceded to the United States (Miller & Almaráz, Jr., 1998), and property claims of now American citizens were unevenly upheld. Between 1846 and 1848, there was an influx of non-Hispanic white Americans to bolster new or transformed military installations, such as Fort Brown in Brownsville and Fort Ringgold in Rio Grande City. Valley leaders who trace their heritage to these times often mention their family's affiliations with the United States military, which in itself is a statement of American value: "[My great uncle] enlisted in the military and was stationed at Fort Brown .... My grandfather ended up coming here, and they pooled their money and started [a business in Brownsville]."

Starting with the American national period (1848–1900), non-Hispanic white immigrants held political office and were able to accumulate wealth, whereas most Mexican Americans were not, due to de facto or legal segregation and other race-based laws. Still, throughout each period of rapidly shifting social and political orders, families mixed and mingled across ethnic, class, and national lines, multiplying and often complicating bicultural and binational identities. Wealthy, landowning Hispanic families continued to be an economic, social, and political force in the area. Leaders from these families associated land ownership with a commitment of the wealthy to philanthropy and education, two more American values. A Hispanic health care administrator and regional business leader connected land, community, and education by saying,

> I was raised amongst giants. It hits the nails on the head. I was raised among people – men and women, who were incredibly motivated by community service, not only political service. Motivated by … "justice be served" …. I grew up with a deep respect for the law, for education, and to give back to my community. We grew up with an incredible sense of pride that my father's side were pioneers in the Rio Grande Valley. They came across in 1850s, ultimately had tens of thousands of acres of ranchland in [a Valley area] …. What's the nexus? What's the catalyst for the success of the family? It's the concentration and the commitment that once you get educated, you can be propelled into success. I think we were raised with a great sense of pride …. Failure wasn't an option.

Enduring land legacies from the Spanish colonial period meant that a few wealthy Hispanic families had substantial power throughout the Valley's history. At the same time, each settlement or development period in the Valley has relied on a large, overwhelmingly Mexican and later Mexican-American underclass of workers who did not have access to economic and political capital. The Treaty of Guadalupe Hidalgo in 1848 and the subsequent U.S.–Mexico boundary establishments ushered in an obvious race-based social order first buttressed by citizenship claims and later reinforced by national racial politics and regional patterns of Valley immigration through the first part of the twentieth century (Nájera, 2015).

During each historical period, land ownership indicated not only wealth and political connection but often also a social and economic reach that extended past the borderlands. In particular, agriculture and cattle ranching have been central to the regional economy and linkages to state and national sites of political power (Amberson et al., 2003; Miller & Almaráz, Jr., 1998). Cotton and trade related to military needs boomed during the U.S. Civil War. Cattle ranching stocked northern markets. Trade and business opportunities during the Civil War attracted more non-Hispanic white Americans to the area (Miller & Almaráz, 1998). While the race-based social order segregated economic and political opportunities, non-Hispanic white newcomers often married into Valley families of Spanish and Mexican descent (Richardson & Pisani, 2017). For today's Valley residents who trace their heritage before the 1910s, i.e., before the introduction of the railroad to the region, last names and other standard American markers of ethnicity are less accurate predictors of language preference, location of residence and business interests in Mexico or (and) the United States, and family land histories in either country. In turn, these leaders often use this historical tie to land as an indicator of current commitment to the state of Texas. One Hidalgo County health administrator told his Valley story in terms of the United States' growing up around his family's ties to the land:

I'm going to repeat it. You've heard this a 100 times already …. The Valley's home. *The Valley's home.* The Valley is a direct representation of my family. [My] family, my roots, have been here 300 years, ok? Since the 1700s. Before Texas was Texas, before the United States was a country, my family has been here. We didn't come to the United States. The United States grew around us. A lot of people from Austin, Dallas, California – they don't understand that. They don't understand that. The whole immigration issue, they don't understand that Texas grew around us. The United States grew around us. I'm a very proud Texan. When I hear misinformed or ignorant people who say, "Go home to Mexico"? Listen, my family has been in this part of the country long before your family ever came to this part of the country. I giggle when I hear people say, "my family is this or that." No. *No.* You don't understand the cultural heritage of the Valley.

The twentieth century saw rapid development and population increases in the region. Both Americans and Mexicans arrived in the region because of mid-nineteenth century military installations along the Rio Grande River, early twentieth century land development programs in the Valley, and upheaval in Mexico during the Mexican Revolution (1910–1920). In 1904, a railroad from San Antonio to the Valley was completed, and the first train arrived in Brownsville (Miller & Almaráz, Jr., 1998). The early 1900s begins the era of Valley cities. While Brownsville's history extends back into the middle to late nineteenth century, most Valley cities were developed early in the twentieth century as a result of the railroad, including Raymondville, Harlingen, La Feria, Mercedes, Weslaco, Donna, Alamo, San Juan, Pharr, Mission, and McAllen. Rapid development of intensive irrigation systems followed the roads, connecting the cities, which transformed the agricultural potential of the area (Gahan, 2013). Often, non-Hispanic white leaders had family legacies that intertwined the military installations and the land developments from that time, as one lawyer and educational leader illustrated in his Valley story:

> My family came here, I think, in [the 1920s]. My grandfather and grandmother were from [the Midwest] on my dad's side. He was a farmer. He came down on the land deal, bringing people down on the trains and showing them around. He didn't buy a farm. He ended up owning a real estate business and an insurance business. My dad was actually born in [a Midwest state]. My mother's side, he was a military man and from [elsewhere in] Texas .... When he joined the military, he was assigned to Fort Ringgold in Rio Grande City ...

Population growth in the four Valley counties almost tripled in the first 30 years of the twentieth century, outpacing state population growth (see Table 6.1).

Early twentieth agricultural development schemes intentionally attracted non-Hispanic white agriculturalists from the midwest United States and low-wage laborers from the interior of Mexico or existing

Table 6.1 Population growth in Valley counties, 1900–1930 (Forstall, 1995)

	1900	1910	1920	1930
Cameron County	16,095	27,158	36,662	77,540
Hidalgo County	41,355	46,760	38,110	77,004
Starr County	11,469	13,151	11,089	11,409
Willacy County	<10,000	<10,000	<10,000	10,499
Rio Grande Valley	<78,919	<97,069	<95,861	176,452
Texas	3,048,710	3,896,542	4,663,228	5,824,715

pools of migrant farm workers. Current leaders also came from each of these three groups. Their Valley stories are narratives of entrepreneurialism or working the land. During the first half of the twentieth century, the railroad into the Valley brought another wave of largely non-Hispanic white Americans from the Midwest, but not exclusively so. Other Hispanic families also migrated to the Valley during this time from northern parts of Texas and the United States, often drawn by promises of year-round agricultural work. A Hispanic educational administrator and physician told a common story:

My family, they've been in the Valley since the 30s. My father and my mom came here. They're from a little city [north of the Valley] …. Their parents come from Mexico. And they moved down here. My parents were very young in the 30s, 40s. As kids, they spent a lot of time as farm workers … and they would track up north. They were in the mid migrant stream. We'd go with them. Eventually, they stayed here. They really believed in the importance of education, which was why they decided at some point: it was more important to become seasonal farm workers [in the Valley] … working cantaloupes, tomatoes, onions, citrus. The reason for that was to make sure [we could stay in school]. As a migrant student, you get pulled out of school in April and don't come back until October, so they focused on the Valley [where they could work year-round as seasonal farm workers and their children could continue to attend the same school].

During this time, agriculture exploded onto the landscape. Cities grew. Valley boosterism (Bowman, 2016) promoted the idea of a California-like arability on thousands of acres of land waiting to be farmed with a ready supply of low-wage workers from Mexico. Ranching families sold off parcels of land to people from northern states while people from Mexico moved north to the Valley for the promise of work on the new farms. By the 1930s, farmers had "cleared 95 percent of the original native brush as well as 90 percent of the natural riparian habitat of the Valley" (Bowman, 2016, p. 32). Land speculators, developers, and commercial farmers led the transformation of Valley land. Citrus, vegetables, and cotton would soon dominate as commercial crops. Cotton and sugarcane came to the Valley in the mid-nineteenth century, and John Shary was responsible for the takeoff of the citrus industry in the 1920s (Bowman, 2016). Intentional recruitment of low-wage workers from Mexico, twentieth century improvements in agribusiness, dams, and a beneficial water treaty with Mexico further increased crop yields and their importance in the regional economy, though freezes and market demands caused fluctuations (Santa Ana, 2017).

The overwhelming majority of farm workers and ranch hands in the Rio Grande Valley since 1848 have been Mexican and Mexican-American. Mid-century immigration policy, notably the Bracero Program (1942–1964), encouraged Mexican immigration for low-wage farm labor by facilitating border crossings for workers. By all accounts, farm work was backbreaking, the conditions inhumane, and pay substandard (e.g., Bowman, 2016; Nájera, 2015; Richardson & Pisani, 2017). Housing for workers was nonexistent or dilapidated. Migrant farm workers concentrated in unincorporated housing settlements called *colonias*, where they purchased plots from unscrupulous land developers who promised infrastructure such as roads and sewage systems but did not deliver (Federal Reserve Bank of Dallas, 2015; Richardson & Pisani, 2017). While cooperation, support, and resilience are fundamental to social life in *colonias*, living conditions were—and are, harsh with poverty. For Valley leaders with farm worker family histories, helping other Valley families engaged in low-wage farm labor or living in *colonias* can become their motivation for service, whether through education, health care, or activism. A leader in both health care and politics said,

I grew up in a *colonia* in [a Valley town] about 20 minutes from here. It's right across the Mexican border. We could even walk to cross into

Mexico …. Then my dad bought a lot in [another *colonia* in a different Valley town]. It didn't have drinking water, roads, or mail service. It didn't have any of the things we needed. I grew up in a farm worker family … different states, different crops, being in a farm worker family. When César Chávez and Dolores Huerta came to organize south Texas, my mom and dad became members of the union. They were at a convention in 1979 here at a local high school. I started working and volunteering after hours there. I became involved with different boycotts, grape, Campbell's Soup … even when I was in [a different Texas city] doing organizing, I felt that some of the experiences that I had had with all of my family, being farm workers, the different states we went to, how we were treated, how we were paid, the housing conditions, the pesticides, they never were far from my mind …. When they started talking about the minimum wage, the pesticides, all the changes we made under the UFW [United Farm Workers], it hit very close to home. I knew the need for them …. I couldn't get myself too far away from [the Valley], just thinking of the people [who] were still left.

Farm work conditions began to improve slowly in the 1960s with Mexican American labor activists and the Civil Rights Movement, especially the emerging United Farm Workers of America movement. For example, where before farm workers rarely had access to water or toilets during the day, by 2011–2012, 98% of farm workers who responded to the National Agricultural Workers Survey had access to a toilet and water for hand-washing, and 86% had access to a toilet and drinking water (Farmworker Justice & The National Center for Farmworker Health, 2015). Such a low baseline for working conditions speaks to the ongoing danger and difficulty of farm work. Leaders from farm worker families frequently referenced their families' histories with farm work, including early efforts to improve working conditions and to pursue education and a later commitment to life in the Valley to help other farm worker families. Frequently, a transnational family moved for work but returned to the Valley, as one regional educational administrator illustrated with his story:

My mom's side of the family came from Mexico but it was one of those, when they were living on both sides of the border, almost as if the river didn't exist. That's how it was back then. My grandmother came from Mexico ... to work in Brownsville .... My grandfather met her ... they eloped .... They went back and forth across the river .... There are small communities around Matamoros, [and] they migrated where the work was. They worked in the cotton fields. Half, six, were born in Mexico. Four were born here, because they travelled back and forth. My mom was one of the ones born over there but raised here. My grandfather bounced around many jobs, farming, migrant work. It was during Prohibition .... They grew up farming, picking. Once you were eight years old, they put you to work picking, okra, tomatoes .... [My dad] decided, "I don't want to do that all my life," so he went to school, and he was the first one in the family to go to college .... My grandparents and the other members went as migrant workers to California. They even marched with César Chávez. Slowly, they all came back [to the Valley]. Hispanic culture tries to stick together ...

Improvements to working conditions have occurred, but not enough. Farm workers remain at high risk for physical injury, exposure-related illness, infectious disease, and mental illness with less access to health care, formal education, and support services (for review, see Arcury and Quandt [2007]). Leaders who trace their family heritage to farm work connect their current commitments to helping Valley communities to working the land in harsh conditions, poverty, and poor access to education. In the following interview passage, a Hispanic health care leader traced his Valley story through the twin principles of family and service:

I think my family has always been here. I'm the second of nine from a migrant farm worker family. We'd leave in summer. My parents would let me finish school .... I was very fortunate that I was one of the younger ones. [My siblings] helped me. I was the only one who went to college, but none of my family is on the system. They didn't grow up with that. I believe the system is there to help you but with the intent to try and see what you can do to be independent. But sometimes you understand the circumstances. I can't imagine what my parents went through when they didn't have these resources, and I think that's why I stayed [after moving back after college]. I want to make a difference. You see these families that don't have anything else.

These two primary values in the larger American story, family and service, remain central to story-framing for Valley leaders even when their Valley origins are much more recent or they left and returned to the Valley after some time. In 1994, the North American Free Trade Agreement (NAFTA) ushered in a new wave of immigration to the Valley. Binational factories, called *maquiladoras* or *maquilas* for short, sprung up in Valley sister cities of Matamoros and Reynosa in the Mexican state of Tamaulipas. The manufacturing industry took off. More Mexicans moved to northern border states to labor in the factories located in Reynosa across from McAllen and Matamoros across from Brownsville. Engineers and other white-collar professionals moved from the interior of the United States to Valley border cities. Their homes and families are often on the American side, and they travel daily across the border for their work. Valley retail and service industries grew due to population increases on both sides of the border. International banking as well as the service and real estate industries also developed, buttressed by increasing investment by wealthy Mexican nationals. People in and around my generation who grew up in the 1970s and 1980s who had left for school and work began to return to the Valley. The Valley population more than doubled between 1980 and 2010 (see Table 6.2).

This group of leaders who moved or returned to the Valley in the last several decades also frame the borderlands region first and foremost as home, family, and commitment to community through work and service. A non-Hispanic white higher education leader and nationally renowned health researcher moved with her spouse to be closer to his family and the opportunity to help craft sustainable, community-based health interventions. She said,

It was an easy move [to the Valley]. It felt like going home, not to my family, but our family was here. It was easy …. I'm happy anywhere …. I love being here. That idea of "oh, I'll never live here"? I've lived to be here. I can't imagine leaving family and this context. I could easily be a [person] that doesn't do work in the community …. I could easily go home and not try to make a difference. That's just not my nature.

Table 6.2 Population growth in Valley counties, 1980–2010 (Roth, 2016)

	1980	1990	2000	2010
Cameron County	209,727	261,693	336,443	407,672
Hidalgo County	283,323	386,777	573,398	779,194
Starr County	27,266		40,873	
Willacy County	17,495		17,690	
Rio Grande Valley	537,811	707,033	983,706	1,270,246
Texas	14,225,512	17,044,714	20,945,963	25,145,561

A social justice activist describes the Valley as a place of family and as a place to continue work to improve housing inequalities and conditions of *colonia* neighborhoods that her parents faced: "I've had the opportunity to leave for school and I came back, because I was homesick. I had always wanted to start a family and raise my kids here. I have been married for six years, and we have a daughter …. Everything that we've been working on, all the struggles that my dad shared with me, I think I do a lot of the work I do for my parents." A leader in banking returned to the Valley after working in a major city, where "I was nobody …. We made a decision as a family: you know what? There is a better place for us. So we decided to move back to the Valley …. You hear these [same] stories over and over again [about people returning for business opportunities]." The director of a community health center also returned for what she believed she could do as a doctor in her Valley community:

> I graduated high school in [the Valley in the 1970s] and at the time, I really didn't feel like there were many opportunities here. I was of the character and of the mind to want to go out and explore [beyond] the Valley. I wanted to get away from the Valley as far as I could.… Then it was time to work in an underserved community [for debt relief from medical school] … and I said, "You know what? Let's go back to the Valley".… [W]e made a decision to stay …. I would not change one bit of my life. I have been so fulfilled with what I've done and what I've been able to accomplish for my community doing this. It's been extremely rewarding …. I get up every single day and I can't wait to get work. Why would I ever want to change that?

When associated with family, community, work, and service, the frame of home offers another way to understand the Valley and border region. The next discursive move in the leaders' stories is to connect that sense of home with "culture." Valley leaders directly attribute cultural resources of family and community to the fact that the region is next to Mexico. Culture becomes shorthand to indicate how the influences from Mexico enhance American values of family, community engagement, land heritage, and work.

Next to Mexico and Better for It

The Rio Grande Valley is a hot, humid, and relatively flat delta. It gets drier and a bit hillier as one gets into Starr County. As a child, I understood winter to be a season that started in December and lasted through January with temperatures occasionally dipping into the 40s (we call these fronts *northers*) but more often averaging in the 60s and 70s. We do not have a fall or spring, really. During the summer, it is best to stay out of direct sunlight, if possible, between ten o'clock and two o'clock because the sun is strongest then. High 90s were common in Harlingen in my childhood summers. Low 100s are not uncommon now. By four or five o'clock in the afternoon, irrespective of season, an onshore wind kicks up from the coast and travels through most of Cameron County. In the warmer months, it cools things down enough to have pleasant evenings by dinnertime. The region has seasonal droughts, and we are subject to hurricanes coming in from the Gulf of Mexico from July through October. While we have had few catastrophic hurricanes in the last 150 years, including Beulah in 1967 and "the hurricane of '33" (before hurricanes had names), most storms get deflected up the Gulf Coast toward Houston and Louisiana.

The benefit of such a climate is year-round recreation on South Padre Island and its national seashore, fishing in the arroyos, bay and ocean, boating, and hunting (deer, dove, and feral hog) in the surrounding ranchlands. One law enforcement leader ticked off on his fingers what he liked best about the environment: "The weather's great. The fishing's great. The hunting's great." Home gardening with tropical foliage, citrus, papaya, avocado, and banana is a favorite pastime, independent of income. The Valley is considered one of the nation's greatest places for bird-watching. The Laguna Madre is one of the world's few hypersaline ecosystems, and it is a haven for birds. Nearby thick, riparian brush is the only United States home to other bird species. Neotropical migrant birds pass through in spring and fall months. Migratory waterfowl and shorebirds winter in the area. Overall, more than 500 species of birds have been recorded in the Rio Grande Valley (Patterson, 2010).

Leaders describe the Valley's physical setting as idyllic. As one thought about how she describes the Valley, she paused and then said, "Oh, and nature! What a haven for nature. You've got the Gulf but yet all these great birding trails everywhere." Leaders describe the Valley as a place with year-round "ability to have fun – go fishing, go hunting, play golf, the weather. Yeah, it's hot, but it's nice year around." Indeed, the year-round warm weather is the number one reason the approximately 95,000 "Winter Texans" from northern climes travel to the Valley for an extended stay (Simpson, 2016, pp. 26, 30). The second reason is the "friendly people" (Simpson, 2016, p. 26) and "culture."

In the Valley, everyone—from older, established leaders to teenagers, spend a lot of time talking about "the culture." We use the phrase "the culture" for both compliment and derision, but not in the same way as the national stories about the Valley. Most Valley leaders interpret culture as two things. First, culture can be a gloss for fine arts opportunities, like live theatre performances or art exhibits. Most leaders agree that opportunities for fine arts have been improving in the last two decades but were rare before. Second, culture is used as a synonym for ethnicity. For both Hispanic and non-Hispanic white leaders, ethnicity refers to something other than "Anglo" or non-Hispanic white. Since the Valley population historically has been overwhelmingly of Hispanic descent, culture becomes shorthand for Hispanic ethnicity. Even this is misleading for today's Valley, however. The binational maquiladora industry and burgeoning healthcare industry have attracted people from a variety of nationalities and ethnic backgrounds. As one health care leader and physician reflected on changes in the Valley in his lifetime, he noted the increasing ethnic diversity:

> The Valley has become very diverse – not very, but more, diverse. When I was growing up in the 60s, it was predominantly Mexican culture, from Mexico, indigenous Indian from Central and South America, but

primarily Mexican. Immigrant whites from up North during the Recon-
struction. A few Europeans that came in with the Spaniards during the
Spanish exploration time …. What I've seen here, is the influx of nationalities from all over the world. We have a very strong Philippine culture,
Asian culture, Chinese culture. We have a very strong Hindu culture
…. You know how I know about it? I see it in our clinics …. It's no
longer that classic "they're from Mexico." We have a larger Ukrainian
population …

Nevertheless, when leaders talk about "culture" as ethnicity, they are
almost always referring to a particular variation of borderlands Mexican
and Mexican-American cultural values and traditions. Both Hispanics
and non-Hispanic whites alike explain this particular brand of culture
with a list of characteristics that are implicitly applied to everyone with
Hispanic ethnicity and often also extended to non-Hispanic whites who
have lived in the region for a long time. A Hispanic health care leader
described Valley culture:

[M]ajor characteristics are family. We say that a lot but I do think
that's true. Identification with family, loyalty to family. Identification
with the living environment, the city, the town, where people live. I find
the friendliness, the warmth are characteristics. I think it's that part of
the Mexican heritage … [where] family comes first when it comes to
resources and when it comes to support, the emotional kind, the material kind …. The psyche revolves around the family. It's what holds them
together. The extended family is very important. Those connections by
and large are maintained once the child leaves the home and has children
of their own.

A non-Hispanic white law enforcement officer reinforced the idea of a
shared culture of family connection and respect:

Here, it's very friendly. It's very family oriented …. Even in my family, it
was farmland. You had my grandparents, the three sons, split up land and
stayed together, and they had kids and built houses …. It was all family.
It's not just my family. You see this with families all over the Valley. My
Hispanic friends had [the] same, generations in the same house. We had

the same concept but in the same community. Families are very tight knit.

That said, no leader spoke as if ethnicity worked only like that, predefining the sum total of a person's values or personality. Recognition of class differences and various outliers was common. As one Hispanic health care leader said, "prejudice is because of economic background, and because those groups have overrepresentation in that, it becomes about them." Rarely did leaders' discussions of culture map onto their daily practice of living and working in the Valley, even if their use of the term did signal real legacies of historical race-based political orders. Leaders' definitions of Valley culture were more about patterns of behavior and value sets shared by Hispanics and non-Hispanics alike; all identified Hispanic culture as the dominant cultural influence. Yet whereas the national renderings of Valley culture are regularly negative, Valley leaders emphasized cultural assets as well as patterns that they believed sometimes hindered economic growth or positive health outcomes. A non-Hispanic white higher education administrator and health researcher describes the cultural emphasis on family as a resource for health interventions:

> The strongest positive infrastructure that we have, insofar as moving health care in any one direction, is the family unit, the culture, and the strength of the family. The closeness, the caring, and using that to motivate and move people forward. I think people are pretty active, also. It's not like they can't be out most of the year. People are able to get out, go to the beach, hunt, walk, golf. I think the environment is a strength. I think pride in their community. Family, pride in their community, the environment, those are all positive in moving our health outcomes, promoting a healthier community. The negative would be that family centers around meals. Food is a big cultural issue. That would be a negative but you could also use it for positive reinforcement for things that are required for a healthier community.

The way Valley leaders explain Valley culture is crucial to how they talk about the future and potential of the Valley, discussed in the next two chapters. In many ways, leaders use culture as the greatest resource of the Valley in their border stories. The impact of the historical and current blending of binational influences cannot be overstated for leaders. Proximity to Mexico is a resource. For Valley leaders, cultural influences from Mexico, from our shared regional history as both Mexico and the United States, make the Valley border region even more committed to American values of family, work, the land, and entrepreneurialism. It also makes the region safer than other areas in the United States. One Hispanic politician explained, "It's a multicultural area that is located almost in the perfect place in the world .... I like the climate. I like the friendliness of people. I think it's an area of opportunity. You know, crime, really .... I go to New York or Paris or London. I feel more uneasy there than I do here." Proximity to Mexico is not the Valley's weakness as per national projections of the border. Leaders call out these outdated ideas about Mexico. As one Hispanic educational leader said, "I think the culture is who we perceive [has] it [and] that [perception] has changed .... Before the culture was seen as deficit. Now it's seen as value added. In our lifetime, this [borderlands] corridor will become the front door of the country, not the back door."

The Valley cultural approach to family instills values of hard work, social support, and faith. Every leader connected this cultural approach to Mexico, and these values map directly onto classic American values, as well. A Hispanic doctor who is also a leader in state healthcare policy was careful to make these kinds of connections in his Valley story:

> I see that nice niche of family, family values in the Valley. It still has that. Kids come first. We don't put our families in retirement homes [or] in nursing homes .... We still show up to everyone's birthday parties. Everybody's tight. That has not been lost. To me, Valley is: everybody's friendly. Helpful. If you see someone broken down on the road, they'll help you .... You don't get that in a big city. Most people when they see somebody down, they help. Family and neighbor, they help each other out. Very loving community. Very religious community. I could care less which religion but they are. They are very engaged. They're not too far left or too far right. They're central. Very upbeat. Very young compared to other cities. They're willing to roll up their sleeve and carry the water. They don't want a handout. They just want to be treated fairly.

For another influential physician and businessman, the Valley has a culture that is "very warm" and "greets you with open arms" because of its roots in Mexico:

> The Valley to me is a very special place. I think that it is a crossroads between two countries. Used to be – this is a safe place to be, this IS a safe place to raise your children. Because it's a very warm community. People greet you with open arms, want to introduce you to their family, make you part of the family. The citrus is the best in the world here. The ranchland and hunting are beautiful .... [The culture is] that sense of family. Of *corazon* [heart], no better word .... *Corazon* is a beautiful thing. That's what it's all about. That's what the Valley is. That's what Mexicans are. We tend to wear our hearts on our sleeves, and it tends to get us into trouble. It's who we are as a culture, and it's a good thing.

The bicultural and bilingual element of Valley culture is primary in its identity as a place and a people. In Chapter 8, I discuss how it was central to the establishment of the new University of Texas Rio Grande Valley. According to one superintendent, the Valley has "deep, very embedded, very deep cultural characteristics. Very family oriented. Very close-knit. I don't know why this word comes to mind, but *respectful*. Respect your culture, respect your heritage." Leaders believe a family concept heavily influenced by Mexican culture is a core component of Valley community ethos. Families live on both sides of the geopolitical borderline to form a foundation of safety. A housing and immigrant rights activist inserted a critique of border militarization within her description of hard-working transnational families:

> It's a wonderful area, an area where families are really important. People are hard-working, where people survive one way or another. For us, the border is just an extension of families on that side to this side. We don't see it's a border to fear. We don't see it's a border where the state has to spend millions for security because we don't believe, as they do, that it's so dangerous that you have to put so much money into state police, DPS [Department of Public Safety officers], glowing lights at night and border walls. You know, we don't see that. We see it as a friendly place where we can visit, and where we have family members, where we go over

every weekend, especially Sundays when people are visiting families and buying staples. When we read the stories where it's so dangerous, we're amazed.

Family is the *sine qua non* of Valley culture. Without fail, Valley leaders talked about the idea of family as central to Valley life sometime during our conversations. Updates on families began our interviews and almost all spontaneous conversations at grocery stores and formal events, such as fundraisers and Valley-wide award ceremonies. Examples including their families sprinkled interviews. People positioned themselves in their professional relationships at least in part through family histories and connections. Family takes on certain qualities in Valley leaders' descriptions of culture in the region: unquestioned support, geographical and emotional proximity, and linkages across families to create a "small town feel." Leaders assert it is a particular quality of the borderlands. When I asked one nationally renowned education leader what Valley or border characteristics she talks about with education leaders from other parts of the country, she replied,

> The culture. It is so different. It is different than any other part of the country or the world that I've been in. We still do have a strong sense of family and that's the beauty of the area .... That's how you instill values in kids, when you can hang out at a table and talk .... Even as [formally] educated as we are, I think there is still a lot of kindness, *noble* [Spanish word emphasizing action based on morality and generosity of spirit], down to earth.

Leaders also associate the emphasis on family with a commitment to community and trust in community leaders and, in particular, in the educational system. Many believe this is an essential characteristic of the Valley orientation, rare in other places in the state and nation in large part because they are distant from Mexico. Educational leaders in K-12 and university settings talked about the power of the family that, if harnessed well, can improve educational outcomes. As one non-Hispanic white university administrator described, "I've never lived anywhere [like the Valley]. People, the general public has a better understanding of what higher education can do for an area. I'm talking not just about the leaders, who uniformly are aware, but when you get down into the population, people are aware that to make a lot of progress, you need a better educational infrastructure and education." A Hispanic educational leader who grew up in poverty in the Valley and returned with his doctorate to improve public education in the region felt the Hispanic culture was the resource that would help solve public education challenges in the state:

> [The Valley has] richness in the Hispanic culture, values of faith and family in Hispanic culture, respect for elders, kindness and friendliness, strong interest in their children achieving greater success than the parents have, pleasure taken in beauty – beautiful plants, flowers, appreciation of people who are helpful to others, a growing sense that education is the way out of problems that they and their parents had to endure, an appreciation for the education system.

Complicating Home and Culture

Of course, home and culture are not so simple. Such formulations as the above are partly rhetorical strategies to get people to think differently, and I would argue that, in part, they succeed precisely because they are relatively straightforward and uncomplicated. I am nevertheless acutely aware of important things left out when claiming the Valley is idyllic, full of hardworking, innovating, family-oriented people invested in a very specific American way of life. While conceptualizing home in the Valley and borderlands in terms of American values has strategic value in challenging the national narrative of the U.S.–Mexico border, there are several risks in doing so. It can deflect conversation from important issues impacting other Valley constituencies, discourage alliances with other scholarship seeking to deborder, and reinforce globalization discourse that often borders the region in traditional ways. Each of these complicates the leaders' story of home in important ways. Rethinking the U.S.–Mexico border requires walking the line between dismantling ideas about borders that become self-fulfilling and recognizing the very real impact of those ideas on the lives of borderlands communities. This is hard work and fraught with pitfalls. As a whole, scholarship on the border has to contend with this, too, just like borderlands leaders do (Heyman, 2017; Ortíz-González, 2004). Indeed, throughout my personal and professional experiences in the Valley, I struggle with how to work toward solving regional problems without reproducing worn out tropes about borders or implying all is copacetic and thus inadvertently contributing to, rather than combatting, entrenched social, economic, health, and political problems. Like other border scholars, I am working to disassemble stereotypes about Mexicans, Mexican Americans, Texans, and immigrants, and the last thing I want to do is reproduce them. I do not want to accidentally uphold the legacy of colonial discourse that the U.S.–Mexico borderlands, especially those of south Texas, are necessarily steeped in backwardness because of their proximity to a purported inherently flawed Global South. Surely, highlighting cultural values that Valley communities associate with Mexico can be accomplished without falling into old stereotypes.

A few Valley leaders, principally activists, faith leaders, and politicians, did address the complexity of home and culture in their framing of the Valley story. A Hispanic immigrant rights activist, for example, integrated the notion of Mexican culture and the ongoing issues of violence in Mexican border cities, all the while suggesting a different border story:

> It's a place you can wrap your arms around …. It's a place where there are so many good people I know … and you run into them. It's a human-sized place. It is a place where, if one has an ethical center, where you are allowed to bear witness to suffering. You can't do that [in other places] …. It's a privilege. It's a place of extraordinary moments of great joy and deep grief. It's the in-between places but it's not a bell curve in-between. It's where the extremes come around. It's a richly complicated place. People come down, and say, "people look so happy" … [but] the public veneer that we carry through life is much thinner here. You get through it much more quickly in friendly conversation … constant creation of communities of people. We get so much of the goodness of the culture of northern Mexico without being shot at when we go out of our homes.

Even here, though, the violence in Mexico is dismissed.[2] The dramatic increase in violence on the Mexican side of the geopolitical borderline was similarly sidelined in other leaders' stories about the Valley. Yet between 2006 and 2011, over 45,000 people were killed in Mexico, stemming from Mexican federal interventions in the drug cartel industry, and the killings were largely localized to northern border states (Correa-Cabrera, 2012, p. 200). It is true that so-called spillover violence is not a problem in the Rio Grande Valley. However, transnational families, businesses, and communities are directly impacted by the violence just on the other side of the river (Correa-Cabrera, 2012, 2014). Without a doubt, violence in neighboring Mexican cities and the deployment of funds, troops, and federal policies further criminalizing unauthorized immigration affect how people in the Valley think about their home and their culture. These are not effective stories, however, in changing the way the nation thinks about the U.S.–Mexico border, because they invariably reinforce the beliefs of a dangerous and porous border. As noted in early chapters, these beliefs impacted policy and contributed to the militarization and securitization and changes in immigrant policy since 2000. The massive investment in an expanded policing apparatus along the U.S.–Mexico border increased the number of migrant injuries and deaths, separated parents and young children, created jobs in borderlands counties with chronic unemployment, and represented external control measures that many borderlanders found unnecessary (De León, 2015; Heyman, 2012; Nevins, 2010 [2002]). Such vastly different effects require more than a sound bite of explanation. It is not surprising that Valley leaders would not incorporate such topics into their framing of the Valley story.

A second risk projecting an American ideal of home is the implied dismissal of alternative conceptions of home, family and community,

---

[2]There were two notable exceptions. One elected national politician and one mayor were upfront with the challenges for transnational families and businesses with the actual violence and perceptions of violence on the Mexican side of the Rio Grande/Rio Bravo River. They used the violence as evidence that our current militarized approach to the border was ineffective, and if we do not work with Mexico to decrease violence on the Mexican side, American revenue from international trade would suffer.

particularly those developed by decades of Chicano/a/x and Latinx scholarship, artistic genres, and literature about experiences of racism, sexism, and classism in the borderlands, including the Rio Grande Valley.[3] They, like Valley leaders, reject persistent colonial discourse about the Global South, and they, too, claim the borderlands region as a home with power and potential. But, many diverge in critical ways, rejecting normative ideas of family, gender, or ethnic hierarchies. Much of this work coalesces around the idea of a homeland, Aztlán, which includes the Rio Grande Valley. Chicano/a/x theorists and activists in the 1960s reimagined Aztlán, the mythical land of Aztec origin, as the lands taken from Mexico during the Mexican–American War of 1846. This more recent version of Aztlán became the source of immense creativity and struggle and alternative social formations of family, gender, and ethnic Mexicans in ensuing decades through today (Arrizón, 2018). In these works, the Valley and other former Mexican territories are a homeland for Mexican Americans and a way to address and redress the profound inequalities from racism and segregation by upending normative values or social orders—not claiming them as strengths of Valley culture.

A third challenge in the leaders' strategy to invoke American values of home, family, community, innovation, and work is that it can dovetail with development discourses common to globalization. Economic development and opportunities in the borderlands are uneven within and between communities and nations (Heyman, 2017), and wealth inequality reproduces itself in binational work arrangements in the transnational maquiladora industry (Ortíz-González, 2004). Promoting the idea that borderlanders are hard workers can parlay into a discourse that low-wage labor is the provenance of the border and acceptable because of unskilled workers nearby in Mexico (Ono & Sloop, 2002). In the burgeoning transnational industries and international trade, Mexican and United States class and gender structures frequently reinforce each other to limit opportunities for women and poor families (Richardson

---

[3]These bodies of works are far too extensive and complex to do them justice here. For the interested reader, I recommend critical analyses (Aldama, 2009; Calderón & Saldívar, 1991; Davis, Fischer-Hornung, & Kardux, 2010; Griswold del Castillo & de León, 1996; Saldívar, 2006) and exemplars (Castañeda, 2007; Gómez-Peña, 2001, 1996; Paredes, 1958; Pérez, 1996; Saldívar Hull, 2000; Santos, 1999) as a way to begin learning about these genres.

& Pisani, 2017). Transnational companies have exploited these hierarchies in hiring practices and working conditions (Simon, 2014). At the same time, transnational companies have brought more wealth to the Rio Grande Valley, even if asymmetrically allocated, and state-level visibility in economic discussions. On the one hand, international manufacturing and its attendant trade, then, call for an innovative, dedicated workforce, and the Valley leaders' border stories fit. On the other hand, the Valley leaders' border stories may also support existing labor patterns that produce further economic inequality in the borderlands. Leaders are in an almost impossible position. They must demonstrate value to an American public and state and national politicians and policymakers in terms and belief systems that make sense, knowing these systems have also produced local problems.

Moving the Valley Story to Border Problems on Their Own Terms

Home and culture are ideas formed from a collection of feelings and experiences associated with places and social relationships. Neither is one thing to all people, and for each of us, our definitions of home and culture change over time and with whom we are speaking. Each manifests in narratives we tell ourselves and each other (Andits, 2015; Escobar, 2001). What we want home to be is as important as what we believe it to be (Andits, 2015). Valley leaders recognize the implicit critique of the national border story that the U.S.–Mexico borderlands cannot represent the American ideal of home as a place of value. They reject that argument. They recast the border, the Rio Grande Valley, as imminently American because of its relationship with Mexico.

This is the point in which the second instance of debordering begins in the leaders' Valley and border stories. They contextualize and reorder border problems presented in the media, such as poverty, poor health, corruption, out of control unauthorized immigration, and drug smuggling. That is, the problems facing the borderlands are not a result of natural social differences but external presumptions of them. Leaders focus on challenges created by these very mischaracterizations, as well as historical struggle over resources between cities, systematic lack of representation in state discussions of resource allocations, and an internal cultural sentiment of "less than" that some leaders feel holds Valley communities back. Culture remains the principal resource by which to address the problem, rather than being the cause. As one activist quipped, "It's the relationships, the caring [of our Valley communities]. We're in the same boat. It may be the Titanic, but we're dancing together and getting the lifeboats over the edge."

Works Cited

Aldama, F. L. (2009). *Postcolonial and Latino borderland fiction*. Austin, TX: University of Texas Press.

Amberson, M. M., McAllen, J. A., & McAllen, M. H. (2003). *I would rather sleep in Texas: A history of the lower Rio Grande Valley and the people of the Santa Anita Land Grant*. Austin, TX: Texas State Historical Commission.

Andits, P. (2015). Rethinking home, belonging, and the potentials of transnationalism: Australian hungarians after the fall of the Berlin Wall. *Ethos, 43*(4), 1348–1352.

Appadurai, A. (2000). Grassroots globalization and the research imagination. *Public Culture, 12*(1), 1–19.

Arcury, T., & Quandt, S. (2007). Delivery of health services to migrant and seasonal workers. *Annual Review of Public Health, 28*, 45–63.

Arrizón, A. (2018). Border and la frontera in the US-Mexico Borderlands. *Oxford research encyclopedias: Literature*, Online publication. Retrieved January 2, 2020, from https://oxfordre.com/literature/view/10.1093/acrefore/9780190201098.001.0001/acrefore-9780190201098-e-397.

Arroyo Colorado Watershed. (n.d.). *About the watershed*. Retrieved July 31, 2020, from Arroyo Colorado Watershed: http://arroyocolorado.org/about-the-watershed/.

Bowman, T. P. (2016). *Blood oranges: Colonialism and agriculture in the south Texas borderlands*. College Station, TX: Texas A&M University Press.

Buch, E. D. (2018). *Inequalities of aging: Paradoxes of independence in American home care*. New York: New York University Press.

Calderón, H., & Saldívar, J. D. (Eds.). (1991). *Criticism in the borderlands: Studies in chicano literature, culture, and ideology*. Durham, NC: Duke University Press.

Castañeda, J. G. (2007). *Ex Mex: From migrants to immigrants*. New York: New Press.

Correa-Cabrera, G. (2012). The spectacle of drug violence: American public discourse, media, and border Enforcement in the Texas-Tamaulipas border region during drug-war times. *Norteamérica, 7*(2), 199–220.

Correa-Cabrera, G. (2014). Violence on the "forgotten" border: Mexico's drug war, the state, and the paramilitarization of organized crime in tamaulipas in a "new democratic era." *Journal of Borderland Studies, 29*(4), 419–433.

Davis, R. G., Fischer-Hornung, D., & Kardux, J. C. (Eds.). (2010). *Aesthetic practices and politics in media, music, and art: Performing migration*. New York: Routledge.

De León, J. (2015). *The land of open graves: Living and dying on the migrant trail*. Berkeley, CA: University of California Press.

Dorsey, M., & Díaz-Barriga, M. (2017). Exceptional states and insipid border walls. In C. G. Vélez-Ibañez, & J. Heyman, *The U.S.-Mexico transborder region: Cultural dynamics and historical interactions* (pp. 65–80). Tucson, AZ: The University of Arizona Press.

Escobar, A. (2001). Culture sits in places: Reflections on globalism and subaltern strategies of localization. *Political Geography, 20,* 139–174.

Farmworker Justice & The National Center for Farmworker Health. (2015). *Farmworkers' health: An analysis of 2011–2012 National agricultural workers survey data*. Buda: Farmworker Justice & The National Center for Farmworker Health.

Federal Reserve Bank of Dallas. (2015, April). *Las colonias in the 21st century: Progress along the Texas-Mexico border*. Retrieved January 2, 2020, from Federal Reserve Bank of Dallas: https://www.dallasfed.org/~/media/docume nts/cd/pubs/lascolonias.pdf.

Forstall, R. L. (1995, March 27). *Texas population of counties by decennial census: 1900–1990*. Retrieved December 1, 2018, from United State Census Bureau: https://www.census.gov/population/www/censusdata/cencounts/files/tx190090.txt.

Gahan, A. W. (2013). *Lower Rio Grande Valley reclamation project*. Washington, D.C.: U.S. Department of the Interior Bureau of Reclamation.

Gómez-Peña, G. (1996). *The new world border: Prophecies, poems & locuras for the end of the century*. San Franscisco, CA: City Lights.

Gómez-Peña, G. (2001). *Dangerous border crossers*. New York: Routledge.

Griswold del Castillo, R., & de León, A. (1996). *North to Aztlán*. New York: Twayne.

Gupta, A., & Ferguson, J. (1992). Beyond "culture": Space, identity, and the politics of difference. *Cultural Anthropology, 7*(1), 1–23.

Heyman, J. M. (2010). US-Mexico border cultures and the challenge of asymmetrical interpenetration. In H. Donnan & T. Wilson (Eds.), *US-Mexico border cultures and the challenge of asymmetrical interpenetration* (pp. 21–34). Lanham, MD: University Press of America.

Heyman, J. (2012). Culture theory and the U.S.-Mexico border. In T. Wilson, & H. Donnan (Eds.), *A companion to border studies* (pp. 48–65). West Sussex: Wiley Blackwell.

Heyman, J. (2017). Contributions of U.S.-Mexico border Studies to social science theory. In C. G. Vélez-Ibañez, & J. Heyman, *The U.S.-Mexico transborder region: Cultural dynamics and historical interactions* (pp. 44–64). Tucson: The University of Arizona Press.

hooks, b. (2008). *Belonging: A culture of place*. New York, NY: Routledge.

Isenberg, N. (2016). *White trash: The 400-year untold history of class in America*. New York, NY: Viking.

Kapchan, D. (2006). Talking trash: Performing home and anti-home in Austin's salsa culture. *American Ethnologist, 33*(3), 367–377.

McWhorter, W. (2010, June 9). *Arroyo Colorado*. Retrieved July 31, 2020, from Texas State Historical Association: http://www.tshaonline.org/handbook/online/articles/rba64.

Miller, H. J., & Almaráz, F. D., Jr. (1998). Four centuries of shared experience in the borderlands. In J. Nirenberg & J. Nirenberg (Eds.), *Borderlands: The heritage of the lower Rio Grande through the art of José Cisneros* (pp. 17–42). Edinburg, TX: Hidalgo County Historical Museum.

Nájera, J. R. (2015). *The borderlands of race: Mexican segregation in a South Texas town*. Austin, TX: University of Texas Press.

Nevins, J. (2010 [2002]). *Operation gatekeeper and beyond: The war on "illegals" and the remaking of the U.S.-Mexico boundary*. New York: Routledge.

Ono, K. A., & Sloop, J. M. (2002). *Shifting borders: Rhetoric, immigration, and California's proposition 187*. Philadelphia, PA: Temple University Press.

Ortíz-González, V. M. (2004). *El Paso: Local frontiers at a global crossroads*. Minneapolis, MN: University oF Minnesota Press.

Paredes, A. (1958). *"With his pistol in his hand": A border ballad and its hero*. Austin: University of Texas Press.

Patterson, S. (2010). Birds. In S. Patterson & L. Lof (Eds.), *El Valle: The Rio Grande Delta* (pp. 228–231). Brownsville: Gorgas Science Foundation Inc.

Patterson, S., & Lof, L. (Eds.). (2010). *El Valle: The Rio Grande Delta*. Brownsville, TX: Gorges Science Foundation Inc.

Pérez, E. (1996). *Gulf dreams*. San Francisco, CA: Aunt Lute.

Richardson, C., & Pisani, M. J. (2017). *Batos, bolillos, pochos, and pelados: Class and culture on the south Texas border. Rev. Ed.* Austin, TX: The University of Texas Press.

Roth, J. (2016, January 5). *Census U.S. intercensal county population data, 1970–2014*. Retrieved December 26, 2018, from The National Bureau of Economic Research: http://www.nber.org/data/census-intercensal-county-population.html.

Ruíz, R. E. (1998). *On the rim of Mexico: Encounters of the rich and poor*. Boulder, CO: Westview Press.

Saldívar, R. (2006). *The borderlands of culture: Américo Paredes and the transnational imaginary*. Durham, NC: Duke University Press.

Saldívar Hull, S. (2000). *Feminism on the border: Chicana gender politics and literature*. Berkeley, CA: University of California Press.

Santa Ana, R. (2017, January 3). *Agriculture tells the history of the Rio Grande Valley* (T. A. Texas A&M AgriLife Extension Service, Editor) Retrieved December 9, 2018, from https://today.agrilife.org/2017/01/03/valley-agriculture-history/.

Santos, J. P. (1999). *Places left unfinished at the time of creation*. New York: Penguin Random House.

Simon, S. (2014). *Sustaining the borderlands in the age of NAFTA: Development, politics, and participation on the U.S.–Mexico border*. Nashville, TN: Vanderbilt University Press.

Simpson, P. (2016). *The Winter Texas report, 2015–2016*. Brownsville, TX: The University of Texas Rio Grande Valley.

Texas Commission on Environmental Quality. (2019, October 10). *Arroyo Colorado: Surveying recreational uses*. Retrieved July 31, 2020, from Texas Commission on Environmental Quality: https://www.tceq.texas.gov/waterquality/tmdl/87-arroyobacteria.html.

Valerio-Jiménez, O. S. (2013). *River of hope: Forging identity and nation in the Rio Grande borderlands*. Durham, NC: Duke University Press.

Vélez-Ibañez, C. G. (1997 [1996]). *Border visions: Mexican cultures of the Southwest United States*. Tucson: The University of Arizona.

7

"Border" Problems: Real and Otherwise

The dominant kinds of portrayal of the Valley and Valley life are in line with portrayals of the U.S.-Mexico borderlands that reach back to the 1820s when the increasing numbers of Euro-American settlers, invitees in many cases, treated local people with varying degrees of disdain and eventually violence ... and even after the episodes of the U.S.-Mexico War and the U.S. Civil War, there was still a way of framing Mexico and the U.S.-Mexico borderlanders in the U.S. literature and popular culture .... The idea of a non-civil society residing on the border is still very prevalent in the mass media ... —professor, The University of Texas Rio Grande Valley

Leaders in the Rio Grande Valley feel the national story about the region gets in the way of the real work that needs to happen to improve Valley communities. Mischaracterizations of the Valley by state and national media and politicians obscure the actual challenges the region faces, including historical inequitable treatment by the state, intraregional competition, and a defeatist attitude among constituents. In this chapter, I continue the analysis of Valley leaders' attempts to deborder the region, specifically how they explain challenges of living and working

K. J. Fleuriet, *Rhetoric and Reality on the U.S.—Mexico Border*, https://doi.org/10.1007/978-3-030-63557-2_7

in the Rio Grande Valley. Remaking the borderlands as a place not of boundaries and difference—debordering, requires a careful deconstruction of accusations embedded in the national border story. They first tackle mischaracterizations in the national news. Leaders across civic, economic, political, educational, and law enforcement sectors identify inaccuracies and gaping holes in the national news story to push for a new way of thinking about the southern border. Leaders then position regional problems as a direct result of how the state and nation have repeatedly treated the borderlands as deficient and in need of control. They contend that what national media and politicians consider border problems are due to imposed inequality from the core, not because of the region's proximity to Mexico. Notably, leaders reject alterity, or the condition of being defined by essential difference.

In earlier chapters, we heard the national story about the Valley. According to the prominent frames, themes, and plots in national news, in particular from 2015 through 2017, the Rio Grande Valley epitomizes all that is presumed to be risky about "the border": a porous, dangerous region rife with corruption, poverty, and illness, in need of external expertise and control to make things better. Valley leaders routinely face this national narrative when they meet with state and national politicians, recruiters for industry, potential employees, federal and private granting agencies, and journalists from national media outlets. Leaders have to balance adequately representing regional problems and not reinforcing border stereotypes. One leader told me that when leaders talk to people outside of the Valley, "you don't describe the Valley, you defend the Valley."

Regional challenges are indeed significant. The poverty rate across the four counties in 2019 was between 22.3 and 31.2% (U.S. Census Bureau, 2019). The medically uninsured rate in 2019 was between 22.8 and 29.7% (U.S. Census Bureau, 2019) in large part because unauthorized immigrants are ineligible for Medicaid. Another regional challenge is the perception of the Valley. In Chapter 4, I discussed some high-profile corruption cases. Due to border security increases in California and Arizona, the Rio Grande Valley became the primary crossing point for undocumented immigrants in the 2010s. And in Chapter 5, we saw how the idea of "the border" as exemplified by the Rio Grande Valley became almost exclusively about drugs and violence from Mexico.

Below, I present how leaders feel the national news has gotten the Valley wrong in three ways: the story is manufactured for political purposes; the story is incomplete; and/or the story is simply inaccurate. Then, we hear from Valley leaders as they describe what they consider the true challenges of living and leading on the south Texas border. First, intraregional competition all too often created impasses that precluded regional representation at the state level. As a result, important initiatives for regional public transportation, education, and economic development stalled. Second, this regional infighting diverted attention from the ultimate cause of health care, educational, and economic problems facing the Valley, which is state funding inequity. Finally, these structural inequities and intraregional competition have frequently combined to create a sense among some Valley communities that they are somehow not as good as the rest of the state. As one elected official said, "When all you write is negative stuff -- you are the 'poverty pocket' of the world, you're the 'most obese' in the world, you can't get out of your hellhole. You can't get out of your situation." While leaders disagree on the reasons for ongoing economic, health care, and educational disparities in the Valley, they all agree that each of these emerged from a specific relationship between the Valley and the state. I conclude with a discussion of the tensions inherent in telling a new border story that can simultaneously deborder social difference created by implicit assumptions about the U.S.–Mexico border and attend to the real effects of those assumptions, such as poverty and violence.

Valley Leaders Say the National Story Is Manufactured, Incomplete, or Inaccurate

Valley leaders do not shy away from talking about and addressing problems. They do, however, strongly disagree with how the media explains problems as integral to the geopolitical border with Mexico and how political rhetoric uses the Valley in ways that reinforce inaccurate, incomplete representations. One exemplar was from a conversations with a business leader in Brownsville and Harlingen that traces his family's roots to Spanish land grants along the Rio Grande River. He looked at the list of themes that I had from my media analysis, set it down on his office table, and rapidly marked off his points and counterpoints. He began with health and health care, his area of expertise:

> [The national story about the Valley is] accurate but incomplete. It doesn't address the things we're doing that no one else is doing south of Houston and San Antonio. We have a stroke and neurology program that has a niche clinical perspective that helps our patients. We are doing joint replacements to a degree almost no one else does. We do cardiovascular care that is either highest quality or differentiator care. We offer our communities some of the best health care in one of the most challenging health care environments. We just don't give up.

He then moved onto recent transformations in public education and workforce training, illustrated by Harlingen but applicable to several Valley cities:

> [The media portrayal] doesn't touch on educational opportunities at all levels. What HCISD [Harlingen Consolidated Independent School District] is doing – I'm incredibly proud of what they're doing. The School of Health Professions, but it goes well beyond STEM [Science, Technology, Education, Mathematics]. It starts in elementary school. I don't care if we compete against Japan or China in terms of STEM attainment unless it relates to our kids' ability to enter the workforce in these areas. That's what I care about …

He next brought in the argument that local, transnational, and hybrid cultures are a regional asset.

> [The media portrayal] doesn't touch on the rich history and multicultural history of the Rio Grande Valley. We are a unique culture down here, and to me, it's beautiful. What we're trying to do is bringing the best of both ethnic cultures together and ignore the rest. You've got the Mexican community that thinks they're the best, the American community thinks they're the best community, but you know, no one's cornered the market.

Lastly, he addressed corruption, drug smuggling, and border security tropes in the media:

> What you don't also hear is about our elected officials that are world class, that are doing their very best, highest integrity. You don't hear how we counter the drug cartels and violence – you don't hear how our violent crimes rate is lower. Just looking at this list [of common media themes] just pisses me off. This law enforcement corruption really chaps my ass. These are men and women who make 30k a year and are putting their lives on the lines each day.

Most leaders agree that corruption is part of public life in all parts of the nation, including the Rio Grande Valley. They also agree that health and health care disparities are significant in the Valley because of poverty, but solutions are not limited to those developed by "parachute researchers" who come from outside the Valley. Most agree huge strides have been made in public education in the Valley but these rarely make the national news. Valley leaders believe undocumented immigration to be a constant but not a single defining element of life across the Valley, and current articulations of border security are often more an obstacle to economic growth than undocumented immigration. Border security instead should be about employment opportunity and industry that works with local businesses to support tourism and trade, they contend. Leaders believe that binational trade, the *maquiladora* industry, the development of the new medical school associated with The University of Texas Rio Grande Valley, and the creation of the SpaceX launch site near Brownsville will significantly grow the Valley's and, by extension, the state's economy, if managed well and not hampered by unnecessary border security expansion.

The Manufactured: Immigration Crises

Manufactured can mean false or produced, and both meanings are relevant to the leaders' critique of how national media outlets and politicians routinely characterize unauthorized immigration. One of my favorite examples of a fabricated media image came from a social justice activist. We were talking in the independent coffee house, El Hueso de Fraile, in Brownsville. I had driven down to the Valley the previous night after teaching a class at UTSA. After meeting with the activist, I was headed less than a mile away to the Brownsville campus of The University of Texas Rio Grande Valley (UTRGV) to talk with a college senior about graduate school possibilities in Anthropology at The University of Texas at San Antonio (UTSA). It was early April and hot. I welcomed both the air conditioning and caffeine of El Hueso de Fraile. Located in historic downtown Brownsville, El Hueso de Fraile opened as a coffee, local music, and Mexican and borderlands art venue. It is a 10-minute walk from the major border crossing into Matamoros. The owners are a well-known couple with a world music band. The coffee house's name refers to an Aztec musical instrument similar to a rattle. The social justice activist with whom I was meeting regularly writes and speaks out about economic inequality and treatment of unauthorized immigrants. He told me the following story. In the mid-2010s, a major media outlet approached him. He had hoped to use the conversation as a platform to discuss American treatment of immigrants. Instead,

> A NBC crew came down and wanted to see people "streaming" across the border. We told them, it didn't happen. They said, yes, it did. So, we went to … [the borderline] and we waited. And I said, "Are you ready?" Suddenly, the weeds part. And it's a Mexican film crew [also looking for immigrants]. I said, "are you looking at something or in the mirror?"

These stories of state and national journalists coming with specific requests for iconic images of the nation's idea of the border were frequent, especially in 2014 after the significant increases in the number of unaccompanied minor children from Central America presenting at the Valley ports of entry to claim asylum in 2014 and the emerging political platform of Donald Trump in 2015.

The 2014–2015 media stories around the Central American refugees were not necessarily incorrect in content, but the uses of words such as "streaming," "crisis," and "surge" suggested an immediate threat (Heyman, Slack, & Guerra, 2018). Politicians, including Donald Trump, used these produced crises, or spectacles, to motivate voters, garner funding for initiatives, or develop policy (Correa-Cabrera, 2012; Kellner, 2009). In 2015, one mayor talked about implications of manufactured crises for the Valley:

> Last summer [in 2014], [we had the] surge of unaccompanied minors, coming primarily from Central America. And the media jumped on this and the national media jumped on it. I started getting phone calls asking about these processing stations .... The media portrayed these kids as running wild through the streets – the Border Patrol didn't have the numbers .... There were things that needed to be fixed. It was not a threat to the security of our communities .... It was really a tempest in a teapot .... We get the black eye. We're the funnel. We're the entry point. The negativity gets thrust on us – in reality, the problems – and there are problems with drugs, drug violence, immigration, but they don't affect just us. Between both issues, the common point is the failure of folks in, the tendency in, other parts of the country and other parts of the state to try to localize the problem so that it just exists here.[1]

The sense of a border out of control and overrun fits neatly into the larger idea of the U.S.–Mexico border that has dominated the United States for the last 150 years.

The Incomplete: Poverty and Health

All Valley leaders with whom I spoke acknowledged that poverty is one of the primary problems facing the Rio Grande Valley, and many connected poverty with poor health outcomes. To be sure, border-lands scholars have long demonstrated that the U.S.–Mexico border is the international border with the greatest economic inequality between two nations, and the economic gaps have been exacerbated by bi- and

---

[1] It is important to note that leaders refer here to the courtesy stigma associated with media stories on asylum seekers, not to the actual conditions imposed on asylum seekers in detention centers. By courtesy stigma (Goffman, 1963), I refer to the phenomenon of negative perceptions of a person, group, place, or activity becoming attached to another because of social or spatial proximity.

multinational trade agreements, such as the North American Free Trade Agreement, and business initiatives, such as the Border Industrialization Program (DeChaine, 2012; Vélez-Ibañez, 1997 [1996]; Wilson & Hastings, 2012). Valley leaders took issue with the assumption that Valley communities are not working actively to reduce poverty or that poverty defines people. One religious leader who had worked alongside community members in a *colonia* to successfully pave the roads and install electrical lines was frustrated by these kinds of assumptions: "We had a guy from CNN come from New York and look around the *colonia*, and said, 'We're not interested. They're not poor enough.' And we said, 'Well, if something hasn't improved in ten years, then something is wrong with us.'" Much depends, a state official from the Valley said, on how the journalist uses poverty to tell the story about the region. He offered an alternative:

> "There is a lot of poverty here." Yes, there is a lack of money. But I would dare anyone in New York City, Houston, and Dallas to live for a year on 5,000 dollars, raise a family of four …. They go to work every day …. They are entrepreneurs …. They may not have luxuries …. Nobody talks about the migrant that goes out every summer and works four to five months and comes back with seventeen thousand dollars for the family, and the family adds a room to the house … buys clothes for the kids, sets aside money for food for the rest of the year …. They always talk about them as needing handouts. That's not what they need. They're success stories. It's just how you spin it.

Leaders recognize the health and health care needs of the region, too, but once again, argue media stories do not account for the context, the improvements, and the potential for improvement. Contexts and progress are crucial to debordering the Valley. Both require an understanding of the history of the region, the allocation of funding for health care by the state and nation, and the transnational resources that are part and parcel of the borderlands.

One cool January afternoon, I met with one of the early leaders in health care in the Valley. We met in a coffee shop tucked in the corner of a bookstore in a McAllen strip mall. A former farm worker, he had intentionally returned with his medical degree to the Valley to help provide better health care access for the poor and underserved communities in the Valley and to lead nascent efforts to get a medical school in the region. He regularly had to contend with state and national legislator and funder misunderstandings about health and health care in the region. I asked him how he described health care in the Valley in these conversations with funders and legislators, when he had to demonstrate need but also the potential of the region. He began, he said, with the issues he felt were more significant:

> Still very medically underserved, physicians per 100,000 population, we have half the national rate .... That presents a difficult situation for us, a very fast growing population, access to care issues, and income based, highly medically underserved ... a confluence of factors ... issues related to health literacy and the other is that we have some health care challenges that are unique to this area, the largest concentration of *colonias* ... around 250,000 living with public health type of risk factors, lacking basic infrastructure, sometimes potable water, sometimes dilapidated homes .... That's a big chunk of our population, a very young part of our population, that represents the future not only of the Valley but our country .... Some public health challenges, TB, an area where dengue fever is endemic. The vector for dengue is ubiquitous .... On the chronic disease side, the ones we always talk about, diabetes, obesity and everything that goes along with it: kidney failure, retinopathy .... The financial costs disproportionately affect this area.

He identified public health, health literacy, health care access, and physician availability as critical health and health care needs. Each is exacerbated but not caused by regional poverty and conditions of the *colonias*. It is significant to note that he is not attributing health and health care disparities to "culture" or "the border" but rather larger political and economic processes that shape both. He then talked about how the demographic profile of the region can be an opportunity to focus more on prevention, support, and management, which will have greater impact on population health:

> But every time I talk about health and health care challenges, I always look at the opportunities as a counterpoint. A young population, a

growing population, the educational opportunities … for research to address challenges, opportunities to look at new models of health care delivery, like medical homes, case management, and new models related to prevention. It's not just about taking care of the acute. We just don't focus enough on prevention, the personal care side, behavior modification. We talk about it, but we don't do it as comprehensively, as effectively as we should …

Finally, he introduced the new UTRGV medical school as the catalyst for major change, concentrating and attracting population health research and intervention in the Valley region. The medical school has a special kind of synergy, he explained, because it attracts researchers due to its location in the borderlands, which increases the depth and breadth of health intervention research that is immediately applicable to Valley communities:

The geographical area lends itself to opportunities, where we're located. That's leverage, the medical school, where it is now. There are other schools that have more resources but they're not here. This is where the population is that needs us. This medical school and university provide opportunities for new models of intervention.

The health intervention research conducted with and within Valley communities may very well provide workable solutions to other areas of the United States suffering from similar health inequalities, such as lack of preventive care and regular care for chronic conditions like diabetes. In each of the passages above, the doctor and educational administrator rhetorically dismantled the assumptions behind the national stories of health and health care disparities. He acknowledged realistic depictions in stories, offered a larger perspective of structural conditions, and then reframed the Valley and the borderlands as a place worthy of educational and health care resources.

The Inaccurate: Violence and Corruption from Drug Smuggling and Unchecked Immigration

Violence is not a central feature of daily life for most people in the Rio Grande Valley. Its persistent portrayal in the media, however, does have economic consequences in the Valley through spending by American and Mexican tourists and Winter Texans. As we saw in earlier chapters, both national media stories and political rhetoric tie violence with drug smuggling. One Hispanic leader rolled his eyes when I asked about it, remarking that the media treat the Valley as "Narcoland. That people are being shot and killed in the street. None of that is happening." A non-Hispanic white elected official said that the portrayal of violence may very well be the most harmful media mischaracterization. He explained,

> My biggest challenge now with the national, the state, and sometimes local media is to do with the negative connotations that we are constantly having to deal with: that the border area is wild and crazy .... It's very, very discouraging to see that the national media, the national leadership and sometimes the state leadership tend to trash the Rio Grande Valley so much. I remember recently when a governor came down here and got on a boat on the Rio Grande with a M16. Now, I don't know who that message was for, but I hope it wasn't for our tourists that come down here, the million tourists that visit the Rio Grande Valley .... This is the kind of media that we can do without.

Regularly, economic leaders such as heads of Economic Development Corporations and Chambers of Commerce, encounter myths of Valley shoot-outs in the streets, kidnappings, and ransoms when they travel across the state and nation.

Violence does surround the Valley, however, and increasingly so. Such violence is due to state and national decisions in both the United States and Mexico, not because violence is an inherent borderland trait. Extreme violence and death occur to the immediate south in Mexico. Significant drug-related violence, including killings, torture, and kidnappings, happens in the neighboring Mexican state of Tamaulipas. Since

2006, Tamaulipas has experienced a dramatic increase in horrific drug-related violence as a result of new Mexican federal tactics to hobble the international drug cartels based in mostly Mexican border states (Correa-Cabrera, 2014). Such violence affects Valley families with kinship and social ties in Mexico, and it constrains international business, especially tourism. Yet, as a Valley political leader noted,

> The spillover violence doesn't really happen in the Valley. It happens in the metro areas. We're not the end point delivery of cocaine and marijuana. The real markets are the metro areas – the real spillover – Atlanta, Houston, Dallas, the big metro areas. People don't – it's convenient for people in other parts of the country [to say], 'it's not my problem. It only happens in that little corner of the world.'

Adjacent and to the north of the Valley's Hidalgo County is Brooks County. Hundreds and hundreds of migrants have died attempting to navigate the harsh brush country in Brooks County. As a result of immigration deterrence policies of the federal government in the 2000s, unauthorized migrants who try to reach the interior of the United States are forced more and more into inhospitable environments of extreme heat with little to no water sources (De León, 2015), such as Brooks County. Between 2009 and 2019, over 650 bodies have been found in Brooks County alone, and it is estimated that there are many more that have not been recovered (Burnett, 2019). Deterrence policies are based on misperception. The majority of unauthorized immigrants in the United States are not ones who crossed the border without documents but rather, people who overstayed their visas (Warren, 2019). Similarly, upward of 95% of illegal drugs that arrive in the United States come through land, sea, and air ports of entry rather than with small groups of people crossing without documents in areas away from legal ports (Finklea, 2019).

Corruption is another defining feature of national and political rhetoric about the border, as I demonstrated in Chapter 4. Leaders' pushback against the assumption of corruption as an inescapable and endemic border characteristic entailed acknowledging some of the more public cases and then recasting them as no different and no more (in fact, often less) than corruption cases in other interior metro areas. One law enforcement official asked me rhetorically, "Is there corruption down here? Absolutely. Is there corruption in Houston and Austin? Absolutely." A state official from the Valley said, "I counter with stories about corruption in other parts of the country …. When I got interviewed by [a newspaper] for the corruption in Hidalgo county, I said, 'have you looked at the corruption in San Diego?'" Others explained the notorious corruption scandals, such as the Hidalgo sheriff and drug running detailed in Chapter 4, as isolated cases. For example, when I asked a mayor how he dealt with a recent corruption case in Cameron County when talking with people around the state, he replied,

> Obviously, that's a bad thing. There's no defense of it. There's *no* defense of it. With the Hidalgo County sheriff and his son, [too]. All I can say is this: google "public corruption." The very first thing that will pop up is the FBI website and all of their press releases around all of the corruption, and it's not just here …. It's not just here. And the notion that it is, is once again one of these insidious misperceptions about the Valley that is unfair.

A hotelier, real estate developer, and elected official used his extensive experience in construction, politics, and business over several decades and across the four Valley counties to establish credibility when he took issue with the corruption stereotype:

> I've been in the Valley over 20 years. I've been in construction. I've dealt with mayors, city councils, politicians in every city. Never has any politician or city employee ever asked me for anything. That's the honest truth …. Is the Valley corruption free? Probably not. I read the papers. But I've never had that problem. People are pro-business … that's what I've encountered. I don't know what they're talking about, "large-scale corruption," just what I read in the papers.

Most leaders did not attribute the corruption cases to cultural influences, but some did. Some of those that associated Valley corruption with "cultural influences" self-identified as Hispanic, others as non-Hispanic white. Even this small group felt the corruption incidence was small and education a relatively simple solution, i.e., it is not a cultural influence that is ingrained and averse to change. Another Hispanic state official from the Valley tackled the corruption trope by arguing corruption is a minor occurrence, solvable with information, but a very real media spectacle:

> Is the Valley a dangerous place? No. Do we have crime? Yes. Do we have spillover violence? No. Do we have spillover corruption? Yes. The solution is education and information …. At the same time, people who have said, "oh, man, you're from the Valley, there is a lot of corruption." I'll turn it around and say, "you're talking about *less than 1%* of public officials who are bad, let's talk about the 99% that are good" …. They accentuate the negative, why? Because bad news sells.

The Real Valley Challenges: Those Friday Night Lights, a Self-Defeating Attitude, and a Voice at the Table

Valley leaders do not shy away from talking about barriers to promoting the economic, social, health, or political well-being of the region. In this section, their voices detail these challenges. Leaders believe the Valley is in a position to be a state leader in economy and politics. According to leaders, there are three internal issues that hurt efforts to improve the region: a divisive competition between cities, a self-defeating attitude in the general Valley population, and historical inaccessibility to state- and national-level political discussions about resource allocation. Most leaders recognize all three as problems but place primacy on one or two. The Valley is not a region full of harmony and agreement about how best to lead and improve its communities. I doubt there is a region in the United States where leaders agree on challenges and their proximate causes. My goal in this book is not to write a work of Valley boosterism, as was standard business practice in the 1920s and 1930s (Bowman, 2016). Nor is it to whitewash very real issues the region faces. My intent is to illustrate why we should try to understand the Valley from the people who live it and lead it rather than uncritically accept a national discourse that uses the Valley as "the border" for political purposes with apparent disregard for the impact of that trope and its assumptions on the region itself. What is particularly striking is that the weaknesses or barriers to improvement according to leaders are not at all what the national news story presents as problems for the area.

As I noted in Chapter 3, Friday Night Lights refer to stadium lights at a Friday night high school football game where community bonding leads to school rivalries that play out far beyond the stadium. For Valley leaders, Friday Night Lights is a metaphor of economic and political competition between nearby cities. By all accounts, this kind of intraregional competition has been part of Valley leadership for decades. In each city, whether Brownsville, Harlingen, Weslaco, Pharr, Edinburg, McAllen, or any other Valley community, I heard about Friday Night Lights as a barrier to Valley growth. I heard it discussed in casual conversations, formal interviews, and focus group discussions. In my interview transcripts alone, I have over thirty, singled-spaced pages of excerpts about the history of intraregional discord and competition. The Friday Night Lights mentality was the most commonly cited reason for stalled regional initiatives, including a Metropolitan Planning Organization (MPO), a regional airport, and a regional public transportation system that would simultaneously promote tourism and better connect *colonias* and other low-income neighborhoods with city amenities and services. One economic leader explained the impact of the intraregional competition on MPO initiatives:

> We have three MPOs here, McAllen ... Harlingen ... Brownsville. The way TXDOT [Texas Department of Transportation] funds projects .... They sit down with MPOs with populations over a million, which are quite frankly, five cities: Austin, San Antonio, Houston, Dallas, Fort Worth ... [and say,] "you guys decide [what to do with the funds]." We don't get a place at that table. If we merged the MPOs [in the Valley], we would now have a MPO of 1.3 million and we have a seat at that table. We have the ability to help determine where that money from

TXDOT goes. So now the MPOs[2] are actually talking to each other about merging as one, because we would get more money. There is still this Friday night football mentality where the undercurrents are. Well, who is going to decide where it gets spent? Is McAllen going to get more than Harlingen? Is Harlingen going to get more than Brownsville? All of a sudden, they get suspicious. But, again, I think that's breaking down.

Some leaders attribute such intraregional competition to fundamental differences in city personalities and priorities. One business leader said, "I would risk to say that there is nowhere else in the country [where] you can have a place called a Valley and each city is completely different .... Every city is culturally different." A state political leader from another Valley city elaborated with a metaphor of immediate needs in a household versus community-at-large needs:

> [Intraregional competition is] absolutely a systemic problem, and I don't even think it comes from a bad place. Someone gets elected to a board, comes in thinking, I want to work regionally, I want to work collaboratively and then they see the needs of their specific bodies that they participate in .... They want them to be an optimal level. It's hard to think outside of the "household." ... If I'm struggling in my household, I'm not going to go out and do community building .... I'm trying to survive .... People are so focused on the inner, most immediate needs, it's hard to see even across town sometimes.

At the same time, most leaders recognize that a regional mindset would help their individual Valley city. They believe the future of each city rests on its ability to work with other cities as a unit. Another political leader said, "I think it starts from the top [at the state level]. And so, I think everyone wants to do what's in the best interest of their particular area. Sometimes, we tend to forget that to qualify for more funding, we need to work together." Most leaders agreed the infighting had created lost opportunities to garner infrastructure resources.

---

[2]In the summer of 2019, the RGVMPO became a reality. Governor Greg Abbott signed the Rio Grande Valley Metropolitan Planning Organization re-designation and consolidation agreement in June of that year (Office of the Governor Gregg Abbott, 2019).

By funding, leaders typically are referring to federal or state resource allocation for infrastructure development, such as public transportation, health care, and public education. A housing activist explained,

> We have not had [public] transportation in the Valley. In the *colonias*, there is absolutely none. They go up Business 83 or the expressway [Inter-state 2]. If we try to get the city to think regionally, it's an issue. The leaders in McAllen or Edinburg may not want to work with the leaders in Brownsville .... The rail can't happen because everybody fights. If there are federal funds, they want to use [them] individually. They think short term and small. We've had regional boards but they haven't been successful. The leaders can't get along. They all go in with their city hats on, and they can't take [them] off.

Leaders share the belief that, historically, the Valley has not received its fair share of state dollars. As a result, this particular Valley brand of internecine conflict arose over the "scraps." Too little funding for public education in an area whose property taxes cannot adequately address needs in the schools leads to regional competition in education, for example. When I asked for her opinion on the primary barrier to addressing public education issues, one non-Hispanic white education leader summarized, "Money, money, money. Inequity of funding from the state level, which is, again, under court review – I don't know how many times it has gone to [state] court. Consistently found to be inequitable." One Hispanic business leader explained,

> [The state] funding's there, [although historically] we have been on the short end of funding ... [but now] there's nothing out there that keeps us from working together. It's by choice. There should be no reason why we aren't working together .... There is a lot of jealousy in south Texas. I don't know if it's because of the Hispanic community, the *machismo* – my pie is bigger. There are still local leaders that love to be on TV. They're managers; they're not really leaders. I really feel that way. There's nothing that keeps people from working together, except they're jealous of one another or people's accomplishments.

At the same time, most leaders also agree that today's higher education funding landscape has changed for the better, notably with the allocation of Permanent University Funds (PUF) from The University of Texas System for the new University of Texas Rio Grande Valley (UTRGV). In the next chapter, I discuss how leaders believe that striving for PUF funds was the turning point in getting Valley leaders to work together in a truly regional collaboration.

Valley intraregional competition may be expected and embedded, but leaders despise it. Older Valley leaders recognize it is their responsibility to change the mentality, but most felt their generation could not conquer it alone. Each one hoped the emerging generation of leaders would see past long-held city rivalries. A higher education administrator influential in the creation of UTRGV felt UTRGV would motivate and model for the younger generation to solve regional transportation issues:

> The reality, [the Valley] was disenfranchised. [laughs] We all have our ideas [why]. There was an idea that the Valley would become one regional mobility authority that determines distribution of TXDOT. We haven't even had a seat on the table. If we did, we would be bigger than El Paso. We could sit at the table, we could determine and distribute more transportation to the Valley. The transformation of UTRGV is that the "regional think" can be more than a theory. People can understand the *poder*, the power, of working as a region .... In my lifetime, it will not be solved. I'm hoping the next generation ... no one's going to have to say that to them, they understand it. They had seen it as an impossible task until UTRGV happened. It can become the model that it can happen .... I think the airport is going to be the next big test .... There is a new group that is thinking about a regional airport.

Each leader had worked hard from their perspective to reduce intercity squabbling, but they implied that other leaders in other cities had not. In interviews, there were different versions of this assertion. One health care leader said, "Frankly, I don't care about boundaries anymore. Perceptions are changing." Another Hispanic health care leader in another city, county, and competing hospital said,

Whoever wants to help us is our friend. I don't care if they're Martians, if they help us get to the goal line, which is building educational opportunities, building the economic infrastructure so people can get ahead, and the health care infrastructure .... For us [in health care in our city], it's about the whole thing, to move the Valley forward, to move [our] County forward. I tend to think regionally rather than provincially .... Barriers to positive change for the Valley? Provincialism. It's provincialism, that's it. And the other thing that is, it's a cultural thing that goes back to in Spanish, *invidia* [Spanish word for envy]. My dad always likened it to crabs in a bucket. It's that it is in our own people: the unwillingness to allow someone else to get ahead so you pull them down. It's a cultural thing. I'm not like that, but others are.

In the preceding quotation, he combined a structural reason, e.g., inequitable resource allocation by the state, with an ethnic/cultural reason, e.g., envy. This was not uncommon among Hispanic leaders. Non-Hispanic white leaders were less likely to cite ethnic cultural behaviors for reasons behind the Friday Night Lights mentality. They felt the city differences were a result of city leadership and historical events, such as the McAllen mayor who was particularly successful at economic growth in the 1980s and 1990s or paths of the railroads and locations of agribusinesses established early in the twentieth century. Only one non-Hispanic white leader in education, relatively new to the region, linked Friday Night Lights to anything cultural, and that was the legacy of the political structure during Spanish colonial times:

I know just enough Mexico and Texas history to think that some of it has to do with some of the ways the populations, the little centers of populations survived early on during the Apache raid and related .... Each [community] banded together, every little city or town had to take care of itself. I think that's where some of what people perceive the intercity rivalry comes from .... City identity is what is most important. You're McAllen, or you're Lyford .... It's changing a bit. UTRGV might be an indicator that there may be some more regional collaboration, thinking. Some people refer to it as a Friday night football identity, but that's stereotypical. You see that in [parts of the Midwest], too. It's a pretty strong emotion here, the city identification you live in, the rivalry, and the competition for resources.

Others focused exclusively on the historical inequalities in treatment by the state of Texas. A long-time business leader with significant influence in the state capitol said, "It's a chicken and an egg thing. First of all, we didn't get any funding, because we didn't have enough population to have political clout. When we did, it was separated into three cities that fought all the time with each other." An elected official wove inequitable state funding and a Global South mentality by the state of Texas into an explanation of Friday Night Lights:

> It is a situation where you have a region that traditionally has not had much resources available to them. And has suffered from a lot of neglect from the state and for that matter, federal governments from both sides, this border issue. Anytime, I don't want to use the analysis because it's not the appropriate one. But. Hungry dogs. If you have a bunch of hungry dogs and you throw out some food, what will they do, right? Really, we're fighting over crumbs. This is just me, but I think it was intentional. I think the state government has always had a certain amount of hostility to the region. Some of it's because we always vote as a Democratic bloc. As a result, we're neglected. I think if we really became a two party area, you'd see more development and attention paid to the Valley than ever before. I think pre-NAFTA [North American Free Trade Agreement], early on, the leadership in Texas saw the border as the end of the world rather than a beginning of the world. They saw it as a buffer zone, a buffer from Mexico polluting San Antonio or other parts of Texas. So, we're going to put just enough money in the area to keep it in status quo. You could see it in the education arena, you could see it in the transportation arena, everywhere. We suffered from benign neglect. As a result, we were hungry. We were always hungry. So when people threw some money down here, they fought over it …. People refer to it here as Friday Night Lights mentality.

One lingering effect of a history of feeling disregarded by the state because of its geography is, to some leaders, a community that does not believe in itself. An activist leader said, "The thought that a location determines your qualities and how good a person is! We in the Valley sometimes have to get past that thinking ourselves." When you are from the Valley, the phrase "in the 956" (area code) refers to self-critiques of Valley culture. Similarly, "only in the Valley" posts spread quickly on social media or begin conversations among people from the Valley as a gloss to insult someone or something associated with Valley behaviors or poverty. Leaders eschew these phrases, because the implicit shame and undercutting undermine efforts to promote the Valley as a place of potential and strength. Internalization of this idea that the Valley somehow produces people who are not as smart or sophisticated can lead to a lack of self-advocacy and a lack of civic participation. Several leaders tied the internalization of alterity with a cultural orientation toward humility, as one public education administrator explained:

> Good, bad or indifferent, our [Valley] culture values humbleness more than it values being in the limelight. So, we don't tell our stories. Instead, these pockets get the limelight. Corruption – this is what gets attention. Health and health care disparities – we are an underserved population, and I will tell you why. We don't exercise our right to vote. We are our own worst enemy. We don't apply pressure to change the systems.

When I asked a county health administrator what he wished for the region, he sighed and said, "For me, what do I wish for the Valley? It'll be a hard one. Let me run it by you first. I wish our youth would be proud to be from the Valley." Several leaders felt the only way to change the national perception of the borderlands and the Valley is to change the defeatist attitude of some Valley communities and be their own story. As a lawyer with state influence in higher education and regional leadership in public education said, "If we don't change that narrative here [in the Valley about the Valley], we don't change the narrative there [at state and national levels]."

Younger leaders and leaders who have recently moved to the region believed it was incumbent upon them to refocus efforts and attention on the potential power of the region. As a younger business leader said, "I think that as one region we can bring so much more money to the area. I think we have to get away from the old school politics, where people think one city will get all of the money. I don't blame them. It's another generation. It's our generation that needs to fix it." The younger and emerging leaders also move through the Valley landscape differently. Many older leaders have an implicit understanding of the Valley landscape similar to mine. When I was growing up in the 1970s and 1980s, driving the thirty minutes to Brownsville from Harlingen was a serious outing. The forty-five minutes to McAllen was an extravagance. Between the cities was expressway bordered by cotton and sugarcane fields or citrus groves. It felt like a long distance to travel. Today, the highway from Brownsville through San Benito, Harlingen, La Feria, Mercedes, Weslaco, and PSJA (Pharr-San Juan-Alamo) to McAllen, Edinburg, and Mission is almost continuously bordered with storefronts. The route now consists of two interstate highways. The younger generation thinks nothing of driving from one city to another for work, dinner, or recreation. In the 1970s and 1980s, most lived and worked in the same city. Not so anymore. As one long-time business leader explained, "there were separations in the communities [in the 1970s]. That is completely gone. You go one end of the Valley to another, and it's like you never left one urban area, there's no separation between them to speak of." A recently arrived health care leader agreed:

> I find the competition between the different cities very interesting. And hard to understand …. People who are from the outside for whom these differences between Cameron County and Hidalgo County just don't mean anything …. I think it will soften with time. And I find it interesting, too, for me travelling between Edinburg and Brownsville, I just don't see it as such as huge of a deal.

Another leader in health disparities research and intervention in the borderlands who moved from a large city to the Valley in the early 2000s says of her work, "I see the work [that I do in health care as] Valley-wide …. Really, the area is one area, characteristics-wise. At every level, it's the same. It's the same everywhere. Yes, you may have some little minor issues, but the issues, challenges, disparities are all the same across the Valley."

Conclusion: Of Metaphors and the Future

[We had a superintendent who] identified the Valley as the "true North" on a compass, which is not a phrase we had heard before. But what he meant by that, he said, was that where the Valley is today is where the rest of the state of Texas will be tomorrow and the United States will be soon thereafter. So, the issues the Valley has been dealing with forever – and is getting a good handle on to deal with them with the help of additional funding and additional resources, can actually be instructive to the entire nation, certainly to Texas. In other words, if we get it right here, we will be the example which can lead the state and the nation as the population changes in the next decade. —education leader

The most common metaphors that leaders used to describe the Valley were *Texas' best kept secret*, *the farm team*, *the future of Texas*, and *Friday Night Lights*. Together, they carry the dominant message that the Rio Grande Valley has the potential to drive the future of Texas, if its communities can work together to address its issues and dispel common Valley and border myths. The Valley's struggles with poverty, chronic disease, and a lack of access to regular and preventive health care, and a fluctuating immigration stream are issues that most would agree do or will face our nation. These have been problems in the Valley for decades, and leaders for several generations have been working toward solutions. It may take time for the Valley public to recognize how much success there has been from within its own communities. As one superintendent told me, "As more of the state begins to look like us and with our challenges and what we grapple with and get ourselves through, we are able to demonstrate [to others] as to how to do it. We don't know how good we are." If leaders and communities can increasingly work across historical divides to represent as a region, then perhaps additional resources will buttress ongoing efforts to improve the well-being of its communities.

Valley leaders see the region "on the cusp of great things." A state journalist sees the Valley as a harbinger of the state's economic and political futures:

We ignore the Valley at our peril. And yet journalistically, we have only paid attention to the Valley when something pokes up either good or bad .... So much of the state's future is whether or not we get the Valley right .... I think the combination of UTPA [The University of Texas-Pan American] and UTB [The University of Texas at Brownsville] into UTRGV [The University of Texas Rio Grande Valley], the onboarding of the medical school, is only the visible part of the iceberg.

Several state and national politicians echoed this sentiment of the Valley as the great predictor. Most often, I heard a variation of "so goes the Valley, so goes Texas. So goes Texas, so goes the nation." One emerging business leader talked about his message to state politicians: "I keep saying, over and over, that the demographics of the Valley are the future demographics of the state, the nation. If we can fix things here, rather than being the laughing stock of the state, the nation, we can be the model." That model is rooted in partnerships, of working intentionally across social, economic, political, and geographic difference, as one public education administrator said,

It helps that the Valley has stopped thinking that the crumbs or left-overs are enough for us. It used to be, "ohhh, at least we got that. Now, [let's] fight over that." There was always this idea that we're not deserving, because we're the Valley. It's still there but it's changing. You know, we can do best practice. We can expect more. We can expect our partners to treat us fairly .... In the last five years, the Valley in some sectors, not all sectors, the Valley partnerships are starting to become stronger. We're seeing with our work, just because of programs we may have in place, partnerships, we're starting to be able to have – there's the part-nerships where you talk to each other, and they're partnerships that you do things together ... towards an improvement goal that creates the next step. Everybody's been talking for years, for good or bad, negative or posi-tive talk, communication. We're seeing now in our work partnerships that are "doing," ... serving, relating, advocating or whatever, thinking about plans. That creates the ground for more conversations.

When I asked one leader what he hoped for the Valley, he said, "I hope that everybody agrees how important it is to work together as a team, to have the same vision, have the same goals .... We're a lot stronger together than we are apart." A leader in philanthropy said that in recent years, "I see people [across the Valley] ... saying how can we connect ... to create a better quality of life and tourism industry, and people are talking and willing to work together."

Different leaders have different ideas about what could help turn the tide toward cooperative regional thinking. One education leader believes it will be public education: "Think about when was the last crusade in the Valley. What was our last crusade, if any? What has united us as a force? We haven't even had a hurricane unite us. We unite for pockets of need, but as a corridor, we're a crusade away .... I think our crusade should be public education." A young business leader agreed there needs to be a regional cause or threat to precipitate regional collaboration: "If it's something that is truly regional, we will come together. If we can see it will benefit the Valley as a whole, the area will come together." Other younger leaders include Mexico in their regional approach to understanding the Valley: "the Valley is all mine, from Mission to Brownsville. I see myself living in an area of 1.3 million, not a town of 72,000. Or maybe 3.5 million people, if we include Mexico."

The most frequent example of the success of regional thinking in the late 2010s was the story of The University of Texas Rio Grande Valley (UTRGV). It encapsulates leaders' definitions, hopes, and analysis of the region. UTRGV symbolizes for Valley leaders the strides the region has made through partnerships in education, community health, and its binational economy as well as its enduring challenges of workforce development, poverty, and insufficient preventive health. A secondary story is the emerging tale of SpaceX's new launch site in Brownsville. Similar to many other leaders, a regional health care and state education leader felt UTRGV was what brought the region to the "adults' table" of negotiation and political power:

The only way I reconcile [the Friday Night Lights mentality] is that we've been so deprived and so needy and so insignificant in so many ways in the minds of state leaders and national leaders that the only crumbs that we had fell off the table .... But it's changing. The population has grown, some of it has been being at the right place at the right time. We're no longer at the kids' table. We're at the adults' table, but we're amateurs at it as a region, so it's still going to take a good bit of time and experience before people really and truly start to work together on issues.

In the next chapter, I demonstrate how the UTRGV story is the primary illustration by leaders of the potential of banding together through regional partnerships and across social difference in order to tackle the historical disregard for the region by the state and nation.

Works Cited

Bowman, T. P. (2016). *Blood oranges: Colonialism and agriculture in the south Texas borderlands.* College Station: Texas A&M University Press.

Burnett, J. (2019, May 21). *After grim deaths in the borderlands, an effort to find out who migrants were.* Retrieved January 3, 2020, from NPR: https://www.npr.org/2019/05/21/724946559/after-grim-dea ths-in-the-borderlands-an-effort-to-find-out-who-migrants-were.

Correa-Cabrera, G. (2012). The spectacle of drug violence: American public discourse, media, and border enforcement in the Texas-Tamaulipas border region during drug-war times. *Norteamérica, 7*(2), 199–220.

Correa-Cabrera, G. (2014). Violence on the "forgotten" border: Mexico's drug war, the state, and the paramilitarization of organized Crime in Tamaulipas in a "new democratic era". *Journal of Borderland Studies, 29*(4), 419–433.

DeChaine, D. R. (Ed.). (2012). *Border rhetorics: Citizenship and identity on the U.S.-Mexico border.* Tuscaloosa: University of Alabama Press.

De León, J. (2015). *The land of open graves: living and dying on the migrant trail.* Berkeley: University of California Press.

Finklea, K. (2019, July 3). *Illicit drug flows and seizures in the United States: What do we [not] know?* Retrieved January 3, 2020, from Congressional Research Service: https://fas.org/sgp/crs/misc/R45812.pdf.

Goffman, E. (1963). *Stigma: Notes on the management of spoiled identity.* New York, NY: Simon & Schuster.

Heyman, J., Slack, J., & Guerra, E. (2018, Winter). Bordering a "crisis": Central American asylum seekers and the reproduction of dominant border enforcement practices. *Journal of the Southwest, 60,* 754–786.

Kellner, D. (2009). Media spectacle and the 2008 presidential election. *Cultural Studies ↔ Critical Methodologies, 9*(6), 707–716.

Office of the Texas Governor l Gregg Abbott. (2019, June 14). *Governor Abbott signs Rio Grande Valley metropolitan planning organization merger agreement.* Retrieved July 30, 2020, from Office of the Texas Governor l Gregg Abbott: https://gov.texas.gov/news/post/governor-abbott-signs-rio-gra nde-valley-metropolitan-planning-organization-merger-agreement.

U.S. Census Bureau. (2019, July 1). *Quick facts: Starr County, Texas; Willacy County, Texas; Hidalgo County, Texas; Cameron County, Texas.* Retrieved January 7, 2020, from United States Census Bureau: https://www.census. gov/quickfacts/fact/table/starrcountytexas,willacycountytexas,hidalgocount ytexas,cameroncountytexas/PST045219.

Vélez-Ibañez, C. G. (1997 [1996]). *Border visions: Mexican cultures of the Southwest United States.* Tucson: The University of Arizona.

Warren, R. (2019, January 16). *US undocumented population continued to fall from 2016 to 2017, and Visa overstays significantly exceeded illegal crossings for the seventh consecutive year.* Retrieved January 3, 2010, from Center for Migration Studies: https://cmsny.org/publications/essay-2017-undocumented-and-overstays/.

Wilson, T. M., & Hastings, D. (Eds.). (2012). *A companion to border studies.* Oxford: Wiley.

8

Crossing Borders: Partnerships and the Story of UTRGV

The University of Texas Rio Grande Valley (UTRGV) was approved as a new university for the Rio Grande Valley in 2013. Its official history as reported on the UTRGV webpage emphasizes its regional focus, distribution of campuses across the Valley, and "transformative" potential for the Valley:

> The University of Texas Rio Grande Valley (UTRGV) was created by the Texas Legislature in 2013 as the first major public university of the 21st century in Texas. This transformative initiative provided the opportunity to expand educational opportunities in the Rio Grande Valley, including a new School of Medicine, and made it possible for residents of the region to benefit from the Permanent University Fund – a public endowment contributing support to the University of Texas System and other institutions.

> UTRGV has campuses and off-campus research and teaching sites throughout the Rio Grande Valley including in Boca Chica Beach, Brownsville (formerly The University of Texas at Brownsville campus), Edinburg (formerly The University of Texas-Pan American campus),

© The Author(s), under exclusive license to Springer Nature Switzerland AG 2021
K. J. Fleuriet, *Rhetoric and Reality on the U.S.—Mexico Border*,
https://doi.org/10.1007/978-3-030-63557-2_8

Harlingen, McAllen, Port Isabel, Rio Grande City, and South Padre Island. UTRGV, a comprehensive academic institution, enrolled its first class in the fall of 2015, and the School of Medicine welcomed its first class in the summer of 2016 (https://www.utrgv.edu/en-us/about-utrgv/history/index.htm, accessed December 31, 2018).

The map at the bottom of the UTRGV homepage in 2020 locates its campuses across the region, reading "A University for the Rio Grande Valley." County lines are absent.

The UTRGV story is the most common story that Valley leaders told in the 2010s to flip the national script about borderlands. Elements in the official UTRGV description above hint at the importance of that story to leaders: the date, the regional reach and identity, the school of medicine, access to PUF (Permanent University Fund) monies for growth, and the partnerships that had to happen. In telling the UTRGV story of potential and hope, leaders do not obscure regional challenges of poverty, unauthorized immigration, and health care and educational disparities. They cite these challenges to indicate the need for and the tremendous potential of a bicultural, binational, and bilingual university to simultaneously improve Valley education, health, and economic conditions and futures.

In the last two chapters, I explored how leaders attempt to deborder, or erase perceptions of difference between the U.S.–Mexico borderlands and the rest of the United States, suggesting that proximity to Mexico makes the region more, not less, American in terms of certain national values. Leaders use the UTRGV story to epitomize a borderlands model of partnership. Their approach to partnership is to work across interregional, language, cultural, industry and nonprofit, and national differences. They talk about how such an approach can help to address educational, economic, and health care inequalities similarly faced by other places in the United States. UTRGV arose from a regional partnership that capitalized on the Valley's unique borderlands strength as a neighbor to Mexico, and it has drawn national and international attention for its successes as a bicultural, binational, and bilingual university. UTRGV offers a different social formation for the borderlands, one of intentional collaboration across imposed differences.

The UTRGV story also extends two dominant scholarly approaches to borders and borderlands, flows and friction. The flows perspective treats borderlands as places of ongoing movements and exchanges of people, ideas, and material and considers how social formations arise as a result (e.g., Richardson & Pisani, 2017; Richardson & Resendiz, 2006). The friction perspective emphasizes what happens when people, ideas, and material run up against assumptions of difference and the kinds of relationships that emerge, e.g., Anzaldua (1987) and Tsing (2005). Both perspectives understand a borderland to be a place of multiple lines of distinction and difference (Wilson & Donnan, 2012). Each approach is interested in the ways in which larger and historical processes, such as wars and international trade deals, influence social relationships, such as kinship, gender, and socioeconomic class. The partnership that leaders use UTRGV to represent suggests a third way borderlands are socially productive spaces: an internal process of debordering within border communities historically pitted against each other due to imposed race, citizenship, class, and other civic identities essential to bordering practices.

The Valley in the leaders' UTRGV story is a different Rio Grande Valley than found in national media and political discourse. It is not a place of dangerous borders and people. Instead, the UTRGV story showcases a region where leaders from different cities, counties, and sectors can work cooperatively, even if not always smoothly, to confront persistent challenges through innovation and to capitalize upon a young, bicultural community invested in its future. UTRGV is not a panacea to entrenched inequalities relative to the rest of the state. There is still much work that needs to be done to help Valley communities, as is noted by leaders. UTRGV is a symbol of what is possible when the state invests in the Valley and Valley communities work collaboratively with each other and with sister communities across the borderline. Local expertise and experience wed with economic and educational opportunities to draw people from other parts of the country to the Valley. One journalist connected the national (mis)narrative, UTRGV, and the Valley's future, saying,

If you're not from here, everyone will tell you this: 'No, no. I can't go down there. It's just not safe.' So the perception is that there's a lawlessness, [that] we're overrun by cartels, drug gangs, illegal immigrants, everything. So, there's a negative image there. People are unaware of what's really happening down here.

There are lots of positive signs. We are getting better grades compared to where we were. Things have improved. With this investment in education, we should be able to grow the middle class .... Business leaders will say we're not going to recognize this community in 20 or 30 years with the seeds being sown, the university [UTRGV], Texas A&M second ... Space X ... LNG [liquid natural gas company] .... They're not leaving school to work in the fields ...

If we can get a good enough percentage of them to stay in the Valley ... if you have an educated population, those better jobs will come. This year, the economist from the Federal Reserve Bank from Dallas says we've overcome El Paso as the fifth largest [Metropolitan Statistical Area].

In this chapter, I bring together not only leaders' renderings of UTRGV from interviews and participant observation fieldnotes but also local journalists' contributions to the UTRGV story. Local journalists like the one above serve as a primary mechanism by which leaders' stories become available to wider audiences. In those stories, Valley leaders are frequent sources. I interviewed eleven former or current writers, editors, and publishers in print and digital media and followed their stories throughout my data collection period. Each was recommended to me by different Valley leaders for their work dismantling border myths. Leaders and journalists alike embed UTRGV stories within an analysis of Valley strengths and challenges to promote health, economic, and educational well-being. Leaders cite regional advantages of culture, border location, demographics, and natural environment. To the very last leader with whom I spoke, the only sure ways to keep moving the region forward are to work and advocate as a region and to engage education, health care, and economic sectors at the same time. Leaders paint a picture of a future of growth and political influence from Valley leadership working in partnership. Often, leaders use UTRGV to transition to discussing other regional efforts, including the SpaceX launch site, that speak to a Valley and borderlands rich with expertise and even greater untapped capacity. UTRGV symbolizes what the Valley is and what it can be.

A Bit of Background: Public Universities in Texas, or Why UTRGV Had to Happen for the Valley

Never in my life did I think you'd have UTRGV and the facilities we have here .... I'll be damned! I know that it's one building [referring to the first medical school building], but it's the cornerstone of what is coming about .... These kids that want to be doctors and nurses, they deserve these resources .... The growth that has taken place [because of UTRGV], they deserve all of it. - journalist in 2014

The creation of UTRGV is intimately tied to funding for public higher education in Texas. Texas public higher education institutions cluster into systems with their own leadership. One system is The University of Texas System, or UT System. Its flagship institution is The University of Texas at Austin. In 1839, the Congress of the Republic of Texas set aside vast stretches of Texas land as a permanent endowment for public higher education. After Texas became a state, the legislature in 1858 approved the first university in Austin and its Medical Branch (medical school) in Galveston (Smyrl, 2010). One hundred and fifty-nine years later in 2017, Texas had 104 public higher education institutions spread out over 37 four-year universities, three public state colleges, 50 community colleges, four public technical colleges, and ten health-related institutions, including medical schools. In the UT System alone, there are fourteen institutions: eight academic and six health sciences institutions. Importantly, medical schools were independent from four-year universities in Texas by constitutional order until the creation of UTRGV and The University of Texas at Austin medical schools in the 2010s (The University of Texas System, 2019).

In the Valley prior to the 2013 creation of UTRGV, higher education opportunities were insufficient for the population and lacked access to adequate growth funds. Graduate and professional degree programs were available at UT Pan American in Edinburg, UT Brownsville and its affiliation with UT Health Sciences Center-Houston's School of Public Health campus in Brownsville, and two Master's in Public Health programs at Texas A&M Health Science Center School of Public Health in McAllen. South Texas College was the only other bachelor's degree-granting institution until Texas A&M opened a regional campus in 2018. There were several community colleges, including Texas Southmost College, Texas State Technical College, and Rio Grande College. Together, Valley higher education institutions in 2019 enrolled 70,000 students (RGV Partnership and Lower Rio Grande Valley Development Council, 2019). By way of comparison, San Antonio's population size is similar to that of the Rio Grande Valley. In 2019, San Antonio had at least[1] three public universities; four private, religious universities; two private, secular universities; and five community colleges. They serve over 125,000 students. Notably, San Antonio's higher education opportunities include a medical school with nursing and allied health professions' graduate degrees, a school of osteopathy, a law school, and easily over 100 doctoral, Master's, and graduate certification programs. If we were comparing access to higher education in surrounding areas for the Valley and San Antonio, we would also need to include Texas State University in nearby San Marcos, a 45-minute drive from downtown San Antonio; Texas Lutheran University, a 35-minute drive; and the universities and colleges in Austin, a one-and-a-half-hour drive from downtown San Antonio. These higher education opportunities would add well over a hundred thousand more students to San Antonio's count. The Valley's next closest universities are Texas A&M Kingsville, a two-hour drive from Brownsville that requires stopping at a border patrol and immigration checkpoint, and Texas A&M International in Laredo, a two-and-a-half-hour drive from the Mission-McAllen-Edinburg area.

---

[1]This number varies depending on whether satellite campuses and campuses on military bases are included. I am reporting only those colleges and universities with a significant footprint in the physical landscape of higher education in San Antonio. This number is also subject to increase with new branches and satellite campuses of other universities opening in San Antonio, e.g., University of Houston. It does not include online universities.

Texas A&M Kingsville and Texas A&M International serve at least 15,000 students.[2]

Valley leaders have used such comparisons of overall capacity and access to graduate programs over the years to push for more state funding for higher education in the region. Leaders advocated to access additional growth funding for both The University of Texas-Pan American and The University of Texas at Brownsville, to provide more and diversified degree programs, and to develop specific professional degree programs, including doctoral, law, and medical degrees. Existing funding for UT Pan American and UT Brownsville was insufficient for that kind of expansion. According to Valley leaders, the issue was lack of access to Permanent University Funds, or "PUF funds" or simply "PUF."

In 1839, the Congress of the Republic of Texas created a land-based endowment for higher education in Texas (Smyrl, 2010), and the Texas Constitution of 1876 established the Permanent University Fund (PUF) as the public endowment. At several points in the nineteenth century, the Texas legislature designated more funds and lands in West Texas thought to have enough yield to fund higher education through PUF. Revenue from grazing leases generated PUF monies for construction and rehabilitation of campus buildings and the promotion of academic excellence. Then in 1923, the Santa Rita well on PUF lands struck oil. The first oil royalty payment was made to the PUF that year. The increase in revenue was astronomical. In 1900, the revenue generated without oil was about $40,000 (Smyrl, 2010). The market value of the PUF at the end of 2018 was 21.5 billion dollars (The University of Texas System, 2018).

PUF monies are principal growth funds for universities who want to expand, especially in areas of research and graduate education. PUF is not available to universities that began as community colleges (The University of Texas System, 2014a). Community colleges and their later incarnations as UT universities instead have access to Higher Education Funds (HEF, sometimes HEAF). According to UT System leadership as well as Valley leaders, HEF monies are inadequate for the growth needed for a major research university and medical school (Perez-Hernandez, 2015; Taylor, 2016). In 1989 and 1991, respectively, The University of

---

[2]Sums are from enrollment data publically available on university websites in 2019.

Texas-Pan American (UTPA) and The University of Texas at Brownsville (UTB) joined the UT System (The University of Texas System, 2019). UTB was originally the Brownsville campus for UTPA, and UTPA grew out of a community college. As a result, the Brownsville and Pan American campuses had access to the HEF but not the massive PUF (THECB, 2009).

Without PUF funds, Valley leaders struggled for decades to find ways to create a medical school and more higher education opportunities in the Valley. Another event precipitated UTRGV. UTB was jointly constituted with Texas Southmost College, but the UT System voted unanimously to separate them in 2010. Many theories abound for what most agreed was a "messy divorce" between the two-year community college, Texas Southmost College, and UTB, which provided upper division coursework and access to graduate programs (Hamilton, 2011). The result was that UTB would need significant investment to build new curricula for the first two years of college, hire new faculty, and find new space. In 2012, then UT System Chancellor, Dr. Francisco Cigarroa, hatched the renowned UTRGV plan (Perez-Hernandez, 2015; Taylor, 2016). Dr. Cigarroa was from Laredo, a few hours up the Rio Grande River from Brownsville. If both UT Brownsville and UT Pan American were abolished and a new UT institution was approved in their place by two-thirds of the Texas legislature, the new UT institution would have access to PUF monies. It could include a medical school. It would have the potential to be a major research university. It would be a Valley-wide institution with three main campuses in three different cities, the first of its kind in Texas.

The UTRGV plan was bold. Figuring out how to productively combine two legacy institutions long embedded in the social fabric of their respective communities would be rocky, at best. Logistically, it would be even harder to navigate. For example, two systems of human resources would have to be disbanded and reconstituted as one, which would include terminating and rehiring faculty and staff and merging all records into one management system. There would be hard decisions about which campus would house which colleges, programs, and departments. Facilities funding and locations of new programs and structures would be controversial. Overall, there would need to be transparency to ensure Valley communities believed there would be equitable distribution of resources and people, faculty, staff, and students at the campuses. Most importantly, Valley leaders would have to convince the Texas legislature that the region was worth the investment.

They did. The Texas Legislature approved UTRGV in 2013 under Senate Bill 24 (SB24, 2103-2014, 83rd Legislature, TX 2013). The initial investment was approximately 500 million dollars, 350 million of which were targeted as construction dollars from PUF monies (Perez-Hernandez, 2015). In fall 2015, UTRGV began with a combined student body of 28,584 students (UTRGV, 2016). UTRGV admitted its first medical student class in 2016. UTRGV is truly Valley-wide. It has campuses, research, and teaching sites in, as noted above, "Boca Chica Beach, Brownsville (formerly The University of Texas at Brownsville campus), Edinburg (formerly The University of Texas-Pan American campus), Harlingen, McAllen, Port Isabel, Rio Grande City, and South Padre Island" (UTRGV, *History of The University of Texas Rio Grande Valley*, n.d.-e).

From its inception, UTRGV embraced a bicultural, bilingual, and biliterate regional identity, seizing on the borderlands as resource where once it was seen as deficit. Students would be encouraged to move expertly through Mexican and American cultures and speak and read fluently in both Spanish and English. The UTRGV vision and mission are explicitly about student and regional success. Four primary priorities revolve around its core priority of student success: educational opportunities, health and wellness in Valley communities, research that impacts the Valley region and beyond, and community engagement. UTRGV styles itself as a "land-grant, sea-grant, and space-grant institution," which highlights its reach across the region (UTRGV, *Core Priorities*, n.d.-c). "Sea-grant" refers to its coastal studies and marine science programs on the Gulf of Mexico. "Space-grant" refers to its nationally recognized and funded Center for Gravitational Wave Astronomy and its more recent public–private partnership with SpaceX in its new "space exploration based technology park" at Boca Chica Beach near Brownsville and South Padre Island (UTRGV, *College of Sciences Office of the Dean*, n.d.-b). "Land-grant" refers to the former UTB and UTPA campuses, its medical school locations in Brownsville, Harlingen, and

Edinburg, and its various satellite sites and community partnerships in many Valley cities.

UTRGV took the excellence in teaching, research and service at UTB and UTPA and magnified them with additional funding, collaboration, and new programs, including the new medical school. By 2017, UTRGV was growing. First generation college students constituted 60.6% of students, and 89.24% were of Hispanic or Latino/a origin. In 2019, UTRGV offered 64 Bachelor's degrees, 56 Master's degrees, four doctoral degrees, 2 cooperative doctoral degrees, and the medical degree (UTRGV, 2019). It is difficult to overstate the impact and potential impact of UTRGV on the Valley. I offer an introductory description of one or two partnerships in each of UTRGV's core priorities as one way to illustrate UTRGV's reach. These examples tell a story of Valley strengths, successes, and expert commitment to improving the well-being of the region through collaboration across diverse constituencies.

UTRGV Core Priority: Education

One UTRGV core priority is educational opportunities for the Valley community. From young children to adult learners, UTRGV educational partnerships are both local and international. UTRGV's P-16 programming, which addresses education from pre-kindergarten through college, partners with five middle schools and 10 high schools across Valley school districts (UTRGV, *Partnerships & Collaborations*, n.d.-h). Here, I focus on the College of Education, which has service learning, community-based learning, and project-based learning partnerships with Valley school districts to promote literacy, encourage education as a professional field, and offer STEM (Science, Technology, Engineering, Mathematics) summer enrichment programming. The College of Education also has developed an innovative, mentored, yearlong teaching rotation for its students as well as leadership development among Valley teachers and administrators in partnering school districts (UTRGV, *Partnerships*, n.d.-g). For all UTRGV students, UTRGV's global partnerships for faculty and student educational and research exchanges numbered over 40 in 17 countries at the time of writing, ranging from Mexico to

Russia to Thailand to Kazakhstan to France and Switzerland (UTRGV, *Global Partnerships*, n.d.-d).

UTRGV Core Priority: Health and Wellness

A second core priority is health and wellness, primarily through research and teaching in its medical, allied health, and health education programs. One example in the medical school is its commitment to provide health care to medically underserved communities. In 2018, the medical school in partnership with the local nonprofit organization Proyecto Desarrollo Humano opened its first student-run clinic in Peñitas. Peñitas is a small town due west of Mission. Sisters of the Immaculate Heart of Mary began Proyecto Desarollo Humano in the early 2000s in and around Peñitas to serve *colonias*. Prior to the UTRGV clinic, members in one *colonia* worked collaboratively with the Sisters to build and improve their neighborhood after a major hurricane caused significant damage in 2003. The community now has organic community vegetable gardens, a community center that offers exercise, English, legal aid, art, and sewing classes, tutoring and a computer room for children, a thrift shop, and clinic space (Mosbrucker, 2014; Salgado, 2016). The clinic space is where the UTRGV medical school clinic opened after Valley leaders, including the Sisters, developed the partnership. The UTRGV medical school clinic offers screening, wellness checks, vaccinations, minor injury care, referrals, and health education. The clinic exemplifies how UTRGV builds on ongoing efforts and successes in Valley communities, in this case adding accessible, affordable health care and education to vulnerable populations already working to improve their communities.

UTRGV Core Priorities: Community Engagement and Research with Local and Regional Impacts and Beyond

The two other core priorities are community engagement and research that affect Valley communities and beyond. An exemplary partnership is UTRGV's interdisciplinary research and outreach center, the Center for Sustainable Agriculture and Rural Advancement (SARA). SARA is committed to promoting agricultural sustainability and rural communities. SARA partners with over 20 local, state, and national public, private, and not-for-profit organizations. Partners include the Food Bank of the Rio Grande Valley, the nonprofit Farm and Ranch Freedom Alliance and HOPE for Small Farm Sustainability, the Texas/Mexico Border Coalition, Texas International Produce Association, the National Immigrant Farming Initiative nonprofit organization, the Service Corps of Retired Executives, the Veteran's Business Outreach Center, the USDA, and the National Science Foundation (UTRGV, *Partners*, n.d.-f). SARA serves as the node for these and other partners as well as offers research and outreach around sustainable agriculture and in rural areas. The table of contents from its first newsletter of 2019 (see Table 8.1) illustrates SARA's regional orientation, scope, and commitment to research and policy that directly benefits regional communities and development.

Other UTRGV units target economic development in binational trade and manufacturing, a staple of the Rio Grande Valley economy. The College of Engineering and Computer Science houses five research and outreach programs, including the Nanotechnology Center of Excellence, the Rapid Response Manufacturing Center (RRMC), the Texas Manufacturing Assistance Center, the University Transportation Center for Railway Safety, and the South Texas Industrial Assessment Center (UTRGV, *Centers*, n.d.-a). Each has its niche in faculty research expertise and relevance to the Valley region. For example, the Rapid Response Manufacturing Center capitalizes on the binational economic zone by supporting the use of new technologies to enhance speed, development, deployment, and production in manufacturing to get products more quickly to market. Rapid Response Manufacturing can also allow for mass customization. UTRGV's RRMC leverages existing Valley assets and the binational maquiladora industry to benefit the region and state. UTRGV's Center for Border Economic Studies (CBEST) buttresses similar efforts. CBEST is an interdisciplinary public policy research center and clearinghouse, whose mission is to work with local, state, national, and international units to identify binational and regional economic trends impacting development and trade, labor and immigration, health and environment policy, and human and social capital

Table 8.1 Table of contents from The SARA Report, UTRGV's Center Sustainable Agriculture & Rural Advancement (Center for Sustainable Agriculture & Rural Advancement, UTRGV, 2019)

Research & education

1. USDA funds Training, Research, and Education in Soil Science (TRESS)
2. Participatory research on sweet potatoes results in research presentations
3. Brownsville Research & Community Garden includes high-tunnel greenhouse
4. BRCG greenhouse to play critical role in student education
5. Research shows conservation tillage improves soil structure
6. UTRGV research garden expands to include high-tunnel hoop house
7. SARA wine research highlighted by UTRGV
8. Citrus wines may be well suited for organic wine production

Outreach & extension

9. UTRGV hosts field day through its Subtropical Soil Health Initiative
10. Church land rezoned for use as a sustainable urban farm
11. SARA's 2017 Annual Report drafted and added to the Center's website
12. SARA works with cooperative to support health and local food systems
13. TRCC* leads cooperative panel discussion for City of Austin
14. TRCC plans summit in support of cooperative-driven food systems
15. TRCC provides technical assistance & leadership training to new cooperative
16. SARA collaborates with the SBA to introduce agriculture opportunities to veterans
17. Video showcases Texas Hispanic Farmer and Rancher Conference
18. NRCS-funded hoop house christened with training event
19. SARA staff assist with student training in sustainable agriculture
20. Rio Farms Grape Growing & Wine Festival scheduled for the end of month

*TRCC = Texas Rural Cooperative Center

(Center for Border Economic Studies, n.d.). Noteworthy, CBEST's mission, like that of other regional initiatives and of Valley leaders themselves, underscores the inextricable connections between economy, education, and health. CBEST brings together scholars in each of these areas to produce policy and policy-related analyses based on research that they conduct, consult, or otherwise support. Moreover, like other UTRGV units, CBEST facilitates partnerships between the private, nonprofit, academic, and government sectors in the region. Its regional

orientation, integrative model of improving economy, health, education, and environment, and its commitment to producing research with
demonstrable impact are hallmarks of UTRGV as a major regional force.

Health-focused efforts by UTRGV are not limited to its graduate
medical education. The medical school draws resources, researchers, and
funds to the region. The South Texas Diabetes and Obesity Research
Institute (STDOI) is an example of what UTRGV was able to attract
with its new funding and medical school. STDOI represents one of
the world's leading research teams of longitudinal, multidisciplinary
studies around genetics and disease. UTRGV first recruited Dr. Sarah
Williams-Blangero, the then chair of the Department of Genetics at the
Texas Biomedical Research Institute in San Antonio. Williams-Blangero
brought with her 21 other Texas Biomedical Research Institute staff and
researchers. It was a huge coup for the new university. Williams-Blangero
and her team had extensive National Institutes of Health funding and
data from large, longitudinal studies on disease and genetics with a
special emphasis on diabetes and obesity. Valley communities suffer
disproportionately from these conditions (Millard et al., 2017). UTRGV
wanted its medical school to have clinical, research, and outreach focus
on conditions afflicting Valley communities. UTRGV was able to offer
funds, space, and technology to expand Williams-Blangero's research
agenda to make the move attractive (The University of Texas System,
2014a). Her team arrived as the first research team for the new School
of Medicine.

STDOI brought prestige, funding, and credibility to the nascent
School of Medicine, setting a high bar. Between 2000 and 2014 in
San Antonio, Williams-Blangero's team received over 200 million dollars
in external funding from the National Institutes of Health. STDOI
brought in an additional 13.8 million dollars during its first 18 months at
UTRGV (South Texas Diabetes and Obesity Institute, 2016). By 2018,
that number had grown to 31 million dollars (Perez-Hernandez, 2018).
Their lab conducts whole genome sequencing, generates specialized cells,
and houses a "high performance computing system with 11,000 proces-
sors dedicated to genetic analysis … it is one of the largest clusters
devoted to human genetic analysis in the world" (South Texas Diabetes
and Obesity Institute, 2016, p. 6). STDOI collaborates with over 70

institutions world-wide, a symbol of its pivotal contributions to studying human genetic variation and health. The development and accomplishments of STDOI highlight what Valley leaders have known for years. With adequate resources, the Valley's educational, research, and clinical opportunities can compete with—and surpass, those in other state and national regions.

Despite its early achievements and commitments to the region, UTRGV from its creation to implementation to assessment is not without its detractors. Nor would I suggest everything runs smoothly and perfectly. It is unlikely that any large higher education institution does. UTRGV has the additional challenges of equitably operating in three counties in a region still fighting for transportation funds to have a regional transit authority for public transportation as well as education dollars to overcome the digital divide for low-income and rural families whom UTRGV serves. Instead, my intent in this section is to illuminate UTRGV's potential to improve and support Valley communities to contextualize Valley leaders' abiding belief that higher education and partnerships are central to changing the region's narrative to itself and for the rest of the nation. I also want to offer a different way to talk about the U.S.–Mexico border region. In the next section, I show how UTRGV as a symbol represents what the Valley can be and should be, according to its leaders and local journalists.

UTRGV as Symbol: Righting Past Wrongs, Bringing the Valley Together

> When we succeeded in the legislature [to approve UTRGV], we tore down the provincial barriers. We spoke as a region. We brought UT Pan Am and UTB into UTRGV and for the first time, we could draw from PUF. Those two things are pivotal to the change in the Valley …. There is great raw talent and intellect down here …. We need to have a Tier 1 university [top national ranking for research universities] here for them.
> - health care leader

Many in the Valley locate the primary cause of regional challenges in historical disenfranchisement by the state, especially evident in the old ceiling for higher education growth in the region. Leaders consider past inequitable distribution of economic, educational, and transportation infrastructural resources as ironic, noting the region's significant economic contribution to the state. The Valley's primary economic contributions to Texas are through its international ports, binational manufacturing industry, retail sales bolstered by Mexican nationals' spending, and agricultural production. Yet again, here is a different story about the U.S.–Mexico border region, the Valley's economic impact through international trade at its ports of entry.

In 2015 for the fourteenth year in a row, Texas was the largest exporting state, in large part due to border ports (Hagar, 2017). Texas has 29 ports of entry, six of which are located in the Rio Grande Valley. Another port, Laredo, is hugely important to U.S. cross-border trade. While not officially part of the Rio Grande Valley, Laredo suffers from the same national image problem despite annually facilitating approximately two hundred billion dollars of cross-border trade, approximately a third of the state's international trade, and contributing over 50 billion dollars of the state's annual gross domestic product (Office of the Comptroller, State of Texas, 2015b). The six Valley ports dot the geopolitical border with Mexico, from Roma in westernmost Starr County to Brownsville at the very tip of Texas in Cameron County. The Valley ports, along with the Laredo port, make up the Laredo Customs District, which is the third largest customs district in the United States after New York and Los Angeles (Office of the Comptroller, State of Texas, 2015a). Rio Grande Valley ports account for 13% of total state GDP (Gross Domestic Product) created by trade in border ports, and Texas border ports altogether make up approximately 40% of estimated state GDP created by trade (see Table 8.2).

Valley leaders feel that the region lags behind other economically significant areas in terms of state support despite the region's contribution to state coffers. They identify several key areas for growth and development, particularly in higher education, that would immediately benefit the region and the state. The Valley before and after UTRGV

Table 8.2 Total trade value and estimated gross domestic product (GDP) created by trade at ports in Texas, 2015 (Office of the Comptroller, State of Texas, 2016)

Port	Total trade value ($US)	Estimated GDP created by trade
Rio Grande Valley Ports		
Brownsville/Los Indios	16,277,507,940	4,129,200,124
Hidalgo/Pharr/Anzalduas	30,045,516,537	7,621,802,493
Progreso/Donna	231,164,095	58,640,599
Rio Grande City/Los Ebanos	261,483,748	66,331,943
Roma/Falcon Dam	59,575,999	15,112,954
Valley International Airport	14,253,546	5,066,823
Total Rio Grande Valley Ports	46,889,501,865	11,896,154,935
Total Texas Border Ports	356,034,186,651	90,322,111,234
All Texas-only Ports	631,014,994,372	224,312,000,000

is their proof. One higher education leader key to the development of UTRGV explained,

> Since 1876 when [PUF] was established, every new UT and A&M school got the distribution of PUF when it started to generate revenue. Everyone got it except Brownsville and UTPA and A&M [campuses in Kingsville and Commerce]. It was Laredo, Corpus, Kingsville, and Commerce. Kind of interesting when you map it out, right? At some point … [the legislature] set up HEAF funds – for all those who don't have PUF funds …. It was a good idea if it could have kept up with PUF distribution … but higher ed, of course, grew faster than [HEAF] funds were available …. So, UTB and UTPA got put into the HEAF fund. It was wrong. We're brothers and sisters [with other UT institutions]. We're not cousins. We're in the family …. They said, "it's because you came on too late." There were lots of rumors as to how and why this happened, and no one knew why. We have been arguing for 20 years for PUF …. We knew how little we were getting. The PUF distribution represented real dollars, and it also represented equity at the table. [It is a] paradigm shift …. PUF gets us at the big kids' table.

Another higher education leader also highlighted the state geographical distribution of graduate degree programs in the UT System:

If you look at the development of degree programs ... you could follow
I-10 [the interstate that enters Texas at Houston, goes northwest through
San Antonio and exits Texas at El Paso] .... There were only three
doctoral programs south of I-10 .... With the continued growth of the
Valley, we're going to develop more professional programs, PharmD ...
Doctorate in Physical Therapy ... Doctor of Optometry .... Our argument is, very simply, there's nothing in south Texas. There are no
educational opportunities for well over a million people. Historically, the
discrimination against the Valley has come in terms of those kinds of
resources .... If you don't have access to those resources ... you go away
to school .... If you go away, you very often stay away .... The biggest
export from the Valley is not citrus. It is brain power .... Part of our job
[at UTRGV] is to keep it here.

As he explained, demonstrated regional need for higher education
outstripped state contribution to develop it. Generation after generation of high-achieving students left, regularly referred to as "the brain
drain decades." Another result was exacerbated regional infighting. As
one political leader explained, "we've always described it as we've fought
each other for the crumbs that fall off the table, trying to get something
from the legislature ... because all the goodies are going to Austin, Dallas
and San Antonio." UTRGV and its medical school, however, opened
up the possibility of collaboration, he noted. A health care leader and
elected official in another city agreed: "And before the UTRGV, what
about [UT] Pan Am? No PUF funds for you .... It's kind of hard to say,
'we treat you equal' when you aren't .... Now with UTRGV, now, they're
tapping PUF funds as they should be. We are all Texans."

While the Texas legislature voted unanimously in favor of the creation
of UTRGV, it also set up roadblocks for regional cooperation, threatening the first prominent regional effort to put aside county and city
rivalries. Leaders tell this part of the UTRGV story to emphasize how
many want to work as a region, but state actions do not consistently
support cooperation. Some Valley leaders suggested that state leaders
intentionally fostered competition as a means by which to control the
developmental process of UTRGV. Others saw state actions, including
that of the UT System, as par for the course. Even in situations with

state support, working cooperatively is not easy for leaders with so many constituencies.

One economic and education leader traced state efforts to foster intraregional competition to the earliest attempts to get a medical school presence in the Valley. The Regional Area Health Center, or RAHC, was a University of Texas Health Science Center San Antonio satellite clinical rotation and medical residency program in the Valley. The leader used the RAHC's history to show how Valley leaders attempted to work together but were stymied by state officials, whether legislators or appointed UT System officials:

> I am so embarrassed by the way UT System does things [sometimes] … and I'm a UT alum …. The history of the RAHC is a perfect example of just absolutely screwing things up. The whole idea of making the communities in the Valley compete over the RAHC and compete with each other in a way that costs the communities so much money, it's abhorrent. It's embarrassing. Then when [the state legislature does] something like create UTRGV and think that worked so well? They asked for competitive proposals from the communities to see where the administrative office should be … and immediately, the cities head to their separate corners … [and then] Guy Bailey [first UTRGV president], comes in from Alabama, a stranger in many ways to this process … and he looks at that and says, "what in the world are we doing here? You want me to be a prophet with the one university message at the same time you have these folks in this throat-slashing campaign with each other?" He put a stop to that.

The state's request for competitive proposals from Valley cities for UTRGV's administrative offices was a common element in the UTRGV story. A political leader from Harlingen said, "UTRGV asks for RFPs [request for proposals] for UTRGV headquarters, sends every community into a big frenzy …. Juliet García, [then president of UTB], said, 'you know, we haven't had any practice working together.' I thought that was profound." An elected official from Brownsville also believed UTRGV's creation was the opportunity Valley leaders needed to cooperate and once they did, the course of the region changed:

UTRGV was a great example of getting united in the community in the Valley. And it wasn't easy. And it was compromise. Not everyone got everything they wanted. The economic portion of that effort is so long-lasting …. The Chancellor [of UT System] and the Board of Regents were very, I thought, they were extremely generous in understanding and recognizing our potential. And, I think once you do that and people believe it, you're going to have a different culture down here. That would be good for the people. I'm just a true believer in that our good Lord didn't make bad stuff.

UTRGV—the idea, reality, and future, became the glue the region needed. As an elected state official from Cameron County described, "I think UTRGV is the greatest unifier right now. The success of that regional effort. Really, it is the purest regional effort we have. It's cross-county, multi-campus, providing a single product, education, that could lay the foundation for future collaborative efforts …. That really is the perfect opportunity to have a success story we can build upon." Leaders who had regularly encountered regional conflicts over resources were surprised by how quickly UTRGV started to reorient leaders to a regional perspective. Some attribute the first major shift with the creation of UTB. UTB, in turn, set expectations for regional collaboration that UTRGV accelerated. One economic leader was involved in the development of UTB as he simultaneously served as an elected leader in another city. He agreed to serve on the Development Board of UTB because he was tired of the Valley's getting in its own way:

I said, I'll do it, [serve on the board for UTB], because I can be somebody from [one city] that gets to know them in Brownsville and we can get over the fighting and start to trust each other. And when I got [into the work], I thought, Holy Christ, this is going to take a long time … [but] it didn't take as long, when [Pan American University-Brownsville] became UTB. It had an immediate impact.

In different sectors, from education to economy to health care, leaders feel that UTRGV will model regional collaboration. One leader involved in community health care centers and the new medical school reflected on the challenges of health care delivery in a medically underserved area in the era of the Affordable Care Act and a state that chose not to expand Medicaid as a political response to the Act. She was hopeful that patient-centered care, electronic medical records, and interprofessional health education would move the Valley's health care "ecosystem" toward an integrative model of health care delivery. She saw UTRGV as providing the model. She said,

> I think in 25 years, we'll eventually get there, where we are all working on [health] care together, where we have lots of information, but information is presented in a way that is easy to utilize to do your job. And working together. As we move toward that ecosystem, I think we can probably do a better job collaborating between cities and counties .... You know, people are living in Brownsville, working in Harlingen, or vice versa. It's all one ecosystem .... Interestingly, at UTRGV, they're putting together their curriculum. They have to be in Brownsville one day, and then in Edinburg. That's not very user friendly .... I'm sure there are some bene-fits to moving back and forth, kind of feeling like everything is one, but at the same time, we have to look at efficiencies, as well.

What is particularly interesting about her reflection is that she started from the assumption that Valley health care leaders would work together; the challenge would be in the logistics of working across systems and levels. Her assumption is typical of a new way of thinking for Valley leaders. Rather than believing the barrier was other leaders' need to hoard too few resources, she talked as if leaders already share a regional commitment to improving health care delivery.

Leaders' commitment to UTRGV produced what many leaders called "regional think." Regional think is just what it sounds like, the ability and willingess to put the region first in strategic decision-making and policy creation. UTRGV represents, stimulates, or otherwise contributes to economic growth and blurring of city boundaries and their stereo-types across the four Valley counties. As an education leader put it, "How do you see the way forward for the Valley to work through their vested, local interests that have historically been at odds? I think there are two things you have to keep in mind. Everybody sees [UTRGV] as an economic generator, and [everybody] wants a piece of it." Another

Hispanic health care leader who lives in Harlingen but works Valley-wide listed city stereotypes and argued that UTRGV would force people to work across city boundaries, which would effectively dispel the old city labels:

[The stereotypes are] Brownsville is Mexico; Harlingen is white; McAllen is rich Hispanics. My reality … is that there are some incredibly good people in Harlingen that are motivated to the same investment in the community. There are also people that still make remarks that are incredibly racist. Brownsville has the same pockets but not the same reputation as racist. Harlingen was controlled by Anglos for many, many years, and the reputation still exists because of the regional infighting. Everyone thinks they're better than the others and would prefer to live in their communities and not leave them. But, that's not how we're going to progress. I think UTRGV will help this …. Frankly, Harlingen is not my only community. My community is bigger than that. Frankly, I don't care about boundaries anymore. Perceptions are changing. I think UTRGV will help greatly in that regard.

A journalist and teacher wondered if UTRGV and regional think could influence the next generation to think first of their regional identity:

I think the Valley's civic leaders have recognized that there is potential in that regional identity and certainly, that's been a big push with UTRGV and the new medical school and the economic development corporations. I don't know, like, definitely, I'm trying to wrap my head around [the question]: do my students think they are Valleyites or are they from McAllen?

Finally, leaders felt that UTRGV was just the first of massive regional collaborations. They pointed to slow-to-grow collaborations in areas that have historically been fraught with intraregional competition, such as transportation infrastructure, especially the possibility of a regional airport and the economic potential of the region as a Metropolitan Planning Organization; hospital and clinic networks; and tourism. Many agreed that regional think required a regional identity.

UTRGV provided that, too, by drawing on unique regional character-istics. UTRGV was intentionally designed as a "bicultural, bilingual, biliterate," or "B3" institution. Upon its creation, UTRGV had the second highest percentage of Hispanic students in all colleges and universities in the United States. It still does. In 2018, 91.4% of students were Hispanic at UTRGV, close behind Texas A&M International in Laredo (94.4% Hispanic students) (Smith-Barrow, 2018). UT System issued 14 "Guiding Principles" for UTRGV at its inception, the fifth of which is "Promote arts and humanities programs to produce state, national and world leaders who are bi-cultural, bi-lingual, and bi-literate" (The University of Texas System, 2013). The ordering is significant. The first and second guiding principles revolve around student success, especially the growth of a Hispanic Serving Institution. The seventh is the establishment of the medical school.

It is no small thing for the state of Texas to prioritize, in writing, a research collegiate identity as bicultural, bilingual, and biliterate in the context of the state and national discourse about Mexico in the 2010s that tended to de-emphasize the economic and social importance of our ties. It is also significant that Valley leaders pushed for that prioritization and identity. This is a region where the norm through much of the 1900s was de facto segregation in public schools and spanking children in elementary schools for speaking Spanish (Nájera, 2015; personal communication with educational leaders). While there were a few significant student demonstrations, such as the 1968 Edcouch-Elsa High School walkout, attitudes and curricula were slow to change. Early bilingual education programs in the 1970s for dominant Spanish speaking children reinforced cultural and national stereotypes with curricula that ultimately limited students academically in both English and Spanish (Guajardo, Esquierdo, & Weimer, 2014).

We have come a long way. Approximately fifty years after the Bilingual Education Act of 1968 that provided funding to schools interested in pursuing bilingual education, The University of Texas System prioritized bilingual, bicultural, and binational programs in the new University of Texas Rio Grande Valley. The "B3" initiative guiding principle that UT System implemented was a Valley idea from a Valley native and the first Mexican-American woman university president in the United States,

Dr. Juliet García (Tyx, 2017). UTRGV is the first intentional B3 campus in the nation. UTRGV's efforts to become a B3 university are concentrated in its B3 Institute. The B3 Institute's mission is to work at multiple levels of the university and community to promote student success and distinguish its students, using

> the vibrant socio-cultural and linguistic landscape that is the Rio Grande Valley … to fashion UTRGV's identity that befits and respects the history and culture of the region …. A theory of change informed by community cultural wealth and an assets based approach to teaching, learning, and service guides the work of the B3 Institute. These [sic] assets based model challenges deficit based perspectives that have historically shaped educational practices vis-à-vis minority students. (UTRGV B3 Institute, *About, Overview and Purpose,* n.d.-a)

The B3 Institute structures its initiatives along three lines of outreach and support. First, the B3 Institute delivers professional development for faculty and staff to offer programming, courses, and course materials that are pedagogically attuned to dominant Spanish and bilingual speakers as well, reinforced with certifications and optional immersion experiences to build Spanish language capacity in faculty and staff. Second, it incentivizes research and scholarship around bilingual education with funding and support for seeking funding as well as a publication venue through *Rio Bravo,* an interdisciplinary peer-reviewed journal. Third, it creates and supports university–community partnerships, workshops, and other forms of collaborative learning and exchange to embed the principles and pedagogies of bilingual education throughout the region and to support existing work in pre-K through 12 settings (UTRGV B3 Institute, *Intiatives,* n.d.-b) To support its binational commitment, UTRGV announced in 2017 its plans to open recruitment offices in Mexican sister cities (Taylor, 2017). In early 2019, the first recruitment office in Matamoros, sister city to Brownsville, opened (personal communication with UTRGV Recruitment Office, February 2019).

UTRGV as Symbol: The Valley's Future

The B3 guiding principle and B3 Institute of UTRGV represent efforts of Valley leaders to reframe historical understandings of weaknesses as regional strengths as they attempt to level the playing field with the rest of the state. Leaders also anticipate that UTRGV will attract new ideas and people to the region to accelerate economic growth, educational initiatives, and improvements in health outcomes and health care. In large part, leaders are equally enthusiastic about building on local expertise and the infusion of creativity and skills to address long-standing economic, health, and educational disparities in novel ways. One health care and education leader talked about the potential infrastructure changes that would influence the region's economy:

> You see the change in the RGV, [the] university that is bringing in a lot of change to the Valley. You see a lot of new people. You see a lot of new ideas. You see a lot of knowledge. You see a lot of infrastructure changing .... You're seeing new business opportunities in the Valley in the medical field and in the small business world, so that's exciting.

Other health care leaders agreed. They believe that UTRGV and its medical school will transform health care in the Valley. It will increase the supply of doctors, nurses, and allied health professionals in general and in specific need areas, such as psychiatric care. The medical school will improve the functioning of healthcare systems through its emphasis on interprofessional education. Both local doctors and future doctors will learn how to manage and deliver care more effectively in terms of patient outcomes and costs. The medical school curriculum is innovative in its pedagogical emphases and structure, its early and diverse engagement with community health, and its team-based learning. A founding medical school administrator described the curricular approach to medical education:

> The basic science curriculum is an integrative model, the whole curriculum is integrative, integrated horizontally and vertically .... Medical school [used to be] parceled out with two years

of basic science and two years of clinical science .... Since [2010 when the president of the American Association of Medical Colleges challenged medical school leaders to improve medical education] and somewhat before, there has been a transformation in medical education, moving away from sitting in an auditorium hour after hour listening to lecture ... to paying attention to students' different learning styles. We hadn't been working in teams, and there are new technologies that need to be embraced .... There are virtual ways to learn in medicine. You can use audience response systems and other new pedagogical methods that are very effective: problem-based learning, self-directed learning, team-based learning. Schools have been going through that transformation.

A Hispanic Hidalgo County health administrator believed UTRGV will be the primary driver behind Valley improvements in health and health care:

The game changer was UTRGV [for health care]. If UTRGV was not here today and I had no inkling it was coming, in 10 years, I wouldn't say [health care] would be better. I would say it would be critical in 10 years .... UTRGV will increase the quality of life in south Texas for the next 20 generations. We're going to see a greater change in our region in the next 20 years, a positive change, a good change ... than we have seen in the entire history combined of south Texas .... It's not just the medical schools. It's the collaboration. It's the interprofessional development ... all of this comes with the medical school. We're no longer seen as Tamale Tech [a common ethnic slur applied to the university both by locals and others in the state], Harvard on the Rio Grande. We're UTRGV. Very soon, it's going to be a distinguished campus.

Health care leaders' conversations often transitioned from the strengths of the curriculum in the medical school and its ability to supply health care professionals to the region to the general impact of improved education. For example, a pharmacist, business owner, and school board member emphasized the new ideas and people that UTRGV would bring, saying, "At the education levels, at the M.A. level, the Ph.D. level, you start talking about cohorts. We want teachers, professors, from outside the area. We don't want to keep teaching the same thing.

You're starting to see that finally with UTRGV." In particular, leaders see the flow of new concepts and perspectives into the area as stimulating the Valley's students to achieve more and to contribute more to the region. The founding medical school administrator cited above believes the increase in higher education opportunities alone will generate more jobs:

> Of course, no question, I'm biased. I make my living in higher education. I am among those that think that higher education is – I think of it as giving people the opportunity to have keys to open doors. Educational opportunities are going to be one of the major influences on reducing poverty. Ultimately, it comes to jobs … and education is one of the main ways people get qualified for those jobs …. I've been tremendously impressed with the impact that UTB and UTPA already had. Hopefully, UTRGV will continue the trend, even accelerate it.

UTRGV was the springboard to talk about other regional changes that will stimulate the economy. One state-level education leader, small business owner, and physician connected the dots from UTRGV to regional infrastructure that will attract more business and "draw down" more state funding:

> If we look at UTRGV, the medical school, SpaceX, the [new] interstate, the second causeway [from Port Isabel to South Padre Island], rumors of a MPO – if these [individual city] MPOs merge, we'll have the fourth largest MPO in the state, which can draw down state funds for infrastructure.

Discussions in 2015 through 2018 about the possible MPO often paralleled discussions about an international Metropolitan Statistical Area, or MSA, designation. The idea of an MPO or an MSA is evidence of the regional think spurred by UTRGV. The Valley's historic city-based identities are shifting to a regional identity. MPOs and MSAs are federal designations that leverage regions to secure federal and state funds for infrastructure crucial to development. Eligibility criteria focus on population size and spread, both of which appear to fit the Valley in the 2010s. Determination of eligibility would require Valley leaders to work in concert with each other and the governor, which would represent significant success of regional think. According to the Federal Transit Administration, which oversees MPOs,

> MPOs are required to represent localities in all urbanized areas … with populations over 50,000, as determined by the U.S. Census. MPOs are designated by agreement between the governor and local governments that together represent at least 75 percent of the affected population (including the largest incorporated city, based on population) or in accordance with procedures established by applicable state or local law. When submitting a transportation improvement program to the state for inclusion in the statewide program, MPOs self-certify that they have met all federal requirements. (Federal Transit Administration, 2016)

In April 2019, Valley mayors gathered to sign an agreement for one regional MPO. They represented the three Valley MPOs: Brownsville, Harlingen-San Benito, and Hidalgo County, which includes the Pharr-Edinburg-McAllen-Mission area. Political and economic leaders increasingly support the Valley MPO, predicted to bring in over 110 million transportation dollars in a 10-year period (Whitlock, 2019). During our conversations, Valley leaders talked about how a regional MPO will secure funds for the development and maintenance of an efficient transportation system region-wide, essential to supporting and growing international trade with Mexico and tourism, both key economic contributors to the state. The regional MPO required collaboration, and UTRGV demonstrated that regional think and success are possible.

Another novel idea is the International MSA, or Metropolitan Statistical Area. An MSA is a Census-defined area:

> An MSA consists of one or more counties that contain a city of 50,000 or more inhabitants, or contain a Census Bureau-defined urbanized area (UA) and have a total population of at least 100,000 (75,000 in New England). Counties containing the principal concentration of population—the largest city and surrounding densely settled area—are components of the MSA. Additional counties qualify to be included by meeting a specified level of commuting to the counties containing the population concentration. (U.S. Census Bureau, 1994)

There are pushes for two kinds of Valley MSAs. The first is a Combined MSA (CSA) which would integrate the two existing Valley MSAs of Brownsville-Harlingen and McAllen-Edinburg-Mission into one Brownsville-McAllen MSA. Similar to the MPO designation, the MSA designation could influence state and federal funding decisions regarding economic development and infrastructure. Although there is some debate over this assertion (e.g., Blum, 2017; Hammond & Osoba, 2008), a regional MSA would conceivably alter the national image of the Valley as a rural outpost dotted with small cities. MSAs represent areas whose economic and social ties overlap. Historically, MSAs often referred to a city and its suburbs, but as urban regions expand and bump up against each other, regional MSAs can emerge.

The second kind of MSA which leaders discuss is the potential of a new designation, an International MSA, or International Combined MSA. The idea is that some international border regions are so deeply intertwined economically and socially, their demographics should be combined into a single demographic profile for an accurate representation of their productivity and population. A banker and economic leader explained the potential economic benefit if the Valley and its sister region in Tamaulipas, Mexico, were identified formally as an international MSA:

All of a sudden, we're one of the biggest players in the nation. But, it will always be discounted by perception, all the violence. I don't know how to measure the [economic] influence of Mexico to us or the bank, but it's big …. I would venture to say it's deeper than Reynosa and Matamoros …. The folks that come on a weekly or monthly basis from deeper in [Mexico] … we've grown and done lots of things [in the Valley], but without [Mexico], I'm not sure it would've occurred. Whether it's trade, transportation into the US, whatever it is, it takes Mexico. And those are the opportunities you hear about all the time [in the Valley]. They're looking at a plant in Mexico or have a plant in Mexico and want to consolidate so they have a closer presence in the US to Mexico … it always seems to have to do with what is happening in Mexico and the opportunities it has. No question, [Mexico] is an economic driver.

Indeed, UTRGV's outreach as a B3 institution to potential students from Mexico and partnerships with industry use proximity to Mexico as an asset, not a weakness. As the head of one economic development cooperation said of rapid response manufacturing,

> What if I offer you as a customer the ability to tell me what you want? I will build it. I will get it to you by ten o'clock tomorrow? What have I just done? I gave you what you wanted .... And what have I done to China? There is no way they can do that. I just cut them out of the market .... That's not only rapid response, it's also customization .... We're going to jump ahead. That's where education and us having the ability of having educational institutions that can respond that way. That's why [having a] Tier One institution [like UTRGV] is so critical. We have the opportunity to become that research entity for manufacturing products. And what they're also finding is that because they're offering you the product exactly the way you wanted it, you'll pay premium for it.

The leader directly tied UTRGV's research emphasis on local communities, its explicit commitment to functioning binationally, and its goal of being ranked as a national research university with the ability of the region to leapfrog over other manufacturing options outside of the United States.

A final theme in the leaders' telling of UTRGV as the future is the means to finally keep and develop its best and brightest, to reverse "brain drain" and jumpstart civic engagement in younger generations. A law enforcement leader sees UTRGV as "a people thing. There is a huge, untapped resource – our people down here, for our state, for our nation .... I think UTRGV is going to have a tremendous impact on this region." Most leaders talked about how many more young people in their twenties and thirties are returning to the Valley by choice, something relatively unheard of prior to the 2010s, except to be close to family. A Brownsville politician told me one effect of UTRGV is that communities now strategically attract young professionals:

> A lot of young people say, "I'm not coming back to the Valley." That's the first thing they say. But the Valley is changing. I think a lot of it has to do with the educational opportunities, the UTRGV system, and they're

looking at what's happening in their cities. It's not only Brownsville. It's Harlingen. McAllen. They're seeing a lot of activities geared toward young people.

Mentioned above, leaders feel like generations of Valley potential and expertise were lost because the region could not offer the most competitive or comprehensive higher education opportunities. In 2016, the Hidalgo County health administrator used the inaugural class of the medical school to illustrate:

> The biggest problem we have in the Valley is that we're losing a lot of capacity, academic capacity, intellectual capacity, leadership capacity. You grew up here [and left]. Everyone is in a hurry to leave the Valley, especially high school kids. I see that changing. I see more and more cohorts of mine who are back. They're back not because they're failures but because there are opportunities .... Half of the [entering medical school class] were from the Valley .... They left the Valley, went to higher institutes of learning away from here, and then applied to come to medical school here. And then you ask them ... you could have gone anywhere, you were a Princeton grad, you got your M.A., your Ph.D. from Princeton and your econ degree from Harvard. Why did you apply to UTRGV? You could have gone to Harvard Medical. And what amazed me was: "I wanted to come to the Valley." Your generation, my generation, we were in a hurry to leave here. But, I see that changing. I see it changing.

Similarly, a journalist believes the medical school will change the way in which students see the Valley. A Valley medical school—which means located on the U.S.–Mexico border in an area that historically and currently experiences serious health and health care disparities, provides local students with the expertise, resources, and skills to truly make a difference:

> To me, I look at the medical school at UTRGV and I see, what potential! If I was an incoming medical student, you have the opportunity to create huge change in our community. There is a lot of services that are offered in other places and models that have been tried in other places that have not been tried here. You can be a leader and an innovator here,

anywhere but particularly here, and with the new medical school, you've got a chance. You have the institutional support.

Others tied UTRGV and its medical school with increasing civic awareness and political participation. A former journalist and emerging leader in politics believed "UTRGV and the medical school are taking it to the next level. That's a big part. Just having people educated enough to learn, to know they can fight a tax discrepancy, to know they have options out there, that makes for a more well-rounded society ... if you have more people voicing their opinions, to know where to go to fight back." Later, he explained further. UTRGV would not only offer more educational opportunity for Valley students but also stimulate other higher educational institutions to open campuses in the region. He tied together the educational opportunities with increased civic engagement, retention of talent, and future political power in the capitol:

> It seems like [the younger generations] are having that feeling of staying, because they're learning so much, always reading, always online, so informed. They'll be of huge value to the growth of the Valley. I think [the Valley] will look very different [in the future]. I think it will change the way in Austin [the state legislature] people think of the Valley as a problem but as a place they want to count on and involve. [The Valley narrative] is going to be very, very different. And that's going to happen pretty soon, I think, in the next 10 years. It's going to happen. It's on the way. I've seen the difference.

The UTRGV story is principal in how leaders understand the Rio Grande Valley region, especially its challenges, the reasons for its challenges, its opportunities, its resources, and strategies to improve the educational, economic, and physical health of its communities. The main message of the UTRGV story is this: *As a region, we have come so far. We still have work to do. We can be a resource for the state and for the nation in the present and in the future.* Striking in its contrast to the national story about the Rio Grande Valley, the UTRGV story is complex but fundamentally positive. It encompasses a long-term understanding of the region that does not overlook histories of inequality, racism, and classism but instead rearticulates the ethnic diversity and relationship with

Mexico as a resource, expertise, and unrecognized potential. Leaders are quite frank about the challenges that come along with such a history and its legacies of poverty and a limited tax base. Conspicuously absent, violence, corruption, and drugs are not part of the UTRGV story.

Conclusion

What the creation of UTRGV has done is simple and very powerful for the Valley. It has reinvigorated hope: hope the region can work together, hope that there are more effective ways to ameliorate poverty and poor health, and hope that more of the Valley's strongest students will stay and invest in their communities. One education leader with more than forty years on local, regional, and state school boards talked about UTRGV as a means to "lift all ships" and attributed her hope to overdue state investment in the Valley's higher education opportunities:

> I believe there is great change afoot as is evidenced by the commitment by the state to UTRGV and the medical school, not just that they will exist. At least, there is conversation in the system that these will be top tier institutions. This will have a profound effect …. "Rising tides lift all ships." We are moving into a rising tide time, thanks to the UT System.

Hope for the Valley is tempered by leaders' nuanced understanding of longstanding challenges in the region. In their predictions about what UTRGV can yield for the region, leaders moved between a strength model and a deficit model to make sense of enduring challenges.

I asked leaders how they understood and talked about regional challenges in ways to justify resource allocation. One U.S. congressman told me, "Look, we're not perfect and we have a long way to go. But, if you go and visit, if anyone goes and visits the brand new facility for the new medical school and realizes that it just started the first class in June, right? You know, if anybody would suggest that we haven't entered into the modern world, they haven't seen that." Other leaders were frustrated by continued infighting, hoping that UTRGV could have more quickly erased old territorial battles over resources. It was a similar refrain to pre-UTRGV Friday Night Lights talk: "Despite my efforts to get us together [to financially support UTRGV], that just isn't happening .... We're always fighting over what we've asked them to give us, rather than doing it ourselves ... so that's why we fight all the time." Still other leaders took the long view, as one leader instrumental to the creation of UTRGV said,

> The deficit model is real. We won't catch up for decades. [The founding medical school dean] has to sit next to the UT Austin dean, and Austin is raising so much more money than we can .... The deficit is real about resources that have come to the Valley. It's not going to be corrected by 500 million [dollars given by UT System to UTRGV] in two years. It will transform us but over years. What's important about PUF money, it doesn't matter who is Chancellor [of UT System], who is governor [of Texas]. To pull [UTRGV] out of PUF [would be] political suicide.

Others talked about regional challenges in terms of how UTRGV has positioned the region to address them. One education leader and journalist acknowledged the difficult road ahead but felt UTRGV's regional orientation, reach and resources might be the turning point for the Valley:

> We have *a lot* of work to do .... I really believe in where this university is going and what the benefits can be. And I think the benefits outweigh any single incident or problem that arises .... I believe we are on the ground floor of helping to educate an historically underserved community. A medical school is coming in! Who would have thought that? Our institutions of higher ed were heartbreakingly referred to as Taco Tech and Tamale Tech. Heartbreaking stuff .... We [at UTRGV] are the agar in the petri dish that is helping the good stuff grow.

Another journalist reflected on how his professional approach to the Valley may be changing. A freelance writer for local newspapers and online political news sources, his audience is both local and state. He saw the central message of his stories evolving over recent years. Like many leaders, he ties together economy, health, and education in his understanding of the region. He, too, considers regional disparities a result of historical, state-level inaction:

You know, education, health, environmental issues that are not *always* brought to the forefront in a way that is entirely negative … [although] sometimes, I find myself pitching the same kind of story over and over, innovative efforts to overcome but not every story has to be that …. Part of the challenge is there is so much that *is* going on. There is tremendous growth. Education is improving dramatically in the Valley. I've seen it …. I've seen dramatic improvements in high school education, higher ed, and those will continue. Obviously, there's economic growth that brings good and bad circumstances, but it's totally transforming the place into an urban place … much more region wide, at least, interest in region wide collaboration … and yet, just looking at numbers, some of the challenges are just so daunting. Issues like substandard housing, health disparities, there is just so far to go to catch up with comparable urban areas …

For other leaders. UTRGV brought a sense of renewed purpose and ability to function as a multi-county urban area by working together. One day, I met with a doctor and economic leader in health care who had been working for decades to advocate for Valley health care resources at the state level through professional and political channels. As we talked about his leadership in health care delivery and innovation in the Valley, he recognized the regional competition as something of a dying breed of leadership. He focused on what UTRGV could and would do for health care in the Valley through its regional orientation and partnerships, ability to draw the right kind of attention by researchers across the nation, and the economic boom that would result from a transformation in health care.

I'm on fire about the future! I've been telling this to our group, our partnerships. They didn't believe me in the early days …. We are, right now, at a crossroads. And, we are in the middle of a transformational crucible that is occurring in this community, right now. It's every week [that] I'm interviewing somebody, talking to somebody who is going to do a [health/medical] study here that is going to revolutionize who we are, transform our community. We don't have to go very far to find parallels. We are where San Antonio was. We will be where San Antonio is, in 25 years. When SpaceX comes aboard, you're going to have a conduit for STEM. You're going to have a marriage of the sciences, the life sciences and the physical sciences and that coming together will lead to innovative discoveries and treatments. We're going to crack the nut on diabetes. We're going to crack the nut of obesity. We're going to crack those things that have decimated our communities .... We're going to be a Tier One university. This medical school will be second to none .... I'm not a Pollyanna person, but I feel the pulse. I get it. It's that energy that drives me .... I'm ready for the next thing.

Other leaders echoed him. UTRGV symbolizes the future and potential for a region to do more and be more for its community members and the state. Often, after a frank assessment of what the problems are in health, education, and economy, leaders would intentionally reroute our conversations, using UTRGV as the pivot. For example, in my conversation with the Hidalgo County health administrator, he returned to talking about the inaugural medical school class's white coat ceremony to shift our conversation from challenges to the future. He saw these students as our future health care leaders, and current Valley leaders need to support and nurture them by modeling a future orientation with an emphasis on potential. At that point in our conversation, he pointed to pictures of medical students during the induction ceremony as they rotated on his screensaver and said, "I have to focus on the strengths .... I'd be lying to you if I said I don't worry about bad things in the past, but [I focus on] what is to come, [how] to influence the positive. You got to, Jill. Otherwise, get the hell out of the way! Either lead or get out of the way."

Works Cited

Anzaldua, G. (1987). *Borderlands: The New Mestiza = La Frontera*. San Francisco: Spinsters/Aunt Lute.

Blum, M. (2017, August 3). *A case for combined MSAs*. Retrieved 28 2019, February, from VBR: Valley Business Report: https://valleybusinessreport.com/news/combining-rgv-msas/.

Center for Border Economic Studies. (n.d.). Retrieved March 9, 2019, from UTRGV: https://www.utrgv.edu/cbest/index.htm.

Center for Sustainable Agriculture & Rural Advancement, UTRGV. (2019, March n.d.). *The SARA report, Vol. 4*. Retrieved 9 2019, March, from UTRGV Center for Sustainable Agriculture and Rural Advancement (SARA): https://www.utrgv.edu/sara/_files/documents/the-sara-report-volume-4.pdf.

Federal Transit Administration. (2016, June 23). *Metropolitan planning organization (MPO)*. Retrieved February 28, 2019, from Federal Transit Administration: https://www.transit.dot.gov/regulations-and-guidance/transportation-planning/metropolitan-planning-organization-mpo.

Guajardo, F., Esquierdo, J. J., & Weimer, A. A. (2014). Composing a new community infused with bilingual, biliterate, and bicultural realities. *Crosspol: A Discursive Journal for High School and College Teachers of Writing, 1*(1), 11–24. Retrieved from https://www.utrgv.edu/b3-institute/publications/index.htm.

Hagar, G. (2017, January 4). *Texas ports of entry: Gateways to the world*. Retrieved March 9, 2019, from Office of the Comptroller: https://comptroller.texas.gov/about/media-center/op-eds/2017/ftd-17-01-04.php.

Hamilton, R. (2011, November 4). *After 20 years, a messy divorce in Brownsville*. Retrieved May 2 2019, from Texas Tribune: https://www.texastribune.org/2011/11/04/after-20-years-messy-divorce-brownsville/.

Hammond, G., & Osoba, B. (2008). The growth impact of the metropolitan statistical area designation. *Annals of Regional Science, 42*, 307–319.

Millard, A., Graham, M. A., Mier, N., Moralez, J., Perez-Patron, M., Wickwire, B., May, M. L., Ory, M. G. (2017). Diabetes screening and prevention in a high-risk, medically isolated border community. *Frontiers in Public Health, 5*(135). https://doi.org/10.3389/fpubh.2017.00135.

Mosbrucker, K. (2014, September 25). *Reap what they sow: Sisters of the immaculate heart of mary*. Retrieved February 21, 2019, from Valley Morning Star: https://www.valleymorningstar.com/news/slice_of_life/reap-what-they-sow-sisters-of-the-immaculate-heart-of/article_a7b44f2a-451d-11e4-b6ad-0017a43b2370.html.

Office of the Comptroller, State of Texas. (2015a). *Economy, port of entry: Hidalgo*. Retrieved February 21, 2019, from comptroller.texas.gov: https://comptroller.texas.gov/economy/economic-data/ports/hidalgo.php.

Office of the Comptroller, State of Texas. (2015b). *Economy port of entry: Laredo, snapshot*. Retrieved February 21, 2019, from comptroller.texas.gov: https://comptroller.texas.gov/economy/economic-data/ports/laredo.php.

Office of the Comptroller, State of Texas. (2016). *2015 Ports tour estimated employment and GDP supported by trade in/out of Texas*. Austin, TX: Office of the Comptroller, State of Texas.

Perez-Hernandez, D. (2015, August 25). *The road to UTRGV: The first university created in 21st century.* Retrieved January 24, 2019, from The Brownsville Herald: https://www.brownsvilleherald.com/premium/the-road-to-utrgv-the-first-university-created-in-st/article_852920de-4ad5-11e5-bd3c-6f829cec6472.html.

Perez-Hernandez, D. (2018, May 20). *A way forward: UTRGV medical research could serve as catalyst to grow billion-dollar industry.* Retrieved February 7, 2019, from The Monitor: https://www.themonitor.com/2018/05/20/a-way-forward-utrgv-medical-research-could-serve-as-catalyst-to-grow-billion-dol lar-industry/.

RGV Partnership Lower Rio Grande Valley Development Council. (2019). *2019 regional priorities Rio Grande Valley: Texas 86th legislative session.* Weslaco: Lower Rio Grande Valley Development Council.

Richardson, C., & Pisani, M. J. (2017). *Batos, bolillos, pochos, and pelados: Class and culture on the south Texas Border, Revised Edition.* Austin: University of Texas Press.

Richardson, C., & Resendiz, R. (2006). *On the edge of the law: Culture, labor and deviance on the south Texas Border.* Austin: University of Texas Press.

Salgado, S. (2016, May 19). *Listening helps sisters build community spirit in Texas border town after storm.* Retrieved February 21, 2019, from Global Sisters Report: https://www.globalsistersreport.org/news/ministry/listening-helps-sisters-build-community-spirit-texas-border-town-after-storm-39906.

Smith-Barrow, D. (2018, July 16). *10 colleges with the most Hispanic students.* Retrieved February 21, 2019, from U.S. News & World Report: https://www.usnews.com/education/best-colleges/slideshows/colleges-with-the-most-hispanic-students?slide=11.

Smyrl, V. E. (2010, June 15). *Texas State Historical Association.* Retrieved January 24, 2019, from Permanent University Fund: https://tshaonline.org/handbook/online/articles/khp02.

South Texas Diabetes and Obesity Institute. (2016). *STDOI: Report on progress during the first 18 months of operation.* Brownsville: South Texas Diabetes and Obesity Institute, School of Medicine, UTRGV. Retrieved January 8, 2020, from https://www.utrgv.edu/som/stdoi/_files/documents/stdoi-pro gress-report.pdf.

Taylor, S. (2016, July 31). *Juliet Garcia writing book about creation of UTRGV.* Retrieved 24 2019, January, from Rio Grande Guardian: https://riogrande guardian.com/juliet-garcia-writing-book-about-creation-of-utrgv/.

Taylor, S. (2017, October 12). *UTRGV looking to open recruiting offices in Mexico.* Retrieved February 28, 2019, from Rio Grande Guardian International News Service: https://riograndeguardian.com/utrgv-looking-to-open-recruiting-offices-in-mexico/.

The University of Texas System. (2013, June 10). *Guiding principles UT Rio Grande Valley.* Retrieved February 21, 2019, from The University of Texas System: https://www.utsystem.edu/news/2013/07/10/regents-app rove-guiding-principles-new-university-south-texas.

The University of Texas System. (2014a, April 2). *UTRGV to be home to NCAA Division I athletic program.* Retrieved January 24, 2019, from The University of Texas System: https://www.utsystem.edu/news/2014/04/02/utrgv-be-home-ncaa-division-i-athletic-program.

The University of Texas System. (2014b, October 13). *UTRGV recruits 22-person research team to establish South Texas Diabetes & Obesity Institute.* Retrieved February 7, 2019, from The University of Texas System: https://www.utsystem.edu/news/2014/10/13/utrgv-recruits-22-per son-research-team-establish-south-texas-diabetes-obesity-instit.

The University of Texas System. (2018, December 31). *Permanent University Fund.* Retrieved January 24, 2019, from The University of Texas System: https://www.utbonds.com/permanent-university-fund/i613.

The University of Texas System. (2019, January 24). *History of the University of Texas System.* Austin, TX. Retrieved January 24, 2019, from https://www.utsystem.edu/about/history-university-texas-system.

THECB. (2009). *Overview: Permanent University Fund (PUF) Higher Education Fund (HEF).* Austin: Texas Higher Education Coordinating Board.

Tsing, A. (2005). *Friction: An ethnography of global connections.* Princeton: Princeton University Press.

Tyx, D. B. (2017, February 8). Inside the nation's first bilingual university. *Texas Observer*, p. online. Retrieved February 28, 2019, from https://www.texasobserver.org/first-bilingual-university/.

U.S. Census Bureau. (1994). *Geographic areas reference manual.* Retrieved 28 2019, February, from United States Census Bureau: https://www2.census.gov/geo/pdfs/reference/GARM/GARMcont.pdf.

UTRGV. (2016, March 3). *UTRGV's fall 2015 student enrollment ranks high in UT System and statewide.* Retrieved May 13, 2019, from UTRGV: University of Texas Rio Grande Valley: https://www.utrgv.edu/en-us/about-utrgv/news/press-releases/2016/march-03-utrgvs-fall-2015-student-enroll ment-ranks-high-in-ut-system-and-statewide/index.htm.

UTRGV. (2019). *The University of Texas Rio Grande Valley fast facts.* Brownsville: UTRGV.

UTRGV B3 Institute. (n.d.-a). *About, overview and purpose.* Retrieved February 28, 2019, from B3 Institute: https://www.utrgv.edu/b3-institute/about/index.htm.

UTRGV B3 Institute. (n.d.-b). *Initiatives.* Retrieved February 28, 2019, from B3 Institute: https://www.utrgv.edu/b3-institute/initiatives/index.htm#item3.

UTRGV. (n.d.-a). *Centers.* Retrieved January 31, 2019, from College of Engineering and Computer Science: https://www.utrgv.edu/cecs/centers/rrmc/index.htm.

UTRGV. (n.d.-b). *College of Sciences Office of the Dean.* Retrieved January 31, 2019, from Physics: https://www.utrgv.edu/cos/departments/physics/.

UTRGV. (n.d.-c). *Core priorities.* Retrieved January 31, 2019, from Strategic Plan: https://www.utrgv.edu/strategic-plan/re-direct-home/core-priorities/index.htm.

UTRGV. (n.d.-d). *Global partnerships.* Retrieved 31 2019, January, from Office of Global Engagement Division of Research, Graduate Studies & New Program Development: https://www.utrgv.edu/oge/global-partnerships/index.htm.

UTRGV. (n.d.-e). *History of The University of Texas Rio Grande Valley.* Retrieved January 31, 2019, from UTRGV University of Texas Rio Grande Valley: https://www.utrgv.edu/en-us/about-utrgv/history/index.htm.

UTRGV. (n.d.-f). *Partners.* Retrieved January 31, 2019, from Center for Sustainable Agriculture and Rural Advancement (SARA): https://www.utrgv.edu/sara/partners/index.htm.

UTRGV. (n.d.-g). *Partnerships.* Retrieved January 31, 2019, from College of Education and P-16 Integration: https://www.utrgv.edu/cep/community-outreach/partnerships/index.htm#item9.

UTRGV. (n.d.-h). *Partnerships & collaborations.* Retrieved January 31, 2019, from P 16 Outreach Office of Student Educational Outreach: https://www.utrgv.edu/p16/about/partnerships-collaborations/index.htm.

Whitlock, B. (2019, January 4). *Valley's three MPOs should merge, say Cameron and Hidalgo county judges.* Retrieved 28 2019, February, from Rio Grande Guardian: https://riograndeguardian.com/valleys-three-mpos-should-merge-say-cameron-and-hidalgo-county-judges/.

Wilson, T. M., & Donnan, H. (2012). Borders and border studies. In T. M. Wilson & H. Donnan (Eds.), *A companion to border studies* (pp. 1–26). Malden, MA: Wiley.

9

Flipping the Script About the Rio Grande Valley and the Border During Turbulent Times

There are so many stories. So many stories that go untold. It breaks my heart. We need to tell the stories. If we don't, someone else will. We in the RGV need to tell our stories …. We can start telling the story of who we are and not be quiet about it. —Rio Grande Valley journalist

It is in your vested interest as a storyteller to tell all the stories, good and bad …. It's very easy to get the bad stories. It's much tougher to get the good stories. —Rio Grande Valley editor and journalist

It is the Christmas season of 2018. I am back in the Valley with my daughter, husband, and our, now, two dogs. Today, December 26th, my husband and I head to the Harlingen Public Library for a quiet place to work. He needs to grade, and I need to work on this chapter. Our daughter is with her cousins, her great aunt and uncle, and my parents. Bill and I climb the library stairs to the second floor, passing original artwork of a crane walking in the bay in Port Isabel and then another of a Valley sunset over agricultural fields bordered by Washingtonia palm trees. It's a classic, oft-repeated rendition of the agricultural era in the Valley. Outside, I can see the crowns of 30-foot palm trees bend with

© The Author(s), under exclusive license to Springer Nature Switzerland AG 2021

K. J. Fleuriet, *Rhetoric and Reality on the U.S.—Mexico Border*, https://doi.org/10.1007/978-3-030-63557-2_9

the strong, balmy coastal wind. I especially love the Valley at this time of year, the ambient feel of it and my memories of family gatherings. The night before, my extended family gathered in my parents' living room around the Christmas tree to open gifts and toss jokes across the room. This morning, we argued around the table about changing gender norms while our pack of family dogs ran around the backyard. Bill bought some fresh breakfast tacos for the family at the Big M Tortilleria down the street. My dad helped my nephew with college applications in the back room. My aunt and uncle went for a long walk around town. This is home, even though I have a settled life and career in San Antonio, Texas, my brother and his family are on both coasts and overseas, and my aunt and uncle live in the Hill Country of central Texas.

At the Harlingen Public Library, I settle down to write, but, as is habit, I clear my phone of notifications first. A news app tells me that President Trump will continue the partial government shutdown until "the Wall" along "the southern border" is funded. On Christmas Eve, he tweeted, "I am in the Oval Office & just gave out a 115 mile long contract for another large section of the Wall in Texas. We are already building and renovating many miles of Wall, some complete. Democrats must end Shutdown and finish funding. Billions of Dollars, & lives, will be saved!" (Trump, 2018). Trump was largely referring to the Rio Grande Valley and its current stretch of border wall built during the tenure of Governor George W. Bush. Trump's border and my border could not be more different. My border, my Valley, evinces deep convictions of home, resilience, and strength, just as it does for Valley leaders.

There is a concept called moral panic, developed over 45 years ago in Sociology (Cohen, 1972; Young, 1971) that captures much of what is going on with the idea of "the border" in the 2010s. A moral panic is, at its most basic,[1] a pervasive sense of a threat against primary social values, most often represented by a dangerous "other" and fueled by mass media, news, political actors, and/or grassroots efforts. Moral panics often weave dominant political discourse with existing inequalities that end up scapegoating stigmatized communities. Think of the

---

[1] For a special journal issue that reviews more recent theories and areas of focus of moral panic research, please see Volume 7, Issue 3 (2011), of the academic research journal, *Crime, Media, Culture: An International Journal.*

Islamophobia of the 2000s (Morgan & Poynting, 2012); the 1990s discourse about violence and crime that focused on the inner-city poor where, in fact, violent crime rates had been falling (Singer, 1998); or the 1980s' HIV/AIDS rhetoric that blamed homosexual men for the spread of HIV/AIDS despite other groups with more rapid transmission rates (Holland, Ramazanoglu, & Scott, 1990). Such patterns of negative press and talk cement our beliefs about what we think we know about an issue and whom we blame.

Knowing the border is a critical task at hand for the United States. In this book, I have argued that people from border communities, especially those long engaged in efforts to improve conditions there, should get to produce that knowledge or, at the very least, have the authority and voice to correct the misperceptions, falsehoods, and inaccuracies circulating in the news and among politicians. As I began this project, I knew this to be essential for the future of the region that I know best, the Rio Grande Valley. Over the course of five years, that one region has become the problematic, misconstrued American emblem for "the border." It is now more important than ever to correct, to contextualize.

In the late 2010s, we saw how border misrepresentations have played out in just a few years. By early 2020, our nation had made it significantly more difficult for people to claim asylum, both procedurally with initial enforcement of family separation (Sessions, 2017) and with the Migrant Protection Protocol (U.S. Department of Homeland Security, 2019) as well as categorically by the reduction of allowable asylum petitions by almost half for 2020 (Presidential Determination No. 2020–04, Fed. Reg. 84[230] [Nov. 1, 2019]). In 2019, a gunman opened fire in an El Paso Walmart after penning an anti-immigrant manifesto that reflected dominant ideas about Mexican immigrants reinforced by the president of the United States (Baker & Shear, 2019).

The 2018–2019 government shutdown affected millions of workers' livelihoods, shaped international perceptions of the American government, and forced the nation to grapple with immigration policy debates grounded in the narrow notion of a wall along the southern border. The shutdown ended on January 25, 2019, marking the longest shutdown in U.S. history. On February 25, 2019, President Trump declared a National Emergency on the southern border. A National Emergency declaration activates certain presidential powers, dictated by which federal statutes are involved. Below is a portion of President Trump's declaration, as published in the *Federal Register*, which operates as a daily official listing by the federal government of proposed and issued federal regulations and presidential documents, including executive orders and proclamations. President Trump's language in the official proclamation reproduced old notions of a dangerous and porous border, an area including the Rio Grande Valley:

> The current situation at the southern border presents a border security and humanitarian crisis that threatens core national security interests and constitutes a national emergency. The southern border is a major entry point for criminals, gang members, and illicit narcotics. The problem of large-scale unlawful migration through the southern border is long-standing, and despite the executive branch's exercise of existing statutory authorities, the situation has worsened in certain respects in recent years …. I hereby declare that this emergency requires use of the Armed Forces … to assist and support the activities of the Secretary of Homeland Security at the southern border … to use or support the use of authorities herein invoked, including, if necessary, the transfer and acceptance of jurisdiction over the border lands [sic] … (Trump, 2019a)

President Trump's claims in this presidential proclamation as well as in a presidential address (Trump, 2019b) that "what our professionals at the border want and need" was in contrast to what I heard and continue to hear from border leaders in the Rio Grande Valley. What I hear is that comprehensive immigration policy reformulation is needed, especially with the recent increase of Central American families legally claiming asylum at Valley border crossings. Specific to border walls and other barriers, I hear a majority of Valley leaders say that what is needed is a nuanced, multipronged security approach that supports our trade relations with Mexico and other long-standing transnational relationships with Mexico. We need, they argue, deft, forward-thinking political and social relationships and networks that bring our countries closer together rather than further apart. Very few advocate for additional wall construction.

Now more than ever, we should listen to the people who lead the Valley's political, economic, health care, education, philanthropic, activist, and law enforcement sectors, in order to understand the daily life of the U.S.–Mexico border region. Their experiences, insights, and work alongside that of other Valley residents should be what define the setting for the border wall story. Those experiences mirror decades of demographic[2] and other social science research documenting the national impacts of immigration trends and policy on our economy and social fabric. My book seeks to contribute to efforts for border communities to tell their own story and to support ways to deborder social divisions in our country.

Perhaps the durability of the negative border concept may change during such a turbulent political time. There are indications that it might. In recent years with the rise of Donald Trump to the presidency, we have seen even more efforts to think beyond national renderings of a geopolitical line drawn in sand, especially with increased news attention to the region during the 2018–2019 government shutdown and National Emergency declaration. As the U.S.–Mexico border stays in the forefront of the news and in the minds of the American public, more news agencies are sending journalists to the Valley for extended reporting, which can lead to more detailed and robust stories. Along with leaders, privately funded public relations initiatives and public grassroots campaigns have stepped up efforts to dispel the myths of the border as a menacing, violent, and insecure backwater of economic development. But efforts to upend inaccurate Valley and border stories have been going on for decades to little effect. Could it now be different?

In this last chapter, I describe local efforts to change the nation's mind about the Valley and borderlands. Leaders now have a far more regional mindset. They work toward partnership across historically embedded differences to create new institutions such as UTRGV that hopefully will benefit the whole region and the state. They tell of a region that embraces and promotes American values of land investment, heritage, family, hard work, and innovation precisely because of its influence from

---

[2]A good place to begin reviewing the demographic and social science research on immigration is the Pew Research Center (pewresearch.org), a nonpartisan, non-advocacy research organization.

Mexico, not despite it. Leaders have largely united across city, county, and political party lines in light of President Trump's portrayals of the U.S.–Mexico border. The analysis of recent narratives about the Valley by Valley leaders and others underscores the national importance of listening to local leaders from the region itself, especially one beset with stereotypes and used as a political football in national movements and policymaking.

Efforts to Flip the Script

Many different people at various levels of influence use diverse strategies to flip the script about the Rio Grande Valley. Mayors, superintendents, elected and appointed politicians, leaders in health care, activists, philanthropists, religious leaders, bankers, heads of chambers of commerce and economic development corporations, and others regularly challenge the dominant negative image of the region. Even more varied attempts have emerged following President Trump's public statements and treatment of the border, immigrants, and Mexico in 2018 and 2019. Valley leaders have to be very careful when they attempt to reshape the story. They have to challenge dominant stereotypes but not paint such a rosy picture that they lose credibility. In their efforts to reframe the Valley story, leaders have to simultaneously validate ongoing work to address health, economic, and educational inequalities, identify successes and potential for growth in each sector, recognize barriers to growth, and invite social, economic, and political capital investment to the area. It is no easy feat. Sometimes, one element gets emphasized over others. Talking about the various kinds of alternative Valley narratives, one Valley journalist said, "you know, there is a disconnect between the rhetoric of economic development and the rhetoric of social justice - and how to reconcile that is difficult." Nevertheless, taken together, different efforts reflect leaders' long-standing engagement with the national Valley story in order to make it more resonant with daily lives in the region. Their depictions suggest something other than physical barriers and fear.

Leaders in the Valley have a variety of ways to combat the national narrative about the Valley. I focus on three strategic efforts to change state and national perceptions of the Rio Grande Valley: legislative tours and lobbying, regional development collaborations, and strategic messaging in the news. I anchor descriptions of various exemplar efforts within leaders' reflections. It is important to note that what I discuss here is only a small portion of work to change ideas about the region. There would be even more efforts if organizations had the public relations capacity to highlight their community successes and innovative approaches to entrenched inequalities. "People ask me why I don't tell the story. It's because we're doing the work," one superintendent told me. There are the innovative partnerships to improve educational opportunities, such as Pharr-San Juan-Alamo Independent School District with the IDEA charter school or Harlingen Consolidated Independent School District's novel approach to in-district school choice and partnerships in teacher training with The University of Texas Rio Grande Valley. In health care, city and county preventive health initiatives regularly win state and national awards for participation and impact. Various clinics are dedicated to serving uninsured populations and patients with specific conditions, such as diabetes. Operation Lonestar in Hidalgo County is a state model for large-scale emergency response. A book alone could be written on the impact of Catholic Charities on the response to the needs and well-being of asylum seekers in Brownsville, San Benito, and McAllen/Edinburg. Other nonprofit organizations and faith-based initiatives in the Valley have successfully partnered with communities to improve working conditions in agriculture, housing in *colonias*, homelessness and hunger, and legal representation for unauthorized immigrants and asylum seekers. These stories regularly go untold, except piecemeal by national news media and often to highlight regional deficits.

Legislative Tours and Lobbying for the Region

In the world of American politics, standard approaches to advocating for a region or issue include political action committees (PACs), legislative tours, and lobbying. What often makes news, however, are legislators' visits to investigate problems. These visits are distinctly different than visits related to PACs and lobbying. The politician's staff plans the visit with a specific purpose in mind, which often does not include showcasing the Valley in a positive light. Such political visits became increasingly common in the Valley in the 2010s. I provide one example to contrast it with the Valley-led and sponsored political visits. John Cornyn, one of the Texas senators in the United States Congress, made repeated visits in the 2010s to the Rio Grande Valley to get first-hand looks at immigration, veteran/military, and education issues. Most Valley leaders with whom I spoke found Senator Cornyn's perception of the Valley to be more informed and robust than that of other senators, but his visits became talking points in Washington which promoted a restrictive, negative view of the Valley. One visit by Senator Cornyn was ostensibly intended to explore health care access issues in the Veteran's Administration. The visit became embroiled in ideas about the border and gun control after the tragedy of the 2012 Sandy Hook elementary school shooting. A mayor told the story:

> Cornyn came down here right at the time of Sandy Hook [Elementary School] and the shooting there, and he had just given a speech on the floor of the Senate. He was opposing Diane Feinstein's gun control legislation … and he was talking about how horrible the border was, how the only solution was getting guns in the hands of the good guys …
>
> He was down here a week later, and [another mayor] and I had a long conversation with him …. He was down here to talk about the VA issues …. I said, "Senator, we've got this incredible VA facility … a couple of them, and we have an ambulatory surgery center that is the envy of every VA regional director, and it's sitting there empty. And the reason … is because the VA can't recruit the doctors and health care professionals to come down here, because they're scared to death that they're all going to get shot or kidnapped or whatever. You're here to help with the VA issues and it doesn't help that folks like you are out there saying you have to have an Uzi down here to avoid getting killed."
>
> [We] gave them our crime statistics …. It looked like a light bulb went on. He did the *mea culpa*, and he said, "You're right."
>
> … He went back to Washington and a week later – I'm a CSPAN junkie, and I was watching the Senate Judiciary Committee markup on

Feinstein's [gun control] bill ... and [the senator] offered an amendment to the bill, a ban on assault weapons, essentially machine guns, an amendment to exempt anybody who lives within 25 miles of the border ... because people that close to the border need to "protect themselves."

And I'm listening [and thinking], didn't we just have a conversation about this?

Less newsworthy to national outlets are the many state and national legislators brought to the region by economic development boards, hospitals, chambers of commerce, industry, and Valley legislators that travel to the capitol buildings in Austin, Texas, and Washington, DC, to lobby collectively for the region. Local news covers the visits, but they rarely bubble up to the national news scene like Cornyn's visit in 2012 or President Trump's visit in early 2019.

The signature Valley political outreach is a trio of events sponsored by the RGV Partnership that includes legislative tours and lobbying in Austin, Texas, and Washington, DC. RGV Partnership acts as a regional chamber of commerce. It organizes the Valley Legislative Tour at the beginning of each two-year legislative session in Austin. In 2019, it sponsored the 22nd Valley Legislative Tour. The Valley Legislative Tour is followed by RGV Day, in which Valley leaders head to Austin to lobby for the region using regionally crafted legislative priorities, and RGVtoDC where they lobby for the region in the U.S. Congress.

In 2019, I attended RGV Day at the Austin capitol building, joining over 200 Valley leaders and representatives for coordinated lobbying for the region. Leadership from each Valley higher education institution lobbied alongside city and county commissioners, business owners from building to international trade companies, county clerks and engineers, CEOs and executive directors of chambers of commerce and economic development corporations, mayors, bank executives, school board members, and marketing and public relations directors from civic, nonprofit, and for-profit organizations. We began the day in the galleys of the House and Senate to stand and be officially recognized as a delegation from the Rio Grande Valley. Afterward, we met for lunch with our elected officials from the region, divided into groups for office visits to every legislator's office, convened with the Lieutenant Governor, who was serenaded by several mariachi bands from UTRGV, and hosted a reception at the Capitol in the early evening for legislators and their staffers.

During our planning lunch that day, our elected officials from the region led a panel discussion as a primer for our afternoon lobbying efforts. RGV Partnership divided us into teams of three to four to represent industry, education, and when possible, some aspect of regional, city, or county governance. Each group was given eight to nine legislators to visit using common talking points. Those talking points mirrored the regional priorities (see Table 9.1) for the legislative session: a brief overview of the region and then priorities in economic development, education and workforce, transportation infrastructure, health care and community services, water and environmental resources, and public safety (RGV Partnership and Lower Rio Grande Valley Development Council, 2019). Each legislative session, the Rio Grande Valley Partnership and Lower Rio Grande Valley Development Council bring together diverse stakeholders to craft these priorities. Table 9.1 lists the ranked priorities as presented in RGV Day's anchor document, "Texas 86th Legislative Session, 2019 Regional Priorities Rio Grande Valley" (RGV Partnership and Lower Rio Grande Valley Development Council, 2019). "Regional Perception," the first bullet point of the first priority in the document, reads,

Inaccurate depictions of border violence, overwhelming immigration, and prominent corruption pose a serious threat to the sustainable economic prosperity of the region. A regional priority is to encourage the portrayal of the RGV accurately by promoting local assets such as the vital binational economy, vast tourism opportunities, affordable cost of living, low crime rates, and the overwhelmingly high quality of life expectancy experienced by residents and visitors.

Significantly, the first bullet point after the Rio Grande Valley overview combatted the negative regional perception. Border security was the third of four bullet points in the *last* priority (public safety). These priorities are intentionally regional, and so was our lobbying. It was up to each team to figure out how to weave the talking points into a narrative

Table 9.1 Texas 86th legislative session, 2019 regional priorities Rio Grande Valley

Area	Priorities
Rio Grande Valley	(Overview)
Economic Development	Regional Perception
	Tourism
	Municipal Regulation
	Economic Development Programs
	Foreign Trade
	Industry Resilience
	Entrepreneurship
	State Bank Investments
Education and Workforce	UTRGV School of Medicine
	General Academic (Four-Year) Institutions
	Community and Technical Colleges
	Dual Credit Programs
	Workforce Education Programs
Transportation Infrastructure	I-69 Interstate
	SPI (South Padre Island) 2nd Causeway
	International Border Trade Corridor
	Port of Brownsville
	FM 1925 (Monte Cristo Rd.)
	East Loop Corridor Project
	Regional Transit Authority
Healthcare and Community Services	UTRGV School of Medicine
	Trauma Network
	Underserved Populations
	Digital Communication Access
	Affordable Housing
Water and Environmental Resources	Flood Management Infrastructure
	Water Supply and Water Quality
	Coastal Conservation
	Environmental Quality
Public Safety	Training and Resources

(continued)

Table 9.1 (continued)

Area	Priorities
	Interoperable Communication
	Border Security
	Disease Response and Preparedness

Source RGV Partnership and Lower Rio Grande Valley Development Council (2019)

that reflected our different involvements with the Valley. In our teams, we did not present by our city affiliations but as people from the Rio Grande Valley. Valley leaders understand that the perception of Friday Night Lights competition in the Valley has extended beyond our four counties into the Texas Legislature. RGV Day is designed to counter that perception, and lobbying efforts are specific in their attempts to reframe our region.

My team included an owner of a large international import company, an owner of a small local business, and a businesswoman. We divvied up our talking points: regional perception, binational trade, UTRGV School of Medicine, and a health care trauma network. As we entered each office, the import company owner began by asking about the bag of Valley grapefruit sent to each legislator's office the week prior. Inevitably, the question served as an icebreaker with a legislative staffer, because Valley grapefruit are famous across the state. Our team lead would segue into the purpose of our visit and ask if the legislator were available. About half were. If not, we met with the legislative aide. Then, my part began. "I'm a professor, originally from the Valley. I'm writing a book about how the nation thinks about the Valley and how it gets the Valley wrong." Invariably, the legislator or aide would nod at this point. I followed with, "My argument is that we should listen to the people who live there, especially its leaders, about what's important." Then, each of my team members would take a turn. Each would introduce their regional priority and bullet point and finish with a quick personal story to serve as a memory hook. At least four of our assigned legislators had been to the Valley on a legislative tour, also arranged by the RGV Partnership. In those cases, the legislator or staffer would talk about how much they "loved" the Valley when they visited. We finished our ten-minute visits with an invitation to a reception at five o'clock in the Capitol to honor elected officials.

The overall response by legislators and their staffers was what one would expect, mostly polite, noncommittal agreement. Overall, RGV Day and its lobbying visits were one more way to promote a different version of the Valley, one rooted in the experiences and expertise of those who lead the region. It was clear that legislative aides and legislators are used to these kinds of visits, a pro forma event that probably does not stand out to most. There was never a moment when a legislative staffer or elected official indicated any major change of mind or political commitment, nor did I expect there to be. But, advertising works. The more we can talk about the Valley in different positive ways, the better.

Still, we were one of many groups lobbying that day. Most days, the legislative session sees a host of Capitol office visits by various constituencies. By way of example, another group making the rounds during our RGV Day was the Sweetwater Jaycees. The Sweetwater Jaycees was advocating for the annual rattlesnake roundup in Sweetwater, Texas. They walked into congressional offices with their rattlesnakes in tow. One of the Jaycees group had the same beat as my RGV Day group. Several times, we passed each other in the halls, we in our professional business clothes with a touch of yellow to represent the Valley, they in their recognizable red vests covered in medals and carrying large wooden briefcases. The first time we passed them, one Jaycee turned to one side to let us pass and nodded to his briefcase, saying "don't worry, they're just snakes." Thirty minutes later we passed an inner, enclosed rotunda, where the Jaycees gathered to bring out their live rattlesnakes for show and tell. Several of our Valley group took selfies with the snakes. The Sweetwater Jaycees with their rattlesnakes put our lobbying into perspective for me. The Sweetwater Jaycees also took an identifiable regional item to represent their priorities. We had grapefruit; they had rattlesnakes. Theirs was also advocacy. We wanted to change the idea about the Valley and encourage thoughtful legislation that would help repair and develop our region. The Sweetwater Jaycees wanted to continue a tradition that has increasingly received critiques. We both went into the same offices with our identifiable props and compelling stories, taking about the same amount of time. Our priorities, of course, were a bit different.

During our office visits, several members reminisced about their legislative tours to the Rio Grande Valley. They spoke about how much they liked the physical landscape and the "culture" of the people. Their appreciation of cultural and environmental beauty were very similar to how Valley leaders themselves describe the Valley (Chapter 6). I wondered about this. Were their comments analogous to the Cornyn visit, where the politician talks about the Valley in one way with people from the Valley and then differently at other times? Was it a political party issue? Except for one member from the Dallas area, all of our assigned legislators were Republican. This is significant, because the Valley has been a Democratic stronghold for decades. My lobbying team steered clear of any partisan politics. In fact, I have no idea how they politically affiliate. We emphasized the relevance of the Valley to state economic and educational priorities. It is hard to imagine any politician disagreeing with initiatives to grow our state economy and improve our educational outcomes. At the end of RGV Day, I was ambivalent. I was honored to be part of such a well-coordinated, large-scale regional effort that promoted a cooperative regional vision with definable legislative actions. I also left feeling there was so much additional work to do in the face of significant barriers to sustained, thoughtful engagement with the region by our state legislature.

Regional Development Collaborations

The suite of lobbying efforts that make up the Valley Legislative Tour, RGV Day in the state capitol, and RGVtoDC is one of a diverse set of strategies to reframe the Rio Grande Valley. Each attempt situates the region in terms of its successes, opportunities, and potential across various sectors. Some focus on economics, such as existing and possible contributions to state and national economic growth. The region as an economic driver, such as the binational trade revenue noted in Chapter 8 or the region as key to American ability to compete in manufacturing, are two primary elements in a different story about the regional economy.

Rather than poverty and unemployment, economic leaders talk about a region booming in international trade and moving from poverty to prosperity. Increasingly, economic leaders speak as a region rather than from competing city and county perspectives. One of the recent and most ambitious economic initiatives is BiNED, or the Binational Economic Development Zone initiative.

BiNED's objective is to develop a seamless, integrated, and advanced manufacturing zone that encompasses Mexican and American industry areas along the entire U.S.–Mexico border (Gonzalez, 2017). When I first heard of BiNED in 2015, it had mixed support. One economic leader in Cameron County leader called the fledgling initiative "a bust." A year later, leaders ranged from cautiously to enthusiastically optimistic. Several leaders believed BiNED might be able to generate the legislative support needed for an International Combined Metropolitan Statistical Area (MSA) designation (see Chapter 8). BiNED and the McAllen Economic Development Corporation began to work cooperatively as, according to one local editor, a "movement" to "create a MSA that acknowledges and recognizes that a border does not necessarily mean anything, and the Valley is proof of that." There had been several prior initiatives to have the Valley represented as a Combined MSA or with its sister cities in Mexico as an International Combined MSA, but they had not been successful. The hope was BiNED could coalesce and jumpstart various efforts to garner Combined International MSA recognition, likely the first of its kind. A Hidalgo County economic leader summarized efforts and his rationale behind full regional support of BiNED's new efforts:

> If you have a border community and you look at the management of a border – believe me, no one in Washington or Mexico City understands the complexity of a border community. They are truly complex .... When you combine Reynosa and McAllen, we're 2.1, 2.2 million people, OK? .... People far away, they see a border. And they think it's a border, [therefore,] that is what's happening. People who live here [in Reynosa, Mexico] say, oh, I'm going to drive over to McAllen or [people in McAllen, Texas, say] I'm going to drive over to Reynosa to work, to go to the doctor, to eat, to shop.

... in the last four months, we have brought in another 17 companies that will bring in another 12,000 jobs – San Antonio is about 45, 46 thousand manufacturing jobs total .... We [in the Valley and Mexican sister cites] are a huge manufacturing area. But because the US only looks at US statistics, those companies don't exist. They don't pay attention to those companies that are employing Americans and the impact on our communities with the Mexican jobs .... When they look at manufacturing on the US side, we have 14, 15 thousand manufacturing jobs in the Valley, and they say, gee, there are no manufacturing jobs, but when you add the [Mexican border cities] we have about two hunder thousand, two hundred and fifty thousand manufacturing jobs ... because of the political boundary, we only look at half the picture.

When you think of a mayor of a border city, they can only budget for what's on their side of the river. They can only plan what's on their side of the river. How can you manage a city, if you can't manage two million but only nine hundred thousand?

The people don't recognize the border as a barrier. It's more of a nuisance. They cross it multiple times a day or multiple times a week. How do you address that? From an environmental issue? From a transportation issue? From a health and health care issue?

Let's take Austin because it has a river running through it. What would happen if tomorrow it was decreed that the mayor could not even consider the south side of the river? How would you even do that? Based on that idea, based on environmental issues, air quality issues ... air quality, pests, diseases, don't stop at the border. DPS [Department of Public Safety] and Border Patrol don't stop those. We need to know what's going on on both [sides of the border].

A few years ago we started floating the idea of the International MSA ... a data system that people use to make business decisions as well as governmental decisions .... And there is no other purpose than to identify what the border is .... It is still a single city. It's just that there are two separate government entities, two currencies, two population centers.

Manufacturing is at the heart of BiNED's proposal. Initially launched in 2014 by Valley engineer and businessman, Dr. Carlos Marin, BiNED takes as its premise that the U.S.–Mexico border region is underutilized as an economic generator for the nation. Marin directly ties his BiNED plan to improving border security (Gonzalez, 2017). Marin contends that current "control and command" approaches to border security do not address the root cause of increased undocumented immigration to the United States across its southern border: deepening economic insecurity. A combined, integrated development of the binational manufacturing region would increase economic stability and growth in the region and for each nation; increased economic prosperity in the binational region would make for a more secure region.

Marin argues that the North American Free Trade Agreement (NAFTA) allowed for the development of a binational manufacturing industry infrastructure at the U.S.–Mexico border but did not necessarily benefit the long-term economic outlook for the Rio Grande Valley (Gonzalez, 2017; Marin, 2016). The binational production cycle in the region needs to be able to incorporate intelligent manufacturing, a kind of advanced manufacturing that supports rapid response manufacturing (see Chapter 8), within one coordinated system across both countries, as well as primary sites for research and development in the binational zones. This kind of binational integration would require additional political and legal articulations between the United States and Mexico, such as an international Combined Metropolitan Statistical Area, that go beyond NAFTA or the 2018 overhaul of NAFTA, the United States–Mexico–Canada Agreement.

In essence, Marin proposes a binational economic zone that allows for enhanced movement of people, technologies, and products within it. The current emphasis by legislators on improving border crossing times and inspection efficiencies, while necessary, builds on the idea of the border region as a pass-through economy. A pass-through economy is a regional economy that moves products through it, rather than a region where the bulk of the production cycle is located. A UTRGV study found that the majority of inputs for manufacturing in the Rio Grande Valley, Texas—Tamaulipas, Mexico, binational maquiladora region is from elsewhere, decreasing the economic revenue for the region (Gonzalez, Kroll, Marin, Rhi-Perez, & Wilson, 2017). Additionally, research and development and their attention to promoting growth of intellectual capital and financial investment occur in other regions rather than in a pass-through economy such as the Rio Grande Valley. Pass-through economies as a result often have a ceiling for economic growth from manufacturing, which Marin contends has negative impacts on educational attainment, poverty rates, and attendant health and health care issues (Fogarty, 2016; Taylor, 2017a, 2017b, 2018).

The regional pass-through economy and increasing militarization of border security locate the Valley at what Marin calls a "crossroads" (Marin, 2016). In his 2016 presentation to regional business leaders, UTRGV scholars, and representatives from the Federal Reserve Bank in Texas, Marin identified regional sectors he believes pivotal to the future of the Valley. The picture is compelling. It tells an unfinished story of a region whose education, leadership, economy, and quality of life are linked inextricably with its national neighbor. Marin suggests that the way forward for the Valley is through economic development based on a mature, facilitated, and twenty-first-century binational manufacturing industry. Industry research and development will require nurturing and retaining intellectual capital, which will encourage educational attainment and growth of a workforce of innovators in technology. UTRGV will become a focal point of research and creative activity. Local production of industry inputs will grow the technical and industrial workforce, generating revenue for the local economy. Leaders will want to work across city, county, and national lines, and the growing population of Valley youth will have the reasons and resources to stay and grow the region alongside the leaders.

By 2017, most Valley leaders with whom I spoke supported BiNED, at the minimum, or were directly involved in the initiative. UTRGV was invested through its College of Business & Entrepreneurship as well as its B3 initiative to promote the benefits of learning and working in a bicultural, bilingual, and binational region. Part of BiNED's appeal to Valley leadership is its fundamental regional orientation. While it originated in Cameron County, BiNED's leadership quickly partnered with public and private organizations in Hidalgo County, including the McAllen Economic Development Corporation. As of 2019, BiNED had an infrastructure, direct support from a host of Valley influencers, and increasing public attention. At the time of writing, BiNED is housed within the Lower Rio Grande Valley Development Council (LRGVDC). The LRGVDC is a "voluntary association of local governments formed under Texas Law to address issues and planning needs which cross the boundaries of individual local governments requiring regional attention" (Lower Rio Grande Valley Development Council, 2019a). Importantly, the LRGVDC has official state recognition as a planning body with an executive committee and board of directors of elected and appointed city and county officials, superintendents, and economic development corporations and nonprofit organization representatives from Cameron, Hidalgo, and Willacy Counties. The LRGVDC additionally plays a pivotal role in lobbying efforts described in the prior section. LRGVDC coordinates a multipronged, regional initiative to draft five-year regional strategic plans updated every two years (Lower Rio Grande Valley Development Council, 2019b). The LRGVDC strategic plans serve as the backbone for the legislative priorities lobbied for during each state legislative session. BiNED also has the public support of U.S. Representative Filemon Vela, who successfully advocated for federal funds to support the development of BiNED (Taylor, 2017a).

BiNED's economic argument might be the kind of rhetorical strategy needed to move the Texas legislature from a narrow view of border security to a more realistic understanding of how trade, economy, and immigration are enmeshed, and the Valley could be the proving ground for innovative new binational partnerships. Certainly, there is national appeal of an economic plan that contributes to the national gross domestic product. The challenge is traction in the national news and, thus, in legislators' voting constituents. Talking about intelligent manufacturing industries, binational economic zones, and a different approach to border security and immigration based on border economic development in two countries is not as easily digestible or, I would contend, as interesting to most American news consumers primed to think of the U.S.–Mexico borderlands as a frightening, drug and crime-filled place with a porous border.

Strategic Messaging in the News

Rio Grande Valley leaders have been publicly outspoken about the misperceptions of the region, especially since 2016. Even before the rise of Donald Trump to the American presidency and his vision of the U.S.–Mexico border, however, Valley leaders have worked individually and in concert to change the American narrative about the south Texas border, but so far to little avail. A Cameron County mayor told me a story about one such effort in the 2000s with former Eagle Pass mayor, Chad Foster:

> The BTA [Border Trade Alliance] hired one of the big media consultants firms like Public Strategies to help stem some of the negativity that was being [made], that the national media was directing toward the border area because of the immigration debate. At the time, the BTA president was a guy from Eagle Pass – Mayor, he's an Anglo guy, kind of, he sounded conservative – Texas twang, perfect guy …. They put him on Fox and on this and on that, and they developed it pretty good.
>
> But it was like the Dutch boy with his finger in the dike, like trying to push the ocean away …. So here's a campaign, sinking a lot of funding, and he was perfect – he wasn't some liberal, couldn't be perceived as a liberal, [but instead] an old country rancher from Eagle Pass trying to say this is a good area, there's a lot of trade with Mexico, keep the borders open, good relations with Mexico. And, it was just impossible.

This passage especially illustrates what most border leaders know. To deborder the Valley, leaders have to work with and against prevailing ethnic, political, and Texas stereotypes and social difference lines in order to break them down. Valley leaders are very strategic in how, when, and through what medium they message. They have to be. They are fighting the public's tendency to confirm, rather than challenge, these social divisions and bias.

One way to shift the narrative is to focus on regional aspects that positively resonate with the national audience, such as benefits to the national economy. Indeed, in early 2019 during the government shutdown over border wall funding, the Border Trade Alliance, a massive grassroots organization with over 4.2 million public and private representatives (BTA: Border Trade Alliance, 2019), recommended that U.S. southern border legislators emphasize the economic importance of their land ports of entry (see Chapter 8) to state and national economies.

At a roundtable discussion with U.S. Senators John Cornyn (R) and Ted Cruz (R) in January 2019 in Mission, Hidalgo County, Texas, the chairman of the Border Trade Alliance advocated for border security discussions around land ports of entry rather than around unauthorized immigrants crossing other parts of the geopolitical borderline, saying,

> More drugs come through all the ports of entry in the United States, more wealth comes through it. Why don't we try to figure the value of what those ports of entry do and start allocating funding on the basis of what supports that wealth ...? And how do we stop rewarding people for taking cash and guns south here and cigarettes to Canada? All sorts of activities go through the ports of entry. If we could sell the ports of entry of the nation, you've got enough votes to pass and get allocations for what you need. (as quoted in Taylor, 2019)

The Border Trade Alliance roundtable with politicians intentionally coincided with President Trump's visit to the Rio Grande Valley that day in January. Local public officials from the Valley did not get the opportunity to meet with President Trump. Instead, Valley leaders used the roundtable as a means to garner news attention to their message to "cut the rhetoric" (Taylor, 2019). Harlingen Mayor Chris Boswell was quoted as saying in the roundtable discussion,

> I have had this concern for a long time: the collateral damage that occurs from all the rhetoric we hear, the crisis on the border, the violence on the border and the perception that creates for our people. Despite that we have made lots of economic gains. Our unemployment rates are the lowest they have been in a decade. But, nevertheless, we are still hampered by the fallout from the constant rhetoric about violence and the crisis on the border. (in Taylor 2019)

Other elected Valley officials at the roundtable talked about the low crime rates in Valley cities and the impact of increased rhetoric about a violent border and the need to secure it with troops and additional physical barriers. Sales were down from Mexican nationals. Veterans' Administration officials in the Valley were having more difficulty recruiting physicians because of families' fears of violence. Economic and law enforcement leaders, including a director of the Customs and Border Patrol field office, talked about trade infrastructure and investment in education instead of additional physical barriers. These comments at the roundtable contrasted sharply with those of President Trump and several Border Patrol officers who accompanied him on his Valley visit. Trump and his team called for more border wall construction for protection. What stays even more in my mind, though, is less the contrasting messages than the irony. The president of the United States stands for a photo opportunity along the Rio Grande River to promote a certain vision of the U.S.–Mexico border while a few miles away, a diverse group of border leaders speak to the local press with their alternative vision, because they were not allowed to speak or meet with the president. The greater national news coverage was with the president, not with the Valley leaders at the roundtable. As long as the national media treats political rhetoric about the border as the border story, national misconceptions will retain their hold.

Valley leaders often attempt to counter the negative perceptions of the Valley border region with strategic public messaging. An exemplar is Dr. Juliet García. García was the president of The University of Texas at Brownsville before UTRGV was created. With multiple honorary doctoral degrees from institutions such as Princeton University, a place in the Texas Women's Hall of Fame, membership on the boards of trustees at the Ford Foundation and Robert Wood Johnson Foundation, and named by *Fortune* magazine as one of the World's Greatest 50 Leaders in 2014, García wields her significant social capital to help change the Valley story. For example, in a 2015 Smith College commencement address, García detailed the important changes in the Valley region over her lifetime of work there:

> My mother grew up in a small south Texas border town, where the Mexicans lived on the south side of the railroad tracks and where they were allowed to swim in the public pool only one day a year. The next day, the pool was drained and cleaned ….
>
> My work began in a place [Brownsville] known best for being one of the poorest and most undereducated in the United States.
>
> Today, that same place is transformed and is home to thousands of young children that learn chess at the age of 5 and are known nationwide for winning chess championships year after year after year. A city that last year was named the Chess Capital of the United States. A city with a

university chess team that attracts players from around the world and who routinely win national and international chess tournaments. And one of the top five cities in the United States that every year sends the most kids to the national chess competition. It is also the city that was recently chosen by SpaceX as the site for the world's first commercial launch pad; chosen for its geography but also for its rich human capital.

And finally it is also the city that is now home to the university that ranks in the top five universities in the United States that graduates the most Latino physics majors, who together last year in our labs, discovered one-third of the pulsars identified and named world-wide. (García, 2015)

Similarly, but at the national political level, U.S. Representative Filemon Vela from the 34th Congressional District of Texas stands out in his forceful, insistent efforts to flip the border script in Washington, DC.

The Vela family of local, state, and national politicians, judges, and servicemen traces its Valley roots back to the 1700s. Filemon Vela, Jr., was elected to the U.S. House of Representatives in 2012. Until 2016, Vela focused on legislative tours to help change the Valley/border narrative circulating in Austin, Texas, and Washington, DC. During the Texas Tribune Festival in 2016, Representative Vela talked about bringing over 100 U.S. senators and representatives to the Valley on legislative tours to dispel border myths. In a *Texas Monthly* article around the same time, he talked about the legislative tours' benefits:

I've had six members of Congress and one senator down in the Valley in the last month, and when you bring people down, they see the trade, they enjoy the culture, they see the new university, they go to South Padre Island. We take them to the international bridges, and they see all this truck traffic, and they start to realize that most of the produce that ends up in East Coast grocery shelves comes from Mexico. It begins to change that perception. And then you start explaining to them that FBI statistics show that the border cities are among the safest in Texas. (as quoted in Benson, 2016)

Vela's approach changed in 2016, however, to incorporate more specific public messaging about the proposed border wall and representations of Mexican Americans and Mexican migrants.

Vela went on the offensive to counter Trump's characterization of the borderlands, Mexican nationals and migrants, and Mexican Americans during his presidential campaign. During his presidential campaign, Trump often used negative stereotypes about Mexican migrants and Mexican Americans in stump speeches to push for additional border security as a campaign issue (see Chapter 5). Vela critiqued Trump's rhetoric openly and aggressively, a surprising move for those who know him.[3] On June 6, 2016, after Trump's verbal attacks on Mexican-American Judge Gonzalo Curiel, Vela issued an open letter (full transcript can be found at: https://latinousa.org/2016/06/06/rep-velas-sca thing-open-letter-donald-trump-full-text/). Vela detailed his opposition to Trump's remarks about Curiel, border wall justifications, and assumptions about Mexicans, ending with the now famous line: "Mr. Trump, you're a racist and you can take your border wall and shove it up your a**." Vela understood the implications of his language, knowing it would receive criticism for the language and the content. Public reaction went much farther. Vela received death threats (Benson, 2016).

Since the open letter, Vela's opposition to the Trump narrative was no less fierce, albeit with less inflammatory imagery. He often points to Valley issues that are ignored or worsened by a limited, incomplete vision of the region. In October of 2018, for example, he pushed back against waiving environmental laws to continue border wall construction. "The Trump Administration's reckless decision to cast aside laws that protect clean air, safe drinking water, public participation and private property is shameful, and will not make anyone safer. These latest waivers of 28 environmental and public health protections are a direct attack on our communities, our wildlife, and our deep economic and cultural connection to our neighbors in Mexico" (Office of U.S. Congressman Filemon Vela, 2018). Vela often followed his commentary with legislation. In February 2019, Representative Vela introduced the Restrictions Against Illegitimate Declarations for Emergency Reappropriations Act of 2019 (H.R. 1293) to block funds released for border security by President Trump's Declaration of a National Emergency on the United States

---

[3]The 2016 *Texas Monthly* article on his decision was subtitled "Congressman Filemon Vela had always kept a low profile – until he told Donald Trump to stick his border fence you-know-where" (Benson, 2016).

southern border. The same day, Representative Vela filed another bill, Preventing the Taking of Americans' Land to Build Trump's Wall Act (H.R. 1234), to ensure that American landowners receive fair compensation when their land is seized to build additional border wall (Office of U.S. Congressman Filemon Vela, 2018).

The retelling of the Valley story is not limited to individuals in elected positions or with national recognition. Valley community organizations have also taken up the call to "tell our own stories." *Explore RGV* is an interactive website developed by the Lower Rio Grande Valley Development Council (LRGVDC), whose mission is to "encourage the exploration of the Rio Grande Valley by highlighting its assets spreading across the four counties: Starr, Hidalgo, Willacy, and Cameron" (https://goexplorergv.com/, accessed April 25, 2019). *Explore RGV*'s website groups these assets by entertainment, outdoor recreation, culture, history, shopping, and transportation and resources. A visitor to the site can design their own Valley trip itinerary or browse ready-made itineraries and featured destinations. Featured destination pages include short video tours of places such as the national shrine of Basilica of Our Lady of San Juan Del Valle, Bentsen-Rio Grande Valley State Park, and Sea Turtle, Inc. on South Padre Island, an internationally renowned sea turtle conservation and research center. The website promotes an entirely different version of the Rio Grande Valley. It offers ecotourism including the world famous birdwatching and sea turtle conservation; cultural entertainment; shopping from farmers' markets to flea markets to outlets; and museums and memorials.

Another community-driven website with a related social media campaign is *Another Side of Us*, created by McAllen community members and PolluxCastor Creative in response to persistently negative portrayals of the Valley in the media (http://anothersideofus.com/, accessed April 25, 2019). The front page of the *Another Side of Us* website reads "Another Side of Us is a movement to challenge misconceptions about life in Texas border cities with positive stories from people of all ethnicities, faiths, identities, and origins." The website offers stories of individual Valley community members, "defying expectations in press," and a description of the city as one of the safest in the United States with a young and growing Latino/a population and a thriving international trade, tourism, and retail economy. Toward the middle of the homepage reads in large font and all capital letters, "ISN'T IT DANGEROUS DOWN THERE?" with the script underneath, "It's a question people from Texas border communities hear when we mention our home to people who've never visited. Some fear our cities are the center of an immigration crisis, or worse, are hardly recognizable as American." The website then offers action:

- **If you're from a community like ours, be heard.** We've quietly been a part of the American story for too long.
- **If you've lived in or visited a community like ours, introduce us to friends.** Your experiences matter.
- **If you're proud of your community, share stories and images** that capture your heart.
- **If you see or hear something false about our communities,** challenge it with facts.
- **If you're inspired by our communities, create art** that inspires others to think about another side of us.
- **Be social.** Share your thoughts with **#anothersideofus** (http://anothersideofus.com/, accessed April 25, 2019)

Another Side of Us is one of several professional and homegrown efforts to showcase the insight, capacity, and heart of the Rio Grande Valley. More exist, such as the *Official Guide to the Rio Grande Valley* on the RGV Partnership's website (http://rgvpartnership.com/guide-to-the-rgv/; accessed April 25, 2019). The *Guide* is similar in content to city guides by chambers of commerce, offering overviews for visitors and newcomers. There is also the established print and virtual magazine, *RGVision: Starting the Conversation* (https://rgvisionmagazine.com/; accessed April 25, 2019), that highlights achievements across the region, especially in education, health, and the economy. These and other community-driven and individual efforts present the Rio Grande Valley and the U.S.–Mexico border according to many of the people who live there. With current technology, it is easier than ever to find those stories that challenge dominant assumptions about the borderlands.

New Stories, Unfinished Stories

[The Valley] narrative is not driven by the broader reality, but it's our fascination with being afraid .... It's been here before 9/11 .... It's the Donald Trump thing .... I think an interesting story is why is that [narrative of fear] so comforting to us .... That's my concluding remark. The Valley is a place of color, not black and white. If you take pictures with black and white film, you're not going to capture the nuances. —activist in the Rio Grande Valley.

Disasters don't hurt us, we have learned to live with them .... It's this culture .... We've been struggling our whole life. You know, I can go back now even a generation, my mom was living on a dirt floor. No one was telling her story. No one .... No matter what, we find a way to survive. We're a faithful community. We accept each other's faults and we move forward. There is no other place like that .... When we need to take a stand, we'll fight tooth and nail. You can't hold us down. We've always been in a struggle. We've always been the least funded area of the state. We've been the most ignored area of the state. We'll fight. —business leader in the Rio Grande Valley.

Since I began this project about the Rio Grande Valley of south Texas, two things have happened that encapsulate a major argument of the book. One, the tall, graceful palm trees that for decades signaled entry into the Valley on the United States have been removed from the center median of the old divided Highway 77 to make way for the new Interstate 69. Two, Donald Trump was elected president of the United States. Places and politics are in constant flux. Some stories persist. When I think of the national story of the U.S.–Mexico border alongside stories from the people who live in the region, I recall the words of Chimamanda Ngozi Adichie (2009): "Many stories matter. Stories have been used to dispossess and to malign. But stories can also be used to empower, and to humanize. Stories can break the dignity of a people. But stories can also repair that broken dignity."

Younger, shorter palms have been planted along each side of the new section of Interstate 69. When I cross into Willacy County now, I see more wind turbines than palm trees. The tree removal, interstate expansion, and development of wind energy represent the change and growth of social and economic significance of the Valley to the rest of the state and nation, as evidenced by the contribution of Valley ports to the GDP (see Chapter 8). Leaders often reference the massive change in the Valley population over the last 30 years as an indicator of regional economic and educational potential (see Chapter 6). A higher education administrator used examples of changes to discuss potential political growth:

> One of the points I like to make about the Valley is because of our population growth, our future is very bright .... We get a lot of negative press from politicians. This crop [of politicians] is really bad ... [but] the end result is that as population grows, the political influence will grow. It is our responsibility to build the social, economic and political infrastructure .... Historically, the Valley for a variety of reasons has gotten the short end of the stick .... We've got a lot to make up to do ...

A national elected leader from the Valley echoed the education leader above but focused on how changes in the Valley over the last few decades put the region "in the game."

> The Valley to me right now is [a space of] extreme potential. It takes a lot to get to the stage where you have potential. How much time does it take years of practice, working on strength and training, to get someone to the NFL, to have the potential to be the quarterback? That's where I feel where we are. We have done so much to be here, where we have potential ....
>
> Where we go from here is the big question. We have key infrastructure in our schools that is very mindful ... the best technology ever .... We have higher education ... that is focused on technical education to fill that gap for kids who want to work in industry but not a college degree. And then you have a university with a medical school attached to it with access to the PUF funds ... to become a Tier One university, to provide the level of comfort and structure for big business to come here, to work with academics .... You have Mexico, with the good and the bad. There are security issues but that led to businesses investing north of the border, that's a very interesting dynamic.

> We've done so much to get into the game. Now we're in the game.
> We're on the roster .... What are we going to do with it?

The Valley story is unfinished, as it should be. It is a dynamic place changing at lightning speed. Much of what happens in—and to, the Valley will depend on the national political landscape, particularly presidential election outcomes. The border, exemplified by the Rio Grande Valley, is likely to continue to figure centrally in campaign platforms. As discussed in Chapter 5, the election of Donald Trump was, in part, due to his ability to draw voters using certain tropes of immigration and the U.S.–Mexico borderlands that already existed. Assumptions abounded about many parts of the U.S.–Mexico border in the national news before Donald Trump. Stories about the Rio Grande Valley rebordered the region with descriptions that suggested a distant place filled with people who constitute risks to the national economy, health, and historical power structure (Chapter 4). That can have its own impact on people who live on the border. As one communications specialist and former journalist said,

> When you live in that shadowland of otherness, when you get off into that land of otherness that mainstream people don't understand, then all of that negativity that is generated by all that fear and all of that sense of being threatened that fear generates .... They throw out names, the names, and those stick.
>
> Naming is powerful. When they start naming [your college or university] Taco Tech, Tamale Tech, they have branded you. You haven't branded yourself. We're hoping to change that narrative into 'we're doing excellent work here. It doesn't matter what color we are. It doesn't matter what side of the border we are from. It's good work, and we are doing it here.'
>
> That's part of my fight here. To get people's minds who were previously closed or threatened or narrow to open up, to start accepting excellence in the RGV.

In his presidential campaign, Donald Trump merely capitalized upon a public primed to believe the U.S.–Mexico border was a bad place and a national news media that predictably emphasized soundbites in its headlines during presidential election cycles. The national media prioritized

President Trump's subsequent actions and words over city and county leaders in a place considered faraway. The election of President Trump and his avowal to build more border wall signalled the increasing importance of the U.S.–Mexico borderlands as a primary symbol which many Americans use as a counterpoint to what it means to be American. The Rio Grande Valley as "the border" became even more unidimensional in the national imagination during the 2015–2016 presidential campaign, a place of unchecked immigration by people who will drain America's resources. By oversimplifying such a dynamic, complex region, President Trump also opened up spaces for national media to explore. The overriding impression of the border as a negative place did not abate, but a few more stories emerged that suggested the border was more than a single story.

Valley leaders tell other stories based on their lives and experiences in the work they do to improve the region. In contrast to the national story of division and difference from the rest of the United States, the leaders deborder the region by suggesting it embodies certain American values and provides a national model of partnership to think through and across historical divides that have hampered efforts to improve communities. Since Chapter 6, I have attempted to let Valley leaders speak for themselves, as much as is possible in a book format. They clearly identify how the national story about the Rio Grande Valley is, at the best, incomplete and, at worst, false and rooted in unequal treatment by the state and nation. As a physician in state leadership in health care leader said,

> The Valley is a place that needs to be treated like any other major metro area like anywhere else in the country. To be told by people who don't know us that we aren't deserving, I'm sorry. I don't think so. We're just as deserving as anyone else .... We have the talent here to do whatever we want to do. We have the educational systems. We have the mentors. We have those people who act as examples to others, to make it possible to inculcate the culture to be what we want to be.

Leaders in the Rio Grande Valley do not avoid talking about the very real challenges in the region, which include poverty and poor health care outcomes and access, especially for asylum seekers and unautho-rized immigrants in the era of family separation policies, and increasing criminalization of immigration and militarization of the border. Valley leaders point to local partnerships and expertise to combat suffering and economic, social, and political challenges. Valley leaders tell stories about people, industries, and initiatives in the region that directly contribute to Texas's economic growth. They speak of their abiding faith in the ability of the Valley and its communities to positively shape the future of the state of Texas and our nation. These stories are inherently political and rhetorical. Leaders argue that the borderlands are essential to the United States. They challenge an enmeshed, long-held set of assumptions about a place that directly impacts how federal and state resources are allocated. These stories unabashedly reproduce American ideals of home, economy, and entrepreneurial spirit. They are also genuine and deeply personal.

Ending the Book When So Much Is Happening

It is hard to end this book. If the U.S.–Mexico border is a primary national symbol, it is essential we get it right. One of the strengths of my profession of anthropology is its commitment to long-term engagements with a community and to learning how members of the community experience the world around them. Anthropologists understand that ideas and meanings about places and people are in a constant process of modification, reproduction, and resistance. At its best, anthropology is a medium by which communities in one place at one point in time speak their truths as a way to question why and how we think about ourselves and others. Anthropologists have to be careful about what we claim our work to represent. I could have written a book about so many other Valley communities' experiences of place. The Valley and the U.S.–Mexico borderlands are an amalgam of experiences, ideas, and physical spaces that changes depending on one's perspectives and positions in society.

The Rio Grande Valley is also a place of extremely rapid change. It is one region in a very long border. I have focused on one community on one side of the geopolitical borderline at one point in time: Valley leaders in the 2010s. I argue that listening to its successes and challenges from the perspectives of those who lead the region offers the nation a different, more productive way to think about common challenges of economic inequality, health care access, and education. The contrast between these stories and the national story of "the border" illuminate our assumptions about the Global South, giving us the opportunity to look to our southern border communities for solutions to problems, rather than causes.

This book offers one way to think differently about the U.S.–Mexico border, as a place of collaboration and resource. But, there are other ways, too. Efforts to flip the script on the Rio Grande Valley and the U.S.–Mexico border have only increased since I began this project. Leaders, grassroots activists, and even the average social media user from the Valley have ramped up efforts. I continue to see, read, and hear almost daily attempts to tell a different story about the Valley. Perhaps one small and welcome irony of political efforts to paint the Valley as a meager, inept, and corrupt place is the increased pushback. The stereotypes are front and center now, not embedded in frames for stories on tired border themes of the Global South. In fact, national journalists more likely to reference the inaccuracies of national ideas about the region in recent years. For example, on January 10, 2019, in *The New York Times*, Ferman and Fernandez wrote,

> The border depicted by the president and the one lived by most McAllen-area residents are two very different places. The collision between the border's reality and how it is being portrayed for those thousands of miles away came sharply into focus on Thursday during Mr. Trump's trip to McAllen, where he met with local, state and federal officials amid protests and counterprotests. (Ferman & Fernandez, 2019)

Social media platforms, too, have created new avenues for other stories to be heard and for protest to dramatically expand its reach. I am hopeful that the national story about the Rio Grande Valley will change. More Valley voices can be heard. One Valley voice is creative artist Gene De La Garza, a filmmaker and educator who regularly crafts Valley memes to circulate on social media. On February 20, 2019, he posted on Facebook a new image that was shared 1,200 times within about a month's time. With his permission, I use it to end the book. In De La Garza's image, the Valley's four counties form its shape, but the internal county distinctions are absent. Inside the four-county area, the Valley speaks. Perhaps, we should listen.

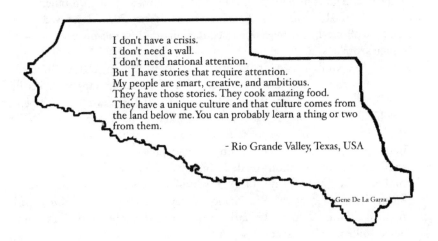

I don't have a crisis.
I don't need a wall.
I don't need national attention.
But I have stories that require attention.
My people are smart, creative, and ambitious.
They have those stories. They cook amazing food.
They have a unique culture and that culture comes from the land below me. You can probably learn a thing or two from them.

- Rio Grande Valley, Texas, USA

Gene De La Garza

Works Cited

Adichie, C. N. (2009, July 10). The danger of a single story. *TEDGlobal*. TED.

Baker, P., & Shear, M. D. (2019, August 4). El Paso shooting suspect's manifesto echoes Trump's language. *The New York Times*. Retrieved January 7, 2020, from https://www.nytimes.com/2019/08/04/us/politics/trump-mass-shootings.html.

Benson, E. (2016, November). Up against the wall. *Texas Monthly*. Retrieved April 25, 2019, from https://www.texasmonthly.com/politics/interview-with-congressman-filemon-vela/.

BTA: Border Trade Alliance. (2019, April 25). *About us*. BTA: Border Trade Alliance. Retrieved April 25, 2019, from https://www.thebta.org/about-us/.

Cohen, S. (1972). *Folk devils and moral panics*. St. Albans, UK: Paladin.

Ferman, M., & Fernandez, M. (2019, January 10). In Texas, Trump's visit offers two views of a border. *The New York Times.* Retrieved January 13, 2019, from https://www.nytimes.com/2019/01/10/us/trump-texas-border-visit.html.

Fogarty, P. (2016, December 10). Borders as economic gateways: A feature on BiNED. *Rio Grande Guardian.* Retrieved April 25, 2019, from https://rio grandeguardian.com/borders-as-economic-gateways-a-feature-on-bined/.

García, J. V. (2015, May 17). *Commencement address 2015.* Retrieved from Smith College: https://www.smith.edu/about-smith/smith-history/commen cement-speakers/2015.

Gonzalez, M., Kroll, M., Marin, C., Rhi-Perez, P., & Wilson, C. (2017). Executive Summary. Backward integration of manufacturing supply chains in the Brownsville-Matamoros region: An approach for creating a competitive binational advanced manufacturing cluster. In S. Taylor, *New BINED study: 15 recommendations made to improve economy. Rio Grande Guardian.* Retrieved April 25, 2019, from https://riograndeguardian.com/new-bined-study-15-recommendations-made-to-improve-economy/.

Gonzalez, R. H. (2017, May). BiNED is brilliant minds shaping south Texas future: The status of the Rio Grande Valley at a crossroads. *Texas Border Business.* Retrieved April 25, 2019, from https://texasborderbusiness.com/bined-brilliant-minds-shaping-south-texas-future.

Holland, J., Ramazanoglu, C., & Scott, S. (1990). AIDS: From panic stations to power relations sociological perspectives and problems. *Sociology, 24*(3), 499–518.

Lower Rio Grande Valley Development Council. (2019a). *Lower Rio Grande Valley development council: 2019 annual work program & budget (draft).* Weslaco, TX: Lower Rio Grande. http://www.lrgvdc.org/downloads/2019% 20Annual%20Work%20Program%20Budget.pdf.

Lower Rio Grande Valley Development Council. (2019b). *2017–2022 Lower Rio Grande Valley regional strategic plan.* Weslaco: Lower Rio Grande Valley Development Council. Retrieved 25 2019, April, from http://www.lrgvdc. org/downloads/2017-2022%20Regional%20Strategic%20Plan.pdf.

Marin, C. (2016, November 9). Binational Border Economic Development (BiNED) action plan. *Border Economic Development & Entrepreneurship Symposium (BEDES).* McAllen, TX: UTRGV Robert C. Vackar College of Business & Entrepreneurship, the Federal Reserve Bank of Dallas and the McAllen Chamber of Commerce. Retrieved November 15, 2018, from Powerpoint available through link at https://texasborderbusiness.com/bined-brilliant-minds-shaping-south-texas-future/.

Morgan, G., & Poynting, S. (Eds.). (2012). *Global Islamophobia: Muslims and moral panic in the west.* Milton Park, UK: Routledge.

Office of U.S. Congressman Filemon Vela. (2018, October 15). *Media center: For immediate release: Vela issues statement on Trump's border wall environmental waivers.* Retrieved April 25, 2019, from US Congressman Filemon Vela: https://vela.house.gov/media-center/press-releases/immediate-release-vela-issues-statement-trump-s-border-wall.

RGV Partnership and Lower Rio Grande Valley Development Council. (2019). *Texas 86th legislative session: 2019 regional priorities Rio Grande Valley.*

Sessions, J. (2017, April 11). Renewed commitment to criminal immigration enforcement. *Memorandum for All Federal Prosecutors.* Washington, DC. Retrieved January 7, 2020, from https://www.justice.gov/opa/press-release/file/956841/download.

Singer, M. (1998). Drugs, violence, and moral panic in Urban America. *American Anthropologist, 100*(1), 186–188.

Taylor, S. (2017a, October 5). BiNED and LRGVDC join forces. *Rio Grande Guardian.* Retrieved April 25, 2019, from https://riograndeguardian.com/bined-and-lrgvdc-join-forces/.

Taylor, S. (2017b, August 27). New BiNED study: 15 recommendations made to improve economy. *Rio Grande Guardian.* Retrieved April 25, 2019, from https://riograndeguardian.com/new-bined-study-15-recommendations-made-to-improve-economy/.

Taylor, S. (2018, July 27). Marin welcomes AMLO's border free trade zone proposals. *Rio Grande Guardian.* Retrieved April 25, 2019, from https://riograndeguardian.com/marin-welcomes-amlos-border-free-trade-zone-proposals/.

Taylor, S. (2019, January 11). South Texas elected officials: Cut out the 'border is violent' rhetoric. *Rio Grande Guardian.* Retrieved April 25, 2019, from https://riograndeguardian.com/south-texas-elected-officials-cut-out-the-border-is-violent-rhetoric/.

Trump, D. J. (2018, December 24). I am in the oval office... *Twitter.* Washington, DC. Retrieved December 26, 2018, from https://twitter.com/realdonaldtrump/status/1077329121745793025?lang=en.

Trump, D. J. (2019a, February 19). Declaring a national emergency concerning the southern border of the United States. *Federal Register, Proclamation 9844* (Billing code 3295-F9-P), 2019-03011. Retrieved March 28, 2019.

Trump, D. J. (2019b, January 8). *President Donald J. Trump's address to the nation on the crisis at the border.* Retrieved July 31, 2020, from The White

House: https://www.whitehouse.gov/briefings-statements/president-donald-j-trumps-address-nation-crisis-border/.

U.S. Department of Homeland Security. (2019, January 24). *Migrant protection protocols*. Press Release. Washington, DC. Retrieved January 7, 2020, from https://www.dhs.gov/news/2019/01/24/migrant-protection-protocols.

Young, J. (1971). *The drugtakers: The social meaning of drug use*. London, UK: Paladin.

Index

© The Editor(s) (if applicable) and The Author(s), under exclusive license to Springer Nature Switzerland AG 2021
K. J. Fleuriet, *Rhetoric and Reality on the U.S.—Mexico Border*, https://doi.org/10.1007/978-3-030-63557-2